SCOTLAND: THE SHAPING OF A NATION

D1635572

SCOTLAND
The Shaping of a Nation

Gordon Donaldson

David St John Thomas Publisher

British Library Cataloguing in Publication Data

Donaldson, Gordon
Scotland: Shaping of a Nation. – New
ed of 2 Rev. ed
   I. Title
   941.1
      ISBN 0-046537-78-X

Printed in Great Britain
by Redwood Press, Melksham
for David St John Thomas Publisher
PO Box 4, Nairn IV12 4HU

Contents

Foreword

The second edition of this book, published in 1980, concluded with a chapter called 'Scotland Today' which recounted what had happened since the first edition was written in 1973, and in it I characterised the five years from 1974 to 1979 as 'a peculiarly significant, if not decisive, period in Scottish history'. This Foreword to the third edition is written in 1992, at the end of another period to which almost exactly the same phrase could apply. At the opening of 1979 it had seemed that the cause of 'Scottish nationalism', as represented by the Scottish National Party, was on the point of achieving results commensurate with the sudden increase in the number of its members of parliament to eleven. But in March 1979 a referendum on a proposed Scottish assembly did not gain the necessary support and in the general election in May the number of SNP members slumped to two.

What happened in the election of 1979 and what happened again in the election of 1992 bears out a remark in the original edition of this book that 'however strong sentiment might be in favour of some kind of home rule, when Scottish voters went to the polling booths they tended to vote on British political issues and support the programme of a British political party' and thus did not vote predominantly on the single issue of Scottish autonomy. Before the 1992 election there were wildly extravagant boasts about 'Scotland free in '93', but at the election on 9 April 1992 the SNP lost one of its four seats. It did not escape notice that the loser of that seat was the militant Jim Sillars, for whom, some thought, there had been built up an image of something like a dictator-in-waiting of a Scottish republic; it seemed an odd coincidence that in Ireland Gerry Adams, the militant president of Sinn Fein, likewise lost his seat. The significance of the sensational about-turn was summed up very neatly by an editorial in *The Scotsman*, which had become strongly 'Nationalist'. The writer presumably recalled the remark attributed to Lord Chancellor Seafield in 1707, when, after the Scottish parliament had voted for the Treaty of Union, he touched it with the sceptre in token of royal assent, 'That's the end of an auld sang'; and *The Scotsman* declared that the election results of 1992 'may be the last verse of what at one time looked like a bright new song'.

There were immediate demonstrations by the disappointed and defeated, who attempted to pluck triumph from disaster. On Monday 13 April *The Scotsman* put on a brave face by devoting most of its front page to a report and photograph of a rally the previous day of about 4000 ScotNats in Glasgow, an event in which it discerned 'a gathering storm'. It did not observe that the day was Palm Sunday ('Hosanna!') and recall what happened the following Friday ('Crucify Him'): has there ever been clearer proof of the fickleness of popular opinion than those events in the first century? Without going so far away in either time or place it would have been relevant to recall that in 1855 the National Association for the Vindication of Scottish Rights had mustered 5000 supporters at a public meeting in Glasgow. More editorial reflection might have tempered the euphoria.

At the present time (1992) there are over a dozen one-volume histories of Scotland on sale in bookshops. One could write an essay – indeed such an essay has been written – on the depressing repetition in so many of those books of factual errors which no amount of correction ever seems to eliminate. But factual errors of detail in one-volume histories are venial in comparison with the false images of Scotland's past which prevail so widely. The *Which? Guide to Scotland* (1992) gets it right: 'The Scotland which has been assiduously sold to visitors is a soft-focus land of high romance, full of fierce but noble chieftains, tartan-clad clansmen and the drama of lost causes. Much of this may be enjoyable, and a good way of selling kilts, bottles of whisky or cuddly monsters, but it bears little relation to the truth about Scotland past or present.'

The image which Scots seem to delight to present to the rest of the world is one which invites ridicule. And as long as they make themselves ridiculous they need not complain of not being taken seriously. If attention could be diverted from false images to the truth about Scottish history the scope for ridicule might be eliminated.

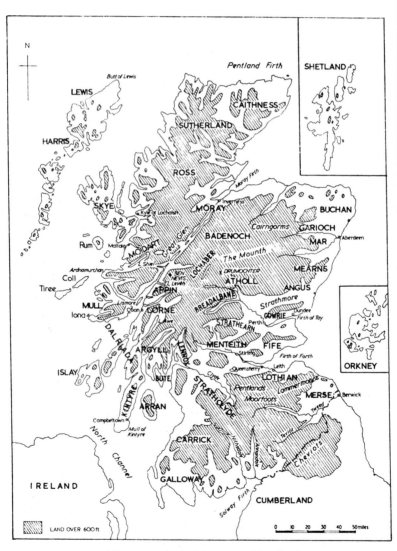

The main physical features of Scotland

CHAPTER 1

Land and People

The two most conspicuous features of the map of Scotland are mountains and the sea, or, to be more precise, high land and water; for there is much high land which is not mountainous and there is much fresh water, in rivers and inland lochs, as well as salt water in firths and sea-lochs. Out of a total acreage of about 19 million, less than 5 million can be reckoned as potentially arable ground or good pasture; nearly one million consist of fresh water and foreshore; the afforested area is at present about two million acres and may have been more in the past. More than half, extending to 11 million acres, is classified as rough grazing. Some of it is very rough: near the rocky shores of north-west Sutherland seven acres no more than suffice for a single sheep, and elsewhere there are tracts of mountainous wastes among which 276 peaks—the 'Munros' of the climbers—exceed 3,000 feet. The areas above the 1,000 foot contour have always been sparsely inhabited, and those above the 2,000 foot contour must always have been uninhabitable, for the habitation of men is much more restricted than the casual operations of shepherds, foresters and stalkers.

A good deal of Scotland was of very little human interest at all until the recent development of climbing and ski-ing as recreations. Even the appreciation of scenic beauty is relatively new. It is true that one English visitor in the seventeenth century described Scotland as 'a legible fair draught of the beautiful creation' and praised its 'deep and torpid lakes, immerged with rivers and gliding rivulets,' but then he was an enthusiastic young angler; until two hundred years ago most people simply loathed looking at mountains.

The high land has always formed barriers to communication. One such barrier is what used to be called 'the Mounth,' a vast massif beginning near the coast south of Aberdeen and stretching through the Cairngorms to finish up with Ben Nevis. Scottish administrators used to think in terms of the more accessible areas south of the Mounth and the less accessible north of it. It is still an important barrier, which can indeed be bypassed along the east coast or through the Great Glen but which is even now crossed by only two routes, both of them often blocked in winter —the pass of Drumochter, taken by the road and railway between Perth and Inverness and rising to about 1,500 feet, and the Devil's Elbow road between Blairgowrie and Braemar, rising to nearly 2,000 feet.

Like 'the Mounth', 'Drumalban' is no longer in current use, but, meaning 'the spine of Scotland', it is a convenient term to denote the series of heights in the west Highlands which form the watershed between the Atlantic and the North Sea. The railways found only three routes through Drumalban—to Kyle of Lochalsh, Mallaig and Oban—one of them rising to over 1,300 feet. Roads are more numerous, but they involve altitudes of 900 feet and more at 'Rest and be thankful' (significant name), Glenogle, The Moor of Rannoch and Glen Clunie. Most people see Highland passes only in summer, and those who traverse them in winter blizzards in a closed and heated car and on roads swept and salted, do not reflect on conditions which a horse would simply refuse to face.

In the Southern Uplands, south of the Forth–Clyde isthmus, a band of high land stretches from the east coast through the Lammermoors, Pentlands and Moorfoots to the Ayrshire–Kirkcudbrightshire border. At their highest they exceed 2,000 feet, they are intersected by river-gorges, and, while there are many roads through them, some of the altitudes again reach 900 feet and are liable to be blocked in winter. The Rivers Tweed and Teviot together almost cut through the Southern Uplands south of that first barrier, but beyond those rivers there rises a second barrier, the Cheviots. While there are some roads through them the easier routes are by the east and west coasts, which alone are used by the railways.

All of these barriers affected military operations. Armies on the march between Scotland and England nearly always by-passed the Cheviots by a coastal road. Most invaders from England avoided the west coast route, because after passing the Solway they were confronted by further upland barriers between Annandale and central Scotland and preferred the eastern route, which circumvented the Southern Uplands and led into the heart of the country. Nor was it difficult to proceed still further up the east coast. But it was a vastly different matter to move west, and this the invaders seldom attempted to do. The high land was thus a refuge for resistance, and helped to preserve Scotland's independence, but it was also an obstacle to government forces pursuing rebels and so made it difficult to consolidate the country.

If high land is one conspicuous feature on the map, water is the other. A seventeenth-century visitor remarked unkindly that a map of Scotland looked like a pillory-coat, bespattered by dirt and rotten eggs. Nowadays it would be said that the country is cut up by arms of the sea and by lochs. But such a remark is misleading. In the twentieth century road transport is fostered at enormous expense and great cost in human suffering, but our wiser forefathers preferred to make use of those natural highways by water which, at no cost to public funds, carried goods and passengers to most parts of Scotland. All through history there is evidence of the use of transport by water. In the sixth century Columba and his island-based colleagues jumped into their coracles exactly as we now jump into a car. In medieval times there was a kingdom of the Isles and a bishopric of the Isles, each extending from the Butt of Lewis to the Calf of Man: there was more unity among those sea-girt islands than between them and places inland. The cathedral for the diocese of Argyll was on the island of Lismore, admirably situated for access by sea. Even on the mainland there were places—and still are, though their number is rapidly dwindling—inaccessible by road and dependent on water-borne transport. All around the shores disused harbours and piers, often with old storehouses nearby, testify to the widespread traffic by small vessels in earlier days. Towns which today are regarded as inland towns used to be reached by sea: Perth indeed is still a port, though the fact is apt

11

to be forgotten, and Stirling was a port until a generation ago.

The mountains and the waterways together defined the communities into which Scotland was divided. Areas which offered arable ground or good pasture contained the bulk of the people in the days before industrialisation; but each such area was cut off from others by high ground and sometimes linked to others by water. There are the valleys and shores of the south-west, on the north side of the Solway, themselves penetrated by navigable estuaries. They contained a clutch of religious houses—Whithorn, Tongland, Dundrennan, Glenluce, Soulseat and Sweetheart, and nine of the sixty-six royal burghs—Dumfries, Sanquhar, Annan, Lochmaben, Kirkcudbright, Wigtown, New Galloway, Stranraer and Whithorn. In the south-east is the fertile Tweed valley, a distinct community which still escapes domination by Edinburgh because of the intervention of a stretch of inhospitable uplands. Here again there was a group of abbeys—Kelso, Melrose, Dryburgh and Jedburgh—and another bunch of royal burghs— Berwick, Roxburgh, Lauder, Jedburgh, Selkirk and Peebles. North of the bleak hills lay the rich soil of Lothian, where there were six royal burghs—Edinburgh, Queensferry, Linlithgow, Haddington, Dunbar and North Berwick; and the Firth of Forth linked Lothian with the harbours of southern Fife, which had, on or near the coast, no less than fourteen royal burghs, a fifth of the total—St Andrews, Cupar, Crail, Kilrenny, Anstruther Easter and Wester, Pittenweem, Dysart, Kirkcaldy, Kinghorn, Burntisland, Inverkeithing, Dunfermline and Culross. Even the Firth of Tay, sand-filled and awkward for navigation though it was, linked the fertile lands on its two sides, for the religious houses of Balmerino and Lindores, on the south side, were in the same nexus as Dundee on the north side and Perth at the head of the estuary. The river and estuary of the Clyde had the burghs of Lanark, Glasgow, Renfrew, Rutherglen and Dumbarton; and on the shores of the Firth of Clyde were the burghs of Ayr and Irvine on one side and Rothesay, Campbeltown and Inveraray on the other. Much further north, the fertile lands on the two sides of the Moray Firth had a concentration of cathedrals—Elgin, Fortrose and Dornoch—and the burghs of Elgin, Fortrose,

Dornoch, Dingwall, Tain, Inverness, Nairn and Forres. That men did think in terms of units like these was shown when the burghs were grouped to send representatives to the Cromwellian parliaments, for the arrangement is almost precisely that just described. The same feature occurs, on a smaller scale, in the Highlands. A modern administrator would use lochs as boundaries; but the old parishes often straddled them, and the church was sometimes on an island, to which access by water was easy from all sides; for instance Eilean Munde in Loch Leven, at the mouth of Glencoe, Eilean Fhinain on Loch Shiel and Inishail on Loch Awe. The only large areas of outstanding fertility which do not straddle waterways are the shallow valley of Strathmore, between the Sidlaw Hills and the Mounth, and the coastal plain of Aberdeen and Buchan.

Yet, while water so often facilitated traffic, it could be an obstacle. It was easy enough for a single traveller, or a small party, to cross the Firth of Forth by ferry from North Berwick to Elie, from Leith to Kinghorn, or at Queensferry, Kincardine or Alloa. But an army, unless it had its own shipping, had to march on until it found a bridge or a ford, and there was neither bridge nor ford east of Stirling. Stirling thus commanded the approach to the northern parts of Scotland, for it was difficult to bypass since the Highland mountains come down not far to the west. Hence the number of nearby battlefields—Falkirk (two), Stirling Bridge, Bannockburn, Sauchieburn and Sheriffmuir. Perth had a similar situation at the head of the Tay estuary, and in its vicinity there were battles at Methven, Dupplin and Tippermuir.

If water was an avenue for traffic within Scotland, the surrounding seas determined the pattern of relations with other countries. Scotland's only land neighbour was England, but even with England communications by land were none too easy before the days of good roads and mechanised transport. For heavy goods like coal the sea was the only possible route, but a great deal of other merchandise was carried by coastal shipping all through the centuries. So late as 1939 there were six ships each week each way between Leith and London, representing over 8,000 tons of shipping, and there were regular services from London to

13

Grangemouth, Dundee, Aberdeen and Glasgow as well. Nor was shipping important only for peaceful commerce. The Romans discovered the value of fleets to accompany and supply their armies when they invaded Scotland, and later commanders, down to the Duke of Cumberland in 1746, followed their example. At times the English were able to hold towns like Dundee, which were capable of being supplied by sea, when they could no longer retain strongholds away from the coast.

Scotland's next nearest neighbour is Ireland, only thirteen miles from the Mull of Kintyre and little more than twenty from the Rhinns of Galloway. Across the narrow North Channel there was always a great deal of coming and going, not only in trade, but in actual migration. There was a Scottish element in north-eastern Ireland long before the Scottish colonisation of Ulster in the seventeenth century, and there was a strong Irish flavour about south-western Scotland long before the great Irish immigration of the nineteenth century. To some extent the two sides of the North Channel formed another of those communities which were linked by water.

France is apt to be considered Scotland's nearest continental neighbour, because people now think primarily in terms of communications overland, and Scots are influenced by the outlook of England, from which France is in truth separated by only a narrow strait. But geographically this is nonsense. From the Firth of Forth, Bremen and Bergen are no further away than Antwerp and Dieppe; from Aberdeen, the Kattegat is as near as the English Channel and the nearest continental country is Norway. Besides, for some centuries the divide between Scotland and Scandinavia was not the North Sea but the Pentland Firth. The Scandinavian lands and the Baltic played the part in Scottish history which geography dictated.

Modern communications, especially by air, go a long way to nullify distance and minimise geographical obstacles, but the Scotland we know today is the product of times in which the configuration of land and water did much to determine the movement of people into and out of Scotland and their settlement within it. Not only the racial composition of the Scots, but their physique and character, their institutions, their means of earning a livelihood, their culture and their pastimes, were all shaped during some sixteen centuries of history, traceable in outline in earlier times and with increasing precision as time passes. Beyond the beginning of history lie centuries of pre-history, and even they must have helped to shape at least the racial composition of the modern Scot. The making of the Scottish nation was thus the result of a long process of which it is impossible to detect the beginning, and even the formation of a single state, with the geographical boundaries we know, had many stages.

Briefly, the kingdom took shape through the amalgamation of five peoples. The first known inhabitants were the Caledonians or Picts, who successfully resisted the attempts of the Romans to extend their empire throughout the whole of Britain. Their origins are uncertain, but for long they occupied the land stretching north from the Pentland or Pictland Hills to the Pentland or Pictland Firth; their main concentrations were in the fertile lands bordering the North Sea and the river valleys running inland from it. In Roman times southern Scotland was occupied by Britons, the people who held the whole of modern England before the Anglo-Saxons arrived and whose Celtic language was the ancestor of modern Welsh. Their territories latterly extended from the lower Clyde basin, with their capital, Dumbarton, on its north side, to the south side of the Solway Firth, and constituted Strathclyde or Cumbria.

The future of Scotland, however, lay in the main with two races who arrived in the sixth century. Emigrants from north-eastern Ireland, who called themselves Scots, crossed the North Channel in about the year 500 to form the kingdom of Dalriada on the islands and shores of Argyll; they spoke Gaelic, a Celtic tongue but one different from the speech of the Britons. A generation later the fertile plains of south-eastern Scotland were, like eastern England, colonised by the Angles or English, a Teutonic people from the continent. Their expansion was at the expense of the Britons, and in the eighth century their territory extended across to Galloway.

Another Teutonic people, the Scandinavians, came to almost

15

all the shores of Scotland between the eighth century and the eleventh. To their expert seamanship it was no problem to cross the 170 or so miles of sea which separated Norway from Shetland and then move on, by the 'stepping-stones' of Fair Isle and Orkney, to the north and west coasts of Scotland. Searching for more kindly conditions than those of their homeland, they made fertile Orkney the centre of a community embracing Shetland and Caithness, in which they effaced most of the traces of earlier inhabitants and preserved their own tongue until the seventeenth century. The west also had some fertile islands where Scandinavians made settlements, to form a mixed race with the native Gaelic speakers. South-eastern Scotland was affected by the proximity of a Scandinavian kingdom in north-east England, and the shores of the Solway were within the nexus of Scandinavian settlements in Ireland, Man and Cumberland. As a primarily sea-faring people the Scandinavians made little direct inland penetration, but their influence was more extensive geographically than is sometimes supposed, and it proved more enduring than that of some of the other peoples. The Scottish state did not gain even formal possession of the main areas of Scandinavian settlement until comparatively late—the western isles by treaty in 1266 and Orkney and Shetland as part of a marriage-dowry in 1468-9.

These transfers of territory from Norway were made by formal written instruments: it is much harder to understand the processes by which the other inhabitants of Scotland had come together in a single kingdom. We do know that in or about 844 the Irish settlers and the Picts were joined together in the kingdom of Alba, comprising most of the land north of the Forth and Clyde. But the circumstances are quite obscure. Accounts of what happened are of Irish origin, and naturally represent the union as one of conquest. This sounds rather unlikely. We can gauge some of the qualities of the Picts from their sculptured stones, which suggest technical skill and efficiency and often show groups of churchmen or warriors in serried and uniform ranks, giving the impression of organisation, the impression almost of a people on the march. It seems inconceivable that the Irish,

16

numerically much inferior and based on a comparatively poor part of the country, could have conquered the Picts, with all the resources of the fertile east of Scotland at their command. Indeed on more than one occasion the Picts had subdued Dalriada and no doubt could have driven the Irish out had they thought it worth while. It is possible that one weakness of the Pictish position had all along been the division of their territory by the Mounth. Conceivably, therefore, Scandinavian pressure, besides weakening Pictland generally, had the specific effect of breaking communications up and down the east coast, while the Dalriadans, with the aid of reinforcements from Ireland, may equally have broken communications through the Great Glen. It is also true that Kenneth, son of Alpin, the Dalriadic king who is credited with the conquest of the Picts, was a great warrior, who six times led an army into Lothian. Yet some mystery does remain. It is not surprising that the suggestion has been put forward that there was already a dynastic link between the two royal houses and that Kenneth was thus acceptable to at least a faction among the Picts.

The acquisition by Alba of the English territory in the south-east seems to have been the result of straightforward military aggression. Probably most of Lothian was conquered in the tenth century, and the battle of Carham, on the Tweed, in 1018, is regarded as marking the consolidation of Alban hold on the south-east. Almost simultaneously, as a result of intermarriage between royal houses, the grandson and heir of the king of Alba succeeded to the British kingdom in the south-west and when he also inherited his grandfather's kingdom, in 1034, his dominions extended to the Tweed on the east and across the Solway on the west. Propaganda to the effect that the Irish 'Scots' had 'expelled the Britons' is no more true than their claim that they had 'destroyed' or 'rooted out' the Picts.

Yet, however improbable an Irish military victory over Picts, English and Britons may seem, the Irish element was influential in the united kingdom. It is true that some of the culture of the Picts survived at least into the eleventh century and that some of their institutions persisted, but it was the Irish 'Scots' who provided the male line of the royal dynasty. Moreover, the Gaelic language of the Irish prevailed completely over the Pictish tongue and even made a short-lived penetration into the former English and British territories south of the Forth and Clyde, where men from Alba no doubt arrived as a conquering aristocracy in the eleventh century. It would appear, too, that some of the institutions characteristic of the Irish church found their way into eastern Alba.

But Irish predominance was soon to be challenged. Ever since the English had settled in the south-east, that area had been a spearhead of influence from the south—influence which had at first been what is loosely called Anglo-Saxon but which, from the ninth century to the eleventh, was more precisely Anglo-Scandinavian, and finally in the late eleventh century became Norman. Scotland's Hastings, if there was one, was an unnamed battle in 1097. Malcolm III, himself half English, had married the English Margaret and introduced innovations from the south, but when they died in 1093 the resentful natives 'drove out all the English who were with King Malcolm before' and raised to the throne Malcolm's brother, Donald, the influence of whom had been Celtic and Scandinavian. Malcolm's sons, however, turned to the Norman king of England for help to oust Donald, and in 1097 an army sent north by King William Rufus finally displaced him by Edgar, son of Malcolm and Margaret, who was to rule Scotland as an English vassal. Of course the event of 1097 did not constitute a Norman Conquest of Scotland any more than Hastings constituted a Norman Conquest of England; but it was, like Hastings, an incident in a process whereby external influence transformed the defeated country.

Under Edgar and his successors Englishmen and Normans flocked into Scotland. It was not an immigration of the same nature as earlier Irish, English and Scandinavian immigrations, for while the newcomers resembled colonists they did not settle in large numbers in a single block of territory. They came primarily as an aristocracy to fill the leading positions in church and state and to add properties in Scotland to those they already possessed in Normandy or England or both. Already in the reign of David I (1124–53), nearly all the valleys of southern Scotland were granted to Normans. Under David's grandson and successor, Malcolm IV, the principal settlement was in Clydesdale; then, under Malcolm's brother, William (1165–1214), the process extended into Angus, Fife, Perthshire and the north-east. The foreigners brought with them kinsmen and clients of their own race and culture, and the influx finally disrupted the kin-based society of Irish tradition, which must already have found it hard enough to digest Picts, Britons and Angles. The institutions and society of at least the south and east of Scotland were largely assimilated to those of Norman England. Probably the Pictish genius for organisation had already determined that the Alban kingdom was centralised from the start, whereas Ireland continued to be no more than a congeries of warring tribes with no permanent central authority and never achieved unity except when it was (somewhat fleetingly) imposed from without. It is significant, if paradoxical, that Scotland, stiffened by the infusion of non-Celtic people, was able to maintain its independence as Ireland and Wales did not. Certainly any possibility that Scotland might be a predominantly Celtic country vanished in the twelfth century.

That there was a new order was unmistakable. The office of sheriff is first heard of in the 1120s, and by 1286, when there were twenty-six sheriffs' seats, a pattern which was to continue for centuries had already taken shape. The sheriffs, seldom of Celtic race, operated from royal castles, and each incoming landowner also had his castle; it might be only a wooden structure on an earthen mound, but there are known sites of over 200 of those 'motte and bailey' castles and it was said that they were 'known to be inhabited by Englishmen'. Burghs were organised— by 1286 there were at least fifty of them—and they too were largely inhabited by men of foreign origin. The church was integrated into the west European system when King David and his successors introduced, sometimes from England, sometimes directly from the continent, the religious orders which had become fashionable, and organised not only dioceses but parishes which, like the sheriffdoms, have continued ever since. Cathedrals and abbeys were in many places the most conspicuous features of the

19

landscape, and the bishops and abbots who ruled them mostly came, like the sheriffs and the landowners, from the south.

All in all, twelfth-century Scotland must, in the eyes of the natives, have had something of the appearance of an occupied country. Tension between the newcomers and the older population sometimes erupted in rebellion. The rebels issued no manifestos which have survived, but we can guess that there was resentment against the introduction of novel institutions and foreign landlords. There was certainly a dynastic element, but 'Pretenders' are apt to be pretexts rather than causes and it is hard to say whether the opposition was to the reigning line's right to the throne or to its innovating policy. It may be that the obsequiousness of some of the kings to their English contemporaries offended patriotism, if such a concept existed. Finally, there were powerful forces of regionalism in a country of heterogeneous race, and perhaps this meant a critical attitude to the increasingly effective activities and agents of the central government. The great province of Moray had a tradition of separatism, and it provided the chief recruiting ground in the north for opposition to the kings and their policy and for support of a rival royal line. Galloway was troublesome too. Throughout past centuries there had been incessant settlement and re-settlement there of Britons, Irish, Angles and Norse, and it is hardly surprising that the people had a reputation for ferocity and unruliness. But the so-called 'native princes' or lords of Galloway were in truth almost as Anglo-Norman as the royal family, and any representation of them as Celtic nationalists would be over-drawn. Yet in 1174, when the king of Scots was unlucky enough to be taken prisoner by the English, the men of Galloway rose in revolt and 'slew all the English and French that they could seize,' while those who escaped found refuge—significantly—in the castles.

The twelfth-century kings acknowledged readily enough that they ruled over diverse races, whom they addressed specifically as French, English, Scots, Galwegians and Flemings. The 'French' were the incoming Normans, whose influence is plain enough in a host of familiar Scottish surnames—Colville, Cuming, Corbet,

Fraser, Gifford, Graham, Hay, Maule, Melville, Montgomery, Moubray, Oliphant, Somerville, Vaus, Vipont, Haig, Sinclair, Boswell, Menzies (de Mesnières), Barclay, Gourlay and Grant, not to mention the royal dynasties of Baliol and Bruce. The 'Scots' were the people of ancient Alba, where the one-time existence of Picts had by now been forgotten. The 'English' were in the main the people of the south-east, but many English were settling in the south-west, in Clydesdale and up the east coast north of Forth, where the place-names they introduced are still to be found. Flemings, too, came in to settle as burghers and as landowners—the Murrays and the Douglases are of Flemish origin—and much of the strong 'Dutch' element in Lowland Scots surely arrived with them. The 'Galwegians' were primarily the inhabitants of Galloway in the extreme south-west, but the term seems sometimes to include most of the ancient British area between the Clyde and the Solway.

The kings who ruled these diverse peoples went back in the male line to Irish ancestry, but from the time of Duncan I (1034–40) their family had generation by generation found wives in the south, and the proportion of Celtic blood in their veins was steadily dwindling. Malcolm III and his English wife, Margaret, who had six sons, ignored native precedent and called them Edward, Edmund, Ethelred, Edgar, Alexander and David; David named his son Henry, and Henry chose the Norman name William for his second son; Malcolm IV was the only member of the dynasty to bear a native name. They had of course no surname, but William, known to Scottish historians as 'the Lion', was most readily identified among his contemporaries as Guillaume de Varenne, from his mother's territorial designation. In the earliest piece of Scottish vernacular which has survived, the name Alexander occurs in the French form Alysaundre. When David I invaded England in 1138, one of his subjects, Robert de Brus, an Anglo-Norman on whom he had conferred the lordship of Annandale, rebuked him for fighting against Anglo-Normans, to whom his family owed its throne and on whom he had had to rely to suppress Scottish rebellions. It was remarked by Walter of Coventry in 1212 that 'the most recent kings of Scots profess themselves to be rather Frenchmen both in race and in manners, language and culture'.

The further statement by the same observer, that these kings admitted 'only Frenchmen to their friendship and service' was, however, less true. In spite of all the innovations, older institutions survived at all levels—in ancient revenues still collected by kings and others, in judicial officers like the *judex* who represented the *brithem* of the older dispensation, and in ecclesiastics who retained old styles if only because they drew ancient endowments. Moreover it has often been remarked that all, or nearly all, of the important magnates styled *comites* (too readily translated 'earls') continued to be Celtic in the male line and that the title could pass to an incomer only through marriage to an heiress. The monarchy itself retained some trappings which demonstrated its continuity from the first Irish leaders to arrive in Dalriada. A king's inauguration centred round a sacred stone which was alleged to have been brought from Ireland and which found a home at Scone, near Perth, a place which became the secular centre of the kingdom of Alba about 900. Some of the ceremonies resembled those for the installation of a pagan tribal chief rather than the investiture of a Christian monarch of western Europe. The inauguration did not take place in a church, but in the open air, on an artificial mound or motte—the 'moot-hill of Scone'—which was perhaps a substitute for a natural rock-fortress like Dunadd, where the kings of Dalriada had had their first headquarters. The central act was not crowning or anointing, but the placing of the king on the stone, and the leading part was played not by a bishop or an abbot but by the principal layman of the realm—the *comes* of Fife.

By the middle of the thirteenth century, separatism and active opposition to the ruling line had petered out. But a more subtle change was taking place. There must have been a phase when a horizontal division into classes was more potent than a vertical division into nations: the Scottish baron, at least partly southern in origin, had more in common with an English baron than with his tenants, whether of Teutonic or Celtic race, and a burgess of Berwick or Perth, of Flemish, English or Scandinavian blood,

had more in common with a burgess of Newcastle than with a
herdsman from the central Highlands, of Pictish or Irish descent.
But at some stage all the people from the Cheviots northwards
came to regard themselves as Scots. By 1200 the church had
gained recognition as a separate province, and it was known as
Ecclesia Scoticana, the Scottish Church. Something very like
national pride in the independence of Scotland had been expressed
as early as 1189 by a monk of Melrose, although he was a member
of an order with its headquarters on the continent and of a community situated in the far south of Scotland, endowed by Norman
landholders and presided over by abbots of English or French
descent. His comment on a transaction whereby the Scottish
king was released from feudal subjection to the king of England
was, 'And so, by God's grace, he worthily and honourably
removed a heavy yoke of domination and servitude from the
kingdom of the Scots'. Kings ceased to address the various races
among their people: all of them were simply subjects of the king
of Scots, and therefore themselves Scots. The time came when a
baron of Norman extraction who spoke French, a bishop whose
tongue took more readily to Latin than to English, the English-
speaking traders and farmers of the burghs and the plains and the
Gaelic-speaking pastoralists from the mountains, all began to
look on themselves not as a collection of different races ruled by a
single sovereign, but as one nation.

In view of the lack of an obvious frontier between north and
south Britain, the existence of physical barriers within Scotland,
the differences of race and language among its people, the contrast
between Highlands and Lowlands and the affinities between the
Lowlands and England, it is remarkable that a separate state,
with its frontier at the Tweed and the Solway, ever came into
existence and preserved its identity. No doubt the persistence
of some native institutions despite all southern innovations had
something to do with it, and no doubt the retention by the
monarchy of its ancient trappings contributed too, but the full
explanation remains mysterious. One element was this: Picts
and Britons, Scandinavians, Angles and Normans, all alike laid
aside their particular memories of the past and adopted as their

heritage the history and mythology of the original Scots, who had come as Irish invaders. What else, it may be asked, but the acceptance of a single history, or of what men imagined to be history, could have made one nation? The mythology was symbolised and enshrined in the royal line, for which a quite unhistorical antiquity was claimed in remarkable flights of fancy which may, however, represent some vestigial folk-memory of early migrations.

It was related that the Scots derived their origin from Gaythelos (whence, allegedly, Gael), son of a king of Greece, who went to Egypt in the days of Moses. He married the eponymous Scota, daughter of a Pharaoh, and led his family from Egypt to Spain. From that country colonies of their descendants moved on to Ireland, and, so the story went on, some of them crossed from Ireland into north Britain, to which they gave the name Scotia. In 330 BC the settlers in Scotland chose as their king 'Fergus I', from whom the dynasty was dated. Under his descendants they remained in Scotland until 360 AD when, after King Eugenius (Ewen) was killed by the Picts and Britons, the Scots, under his brother Ethodius and his nephew Erc, were driven back to Ireland. Then in the fifth century they returned to reoccupy Argyll under Fergus, son of Erc. From him the succession continued to Kenneth, son of Alpin, who united the Picts with the Scots in the kingdom of Alba. Needless to say, the forty-five kings from 'Fergus I' to Fergus, son of Erc, were a fabrication, typical of the Irish readiness to present claims to territory and allegiance in genealogical form. The point of the story was the claim of the Scots to have been in Scotland before Picts, Britons, English, Scandinavians and Normans. The remarkable thing is that before the end of the thirteenth century most of the inhabitants of Scotland believed all this, and were convinced that the dynasty represented a line of upwards of a hundred kings. In 1249, after Alexander III had been inaugurated on the sacred stone, a *seanchaidh* or bard from the Highlands recited the new king's pedigree in Gaelic, going back, generation by generation, to 'Fergus I', the mythical founder of the Irish kingdom in Scotland. What impression did this rigmarole make on the entourage of an anglicised, French-speaking king, only two of whose thirty-two great-great-great-grandparents could claim Irish blood?

The integrity of the kingdom was long to be sustained partly by a belief in all this mythology, embodied in the dynasty. And after the union with England in 1707 history—not even yet purged of legend—continued to maintain the identity of a nation which lacked the political framework of a state and many other attributes of national unity. R. L. Stevenson wrote:

Scotland is indefinable: it has no unity except upon the map. Two languages, many dialects, innumerable forms of piety, and countless local patriotisms and prejudices, part us among ourselves. ... When I am at home, I feel a man from Glasgow to be something like a rival, a man from Barra to be more than half a foreigner. Yet let us meet in some far country, and, whether we hail from the Braes of Manor or the Braes of Mar, some ready-made affections join us on the instant. It is not race. Look at us. One is Norse, one Celtic, another Saxon. It is not the community of tongue. We have it not among ourselves: and we have it almost to perfection with English, or Irish, or American. It is no tie of faith, for we detest each other's errors.

The answer to Stevenson's quest for the origin of the 'ready-made affections' which join Scots in a nation is to be found, at least in part, in the acceptance of a common history in the thirteenth century. Yet at that time, despite emergent nationalism, class-divisions were still strong enough to cut across national boundaries. A more effective welding together was to come not from further developments inside Scotland but as a result of a challenge from outside.

CHAPTER 2

Scotland and England

Something of a pattern in the relations between south and north Britain was established long before there were kingdoms of England and Scotland. Any power in control of the larger and wealthier part of the island almost inevitably had ambitions to extend its sway over at least the whole east coast, where there was no definitive natural barrier. This happened in Roman times. Late in the first century Agricola operated up the eastern coastal plain, possibly as far as the shores of the Moray Firth. Much the same thing happened early in the third century, when the Emperor Severus was in command in Britain. Between these two aggressive phases the frontier between the Roman province in the south and the untamed peoples of the north was twice (from about 85 to 95 and again from about 140 to 180) across the Forth–Clyde line, but these attempts to include southern Scotland in the Roman empire were not successful, and it was the Tyne–Solway line, where the Emperor Hadrian built his wall in about the year 130, which was the frontier from about 95 to 140 and again from about 180 until the collapse of Roman government after 400. Yet, while not even southern Scotland was held in a military sense, the unobtrusive influence continued of the settled Roman province, and the tribes beyond its frontier received a tincture of Romano-British civilisation. This again was a feature which was often to recur, for throughout succeeding centuries military operations were only part of the story of the relations between south and north Britain.

In the seventh century the Anglian kingdom of Northumbria was probably the most powerful state in Britain, and it attempted not only to consolidate the area from the Humber to the Forth but to establish at least a sphere of influence over Pictish territory

26

further north. Efforts to dominate the Picts by military force came to an end in 685, when King Egfrith of the Angles was enticed by the Pictish king Brude to lead his army north of the Tay into Angus, where he met with disaster at Nechtansmere. But once again peaceful penetration continued despite military reverses, and within half a century Pictland was coming under Anglian influence in the ecclesiastical and cultural spheres.

Presently aggression came from the north, for the united kingdom of the Picts and Scots, Alba, was eager from the outset to expand southwards. It confronted an England which was itself achieving unity under the kings of the house of Wessex, but these kings were either unwilling or unable to play a very active role in the north, where in any event Scandinavian-occupied territory sometimes formed a buffer. Consequently they acquiesced in a considerable amount of Alban expansion in the tenth century, into both the south-east and the south-west, in return for recognition of some kind of English overlordship. Malcolm II (1005-34) profited from the disturbed state of England when it was over-whelmed by the heaviest of all Scandinavian invasions, which for a time placed a line of Danish kings on the English throne. He was heavily defeated in 1006, possibly on besieging Durham, but after a Scottish victory at Carham (1018), English rulers seem formally to have accepted Alban domination over Lothian.

Scotland, as we can now call it, was still not content, for Duncan I (1034-40), the first Alban king who ruled Strathclyde and so had a frontier reaching beyond the Solway, besieged Durham in 1040. No aggression is recorded of Macbeth (1040-57), but Duncan I's son, Malcolm III (1058-93), made five raids into England, apparently mainly out of a desire for loot. Malcolm was the son of a Northumbrian lady; he spent his adolescence, during the reign of Macbeth, as an exile in the England of Edward the Confessor; he recovered his father's throne only with southern help, and he married the Confessor's grand-niece, Margaret, who took refuge in Scotland when her family was excluded from the English throne by William the Conqueror. It is hard to see any intelligent link between Malcolm's foreign policy—if it can be dignified by that name—and either a sense of

27

gratitude to the English who had helped him to his throne or a desire to commend his wife's family to the people of England in preference to Norman William. English retaliation for Malcolm's raiding followed something of the pattern established in the previous century: there was no serious attempt to recover territory except by mopping up the land Scotland had acquired south of the Solway, but in 1072 William the Conqueror marched as far north as Abernethy, not far from Perth, and compelled Malcolm to become his 'man'.

After the death of the troublesome Malcolm, in 1093, the Conqueror's son, William Rufus, turned to the policy, imitated by several later English kings, of enthroning an English vassal in Scotland. His first experiment was with Duncan II, a son of Malcolm by his first marriage, but Duncan found that the Scots would accept him only if he dismissed the English and French who had set him on the throne, and this rendered his position untenable. An experiment with a second client, Edgar, a son of Malcolm and Margaret, was successful. The relations between the two royal families became ever closer. One daughter of Malcolm and Margaret married Henry I of England, another became the mother-in-law of Henry's successor, Stephen. Edgar never married, but his brother and successor, Alexander I, was—it is hard to avoid the conclusion—deliberately humiliated by being espoused to an illegitimate daughter of Henry I who had, it has been said, neither good looks nor courtly manners. Alexander was thus at once brother-in-law and son-in-law of his English contemporary. David, the next king of Scots, married a grand-niece of the Conqueror; her father had held the earldoms of Northumbria, Northampton and Huntingdon, and she was, besides, a wealthy widow, so that her vast inheritance made David the greatest magnate in English society.

But these ties did not deter the Scots from aggression. David took advantage of the unsettled state of England when Stephen and Matilda were competing for the throne after the death of Henry I in 1135. He might be credited with a wish to secure the rights of Matilda, his niece, but he was also the uncle by marriage of Stephen, and he cannot be acquitted of territorial ambitions. In

1138 he was heavily defeated at the battle of the Standard (North-allerton), but in the next year Stephen ceded Northumbria to David, who seems in practice to have controlled territory as far south as the Tees. Then in 1149 Henry, son of Matilda, promised the Scots the counties of Northumberland, Cumberland and Westmorland in return for help to establish him on the throne. This was the high-water mark of Scottish power for, territorial gains apart, when David was almost playing the part of a king-maker in England he could hardly be thought of as an English vassal.

However, by the time Henry became king of England, he had to deal not with David but with David's grandson, the boy Malcolm IV, and he coolly repudiated his promise. It was at this point (1157) that the Border in its essentials took shape. Malcolm reverted to a position of vassalage, but his brother, William (1165–1214), was more militant. In 1174 he agreed to support an English rebellion in return for a promise of Northumberland, but he was taken prisoner and compelled by the treaty of Falaise to acknowledge Henry II as his feudal overlord for the kingdom of Scotland. This agreement lasted for only fifteen years, for in 1189 Richard Coeur-de-Lion, engaged in raising money for the third crusade, sold back to Scotland what William had sur-rendered. But this merely restored the old ambiguity, which was not ended even when, in 1237, by the treaty of York, the Scots finally relinquished their claims to the northern counties and received, as partial compensation, estates in north-west England. Whether homage was due only for English estates, or perhaps for Lothian, or for the whole of Scotland, no one could say, or at any rate no one could prove. Yet those who saw the king of Scots from time to time on his knees before the English king must have doubted whether he was a fully sovereign prince.

Nor did it escape notice that although the Scottish kings, at least from the time of Edgar, had worn a crown, they were neither crowned nor anointed at their inauguration. The Scots more than once sought from the pope permission to have their kings anointed, but he declined to offend the English by conceding a rite which was the mark of full sovereignty. Similarly, although he conceded that the Scottish church was a separate province, he would not go so far as to appoint an archbishop in Scotland as he had done in Denmark, Norway and Sweden.

But all the ambiguity did not interrupt the close relations between the two royal families. Alexander II (1214–49) married as his first wife the sister of Henry III, though his son Alexander was the child of a second marriage, to the daughter of a Picard lord. The mother of the children of Alexander III (1249–86) was the sister of Edward I. But Alexander's children predeceased him and on his death the direct male line of the dynasty came to an end. The heiress was the three-year-old 'Maid of Norway', offspring of his daughter Margaret and King Erik of Norway. Edward of England, her great-uncle, had a son and heir a year younger than the Maid, and the precedents of the two previous generations suggested yet another marriage, one which this time would bring about a peaceful union of the two kingdoms. The Scots knew Edward as the trusted brother-in-law of their late king and as the nearest kinsman in Britain of their young queen; not one of them remembered a time when there had been war between the two countries; many of them were products of a civilisation which straddled national boundaries, and some were vassals of Edward as English landowners. One of the Anglo-Scots thought his English estates equivalent to a third of the kingdom of Scotland. Edward's plan was not unwelcome, and had it matured there would have been a union closer than that achieved in 1707 and closer than that existing today, for Scottish institutions would probably have been completely assimilated to those of England.

On the death of the child-queen in 1290 there were thirteen claimants to the Scottish throne, and the most convincing cases were those of John Balliol, Lord of Galloway, and Robert Bruce, Lord of Annandale. Edward undertook to adjudicate. He had not asserted feudal overlordship on the death of Alexander III, when he might have claimed that Scotland had fallen to him because the heiress was his ward and that her marriage was at his disposal; but, leaving aside both feudal law and his relationship to the Scottish royal family, it was no novelty for England to act as a king-maker in Scotland, as the instances of Malcolm III, Duncan II and Edgar had shown. Edward agreed to give a decision provided that the competitors acknowledged him as overlord of Scotland. In 1292 he decided in favour of Balliol.

There is no reason in principle why the familiar experiment of a puppet king should not have been a success. Balliol and several of his subjects were already vassals of Edward for English estates, and it did not make much difference when they became his vassals for Scottish properties as well. But possibly Edward had no sincere desire to make the experiment work. If he wanted to goad Balliol into rebellion and provide an excuse for the armed conquest of Scotland, he succeeded. Balliol's subjects, and King John himself, were summoned to English law courts, and Edward demanded Scottish contingents for his armies. However, France, threatened by Edward, procured the alliance of Scotland, and also of Norway, at the end of 1295, and this was the signal for Scottish revolt. After an army had been routed at Dunbar (1296), Balliol was forced to abdicate and Edward progressed at the head of his army over routes previously traversed by Romans and Angles. Scotland's future constitution was not defined, but an English administration was meantime introduced. The unification of Scotland and England simplified the position of the magnates and shelved problems of divided loyalties. Besides, some of them had expectations of a throne on Edward's terms should he appoint another vassal king.

Within a year, however, local rebellions had begun and they coalesced under the leadership of Andrew Moray and William Wallace. Neither was a claimant to the throne, but both regarded themselves as subjects of Balliol, and while Moray belonged to one of the important baronial families, Wallace was no more than a Renfrewshire country gentleman. His name means 'Welsh', but any tendency to regard him as a Celtic nationalist is checked when we learn that the contemporary Lord Mayor of London was a Sir Henry Wallace; King Edward can be pardoned for seeing nothing in Wallace's name to distinguish him from his English subjects. It is Wallace who lives in popular memory, partly because Moray's career was soon cut short by death and partly

31

because Wallace's story was embroidered in the popular verses of Blind Harry two hundred years later. Yet, whereas the battle of Stirling Bridge (1297) was a victory for Wallace and Moray, next year Wallace, without Moray, was no match for the English when he met them under Edward himself at Falkirk. Between the battles Wallace had been raised to the office of guardian, or regent, but he may well have been regarded as a *parvenu* and at the best he could expect the support only of the pro-Balliol faction. The defeat at Falkirk caused Wallace to lay down his office, but guardians of higher rank maintained resistance for some years and only in 1305 did Edward believe that Scotland was subdued.

The national cause was next year revived under the leadership of Robert Bruce, grandson of the Bruce who had been a competitor in 1290. Bruce had hitherto sometimes supported the cause of resistance, but he had been ready enough to mount the Scottish throne as an English vassal and he had never been able to collaborate comfortably with those who upheld the claim of Balliol. His relations were particularly strained with John Comyn, whose father had been a candidate for the throne in 1290 and whose mother was a sister of Balliol. In 1306 Bruce murdered Comyn in a church. This violent and surely unpremeditated act, perhaps coupled with the knowledge that he had incurred Edward's unrelenting suspicion, made him a desperate man who had nothing to lose by claiming the throne. Hastily inaugurated as king at Scone (though not on the historic stone, which Edward had removed to Westminster), he was almost at once defeated, lurked in obscurity for a time and then emerged to conduct campaigns against English garrisons and gradually recover castles until, on 24 June 1314, he won a resounding victory at Bannockburn over Edward II, who had succeeded his father in 1307.

Edward I lives in popular memory as 'the hammer of the Scots'; but a hammer, properly used, is a constructive tool, and English attempts at conquest did much to weld the Scots into a nation. Yet the process was a long one, and the issue, in a land divided into factions, was never clear-cut between national independence and submission to England. If one claimant to the throne declared for resistance, the faction supporting another was apt to side with England. It is impossible to isolate patriotism, for no one could

Page 33 Pictish cross-slab, from Rossie Priory, between Perth and Dundee, with typical symbols, animals and warriors in array

Page 34 (left) Round Tower, Brechin, showing Irish influence in the tenth century; *(right)* Tower of St Regulus, St Andrews, showing English influence in the eleventh century

fight for independence without also fighting for a claimant to the throne. No more than Balliol could Bruce be regarded as a nationalist candidate. Balliol's ancestors had come from Bailleul in Normandy, Bruce's had come from Brix in the Cotentin, and both were vassals of Edward. Presumably both conversed most freely in French, and if Bruce's mother was Countess of Carrick (giving him a place in Celtic society), Balliol's mother was the Lady of Galloway, an area probably more Celtic than Carrick.

The claim sometimes made that 'Celtic' regions were especially 'patriotic' cannot be sustained. Although the predominantly Anglian south-east was constantly harried and occupied by the English, yet plenty of Lothian men of all ranks fought with Wallace and Bruce, and more Scots aligned themselves with English garrisons beyond the bounds of Lothian than within it. The fertile lands from Fife to Moray had been so heavily penetrated by southern influence that it is preposterous to regard them as 'Celtic', and Professor Barrow has pronounced: 'The notion of the Celtic north, under the leadership of its "great earls", rallying to Bruce in 1306 is a myth best classified in stud-book language as "by Prejudice out of Imagination".' The truth is that disunity permeated the whole country and it was in what are sometimes reckoned Celtic areas that Bruce had to conduct civil war against English collaborators—the Comyn supporters in Buchan, the MacDougals of Lorne, the Macnabs in central Perthshire and the MacDowells of Galloway.

Bruce, therefore, had not only to win military victories; he had to win the hearts of a people, and this was perhaps the harder task. Like eighteenth-century Hanoverian monarchs, he had a rival in a King over the Water—Balliol, who had retired to his French estates—possessed of a superior claim by hereditary right. Propaganda was the task of Bruce's clerical supporters, who were skilled in literary composition and legal argument, and it took the shape—it often does—of fable and counter-fable which, though lacking in factual content, were far from pointless. Years before, the Scottish Guardians had appealed to the pope against Edward, on the ground that Scotland had been converted to Christianity centuries before the Saxons or Angles and was subject only to its patron, St Andrew, and his brother, St Peter. But Edward sent off his rival mythology to 'clear the conscience', as he put it, of His Holiness: Britain derived its name from Brutus the Trojan, who gave England to his eldest son, Locrinus, Scotland to his second, Albanactus, and Wales to his third, Camber. When the pope had to condemn Robert Bruce as a sacrilegious murderer, English propaganda appealed to him. The Scots had therefore to state their case afresh: they recounted their origins in Scythia and boasted not only that their conversion could be entrusted to no less a person than St Andrew, the first apostle to be called by Our Lord, but that their kingdom had been ruled by a succession of independent kings, a hundred and thirteen in number, all of native stock and without interference from foreign powers until the advent of the tyrannical Edward I.

This was a good enough retort to English pretensions, but it did not prove Bruce's right to the throne. Further arguments were therefore advanced in a letter sent by the barons of Scotland to Pope John XXII in 1320 and known as the Declaration of Arbroath or the Scottish Declaration of Independence. It was alleged that the Scots had always preferred the Bruce line and that Balliol had been forced on them by Edward I. Bruce, it was said, had the best claim by right of blood and also—not very consistently—because he had been selected by the people. The emphasis on selection was forcefully expressed: the Scots, that Chosen Race, had been led to victory by King Robert as Joshua and Maccabeus had rescued an earlier Chosen Race; but should he give up the struggle they would repudiate him and make another king, 'because so long as a hundred of us remain alive we will never be subject to the English, since it is not for riches, or honours, or glory that we fight, but for liberty alone, which no worthy man loses save with his life'. They were protesting that they were patriots and not merely supporters of Bruce.

The pope finally gave way, not only by withdrawing the ban on Bruce but, after England had conceded Scottish independence by the treaty of Edinburgh-Northampton in 1328, by granting the long-sought privilege of anointing, so that there could be no doubt in future about the complete sovereignty of Scottish kings.

This privilege—for which the Scots paid the great sum of £2,000 —arrived to find the liberator king dead, and his son David II was the first Scottish king to be crowned and anointed. Yet all this did not secure the Bruce dynasty, because David was for a time displaced by John Balliol's son Edward. It is true that Edward Balliol had English backing and therefore represented another experiment in puppet kingship, but many Scots supported him, either because they thought the Balliol claim superior or because they preferred an adult to the child David II. In the 1330s there had to be another war of independence. David was sent to France for safety and, five years after he returned, he invaded England as his father had sometimes done, only to be captured at Neville's Cross near Durham, in 1346, and kept a prisoner in England for eleven years, when he was released on promise of a heavy ransom.

For over two centuries more no generation passed without serious military operations, and hardly a decade without disturbed relations. The two peoples became habituated to enmity. A traveller in Scotland in 1435 remarked that 'nothing pleases the Scots more than abuse of the English', and when the English taught their children archery they encouraged them to take good aim—so at least a Scot believed—by saying, 'There's a Scot. Shoot him!' Yet from time to time thoughts did turn again to the possibility of peaceful union through marriage. When Robert Bruce stipulated for the marriage of his heir, David, to one of the four children of Edward II, he showed that he considered such a union not inconceivable. David, as it turned out, was childless, and, as he learned to appreciate English ways during his captivity and had no love for the nephew who was his designated successor —his half-sister's son, Robert the Steward—he was prepared to entertain the possibility that he might be succeeded by another nephew, one of the sons of his brother-in-law, Edward III, perhaps even by the heir to the English throne. It has been suggested that David's manoeuvrings were no more than a device to defer or evade the payment of his ransom, and the Scottish estates rejected the proposal. Yet the discussions were not unstatesmanlike, because, in return for accepting an English prince as his heir, David could have obtained terms (including the return of the Stone of Scone) in some ways more favourable to Scotland than those ultimately obtained in 1707.

A century later, in the reign of James III (1460–88), almost every conceivable marriage was proposed between his family and the English royal family—or rather families, for Yorkists and Tudors were both involved. But English marriages for Scottish princes had ceased to be usual: David II's second marriage and the marriages of Robert II and Robert III had been to Scotswomen, while James II and James III had found their wives on the continent. Besides, bitterness against England was stimulated by 'Blind Harry's' verses commemorating the deeds of William Wallace. Therefore, one of the counts against James III, who so assiduously sought English marriages, was that he had counselled 'the inbringing of Englishmen to the perpetual subjection of this realm'. However, James IV, for whom his father had proposed an English bride in his infancy, did ultimately marry Margaret, the elder of the two daughters of Henry VII. When it was pointed out that such a marriage might lead to a union of the kingdoms, Henry sagely observed that the greater would always draw the less and that England would be the predominant partner.

Throughout generations of hostility, tempered only by occasional marriage plans, England was never without friends of a kind—it might be better to call them agents—in Scotland, for, from the time when Edward I relied on one claimant to the Scottish throne against another, each country cultivated the other's dissidents. Edward Balliol, contesting the throne with David II, had the support of 'the Disinherited', those Anglo-Scots who had lost their Scottish estates because they had taken the English side against Robert Bruce. In about 1400 there was another instance. When Robert III's son, the Duke of Rothesay, jilted the daughter of the Earl of March, March went over to the side of Henry IV; on the other hand, the Percies of northern England, at loggerheads with Henry IV, sought help in Scotland, where there appeared an English pretender, claiming to be Richard II, whom Henry had displaced and was supposed to have murdered. When England was distracted by the strife of York and Lancaster, the Scottish government supported the Lancastrian Henry VI, and in 1461 he obtained a promise of Scottish help in return for the cession of Berwick. Edward IV, the Yorkist who had supplanted Henry VI, retaliated by making a treaty with the Earl of Douglas and the Lord of the Isles for the conquest and partition of Scotland, and twenty years later he took up the cause of James III's troublesome brother, the Duke of Albany, whom he acknowledged as 'Alexander IV, King of Scots'. In the next decade, after the Tudor Henry VII had displaced the Yorkists, James IV supported Perkin Warbeck, who claimed to be the younger of the two princes who had been murdered in the Tower and therefore the rightful possessor of the crown worn by Henry.

France, if only because she was also a target for English attempts at conquest, was Scotland's 'Auld Ally', by a treaty first formally made in 1295 and many times renewed. The treaties generally committed the two countries to mutual assistance against English aggression, and in practice many Scots gave military service in France, while French forces occasionally came to Scotland. But the French were on the whole less ready to come to the assistance of the Scots in defensive operations than to invoke the treaties when it suited them to stimulate the Scots into making attacks which would divert English attention from the continent.

When James IV married Henry VII's daughter in 1503, he refused to accede to Henry's request that he should renounce the French alliance, for that would have meant the loss of freedom of action and the danger of complete domination by England. However, he refrained from formally renewing it, and a 'treaty of perpetual peace' between Scotland and England was strengthened by a papal confirmation, so that, should either party break the engagement, he would incur excommunication.

James could hope to reconcile his new, formal undertaking to England with his old, moral understanding with France, only as long as England and France did not go to war. The cautious, peace-loving Henry VII was succeeded in 1509 by Henry VIII, who was ambitious to play a part on the continental stage. James was not averse from foreign adventure either, but his mind ran on a crusade by the princes of Christendom against the Turks, who were by this time threatening central Europe. Enthusiastic for his navy, for which he built the great *Michael*, the largest ship of the time, he probably fancied himself as the admiral of such an expedition, for which he naturally expected the papal blessing. To his immense chagrin, to put it no higher, he found that Pope Julius II's chief aim was to exclude the French from Italy. The 'Holy League' which the pope formed was therefore directed not against the infidel but against the Most Christian King of France, ancient ally of the Scots. When Henry VIII joined the Holy League, King Louis was lavish with promises of what he would do to further James's crusade, and the Scots formally renewed their alliance with France (1512). Next year an English army invaded France, and James could not stand aside. The outcome was a disastrous defeat at Flodden (9 September 1513). Although James IV was under papal censures for opposing the pope's league and for breaking the English treaty, Scottish bishops and abbots stood by him as they had stood by Robert Bruce, and some fell at Flodden alongside king and nobles.

Flodden, as it turned out, was the last occasion when the Scots willingly acted as a tool of France to mount a large-scale invasion of England. The truth was that the international setting was changing and the Auld Alliance out of date. It had been appropriate in a period when England threatened to conquer France, but the threat to France now came rather from the house of Hapsburg, which ruled Austria, the Netherlands, Spain and parts of Italy. To counter this encircling power, France from time to time sought the alliance or neutrality of the English, and in order to court them did not hesitate to sacrifice her old allies the Scots. Some Scots began to reflect that the old alliance had been a one-sided affair, and never again would Scottish nobles show any enthusiasm for crossing that fatal frontier and risking repetition of the disaster of 1513. Thus there emerged a party which, if not yet pro-English, at least thought that Scotland's foreign policy should be reconsidered.

The growth of a pro-English party was soon encouraged by the Reformation. Scots who, from the 1520s, were influenced by the teachings of Luther, welcomed Henry VIII's example in repudiating papal supremacy, and some of them, at odds with the authorities in their own country, found a refuge in England. By the late 1530s there had taken shape a party which thought that Scotland should side with England against the papalist powers of the continent. On the other hand, those whose ecclesiastical views were conservative upheld the alliance with France and were ready to see Scotland used in a crusade against the schismatic Henry VIII.

James V (1513–42), although not unaware of the unrest caused by the moral shortcomings of the clergy and their financial exactions, was by upbringing and policy inclined to the French alliance. Yet he wanted a price for his adherence to France and Rome, and circumstances played into his hands. The pope, fearful that Scotland might follow England's example, was ready to concede anything James asked; at the same time, France and the Empire, in their phases of hostility to England, sought Scottish support, while England, anxious to avoid encirclement, also wooed the Scots. For a few years Scotland played a part in the international scene in almost ludicrous disproportion to its real importance. Negotiations with the emperor, which brought James the order of the Golden Fleece, so raised his price in the English and French markets that he received the orders of the Garter and St Michael as well. Similarly, negotiations for other marriages ultimately induced the French king to concede his daughter Madeleine, and on her death James contracted a second French marriage, to Mary of Guise.

Henry VIII retorted by urging on James the financial advantages of dissolving the monasteries, and in 1541 he brought him to the point of agreeing to a meeting at York. James, however, thanks to papal complaisance, was getting all he wanted from the church already, and the Scottish clergy, alarmed at the proposed meeting, offered a subsidy and pointed out how their king could profit by prosecuting wealthy Scots for heresy. James therefore did not turn up at York, to the fury of Henry, who had made the long journey for the only time in his life. In the war that followed, James could not carry his people with him. The memory of Flodden checked enthusiasm for an attack on England, Scots who favoured reform were critical of the use of their country as a French and papal tool, and James's domestic policies had alienated many of his subjects. The Scots were routed at an engagement at Solway Moss (24 November 1542). James died in the following month, leaving as his heir a week-old daughter, Mary.

Scotland, divided internally, was now to be subjected to external pressure as France and England each sought, sometimes by war and sometimes by diplomacy, to turn it into a satellite. England was first in the field. Ever since James IV had married Margaret Tudor in 1503, the union of the crowns had not been an entirely remote contingency, but at this point, when Henry VIII had three children living—Mary, Elizabeth and Edward—it seemed more unlikely than at any other time in the century that the Scottish line would succeed to England. However, it was 1286 all over again. A Scottish king had died leaving a little girl to succeed him; the English throne was occupied by an ambitious king who was great-uncle to the infant queen, this time Henry VIII, who, like Edward I, had a son and heir, Edward, a boy of five. Again it was proposed that Scotland and England should be united by the marriage of the two children. Whereas Edward I's marriage scheme had come at the end of two centuries during which the two countries had been drawing together, Henry's came after two and a half centuries during which war had been almost incessant. Yet Henry, like his predecessors, had agents in Scotland. Scottish lords who had been taken prisoner when fighting—reluctantly—at Solway Moss were released on giving undertakings to Henry. Gaining ascendancy over the Earl of Arran, the governor, they began negotiations for the English marriage, imprisoned Cardinal David Beaton, head of the Scottish hierarchy, and authorised the circulation of the Bible in the vernacular. Henry's envoy reported that if a cartload of Bibles were sent to Scotland 'they would be bought every one'—a remark which has sometimes been misquoted to suggest that the English sent cartloads of Bibles to convert the Scots. However, within a few months Beaton was again at large to rally the French party, and he prevailed on the governor to withdraw from the marriage treaty.

Henry, in his fury, launched two invasions on Scotland

(1544–5), and the Earl of Hertford, who led them, returned in 1547, as Duke of Somerset and Protector of England in the minority of Edward VI, to defeat the Scots at Pinkie and plant garrisons at a number of strong points in the south-east. In this action for breach of promise, known as the Rough Wooing, the English devastated the land from the Tweed to the Forth. What it meant in human misery when most people were dependent for their survival on food grown at their own doors can only be guessed, and it did nothing to endear the English cause to the Scots. England, however, could as usual find fifth-columnists. Henry encouraged plots against Beaton, who was murdered in 1546. He revived the policy of appealing to Celtic separatism, and an English-sponsored administration appeared in the west Highlands. He also tried hard to gain the support of nobles by direct bribery, but in this he was outbidden by the Scottish and French governments. More was done by religious propaganda, for to some Scots the attraction exerted by a country which had broken with Rome outweighed patriotism. Nor can it be overlooked that many lairds and burgesses saw economic advantages in Anglo-Scottish peace.

As Scotland was distracted by disaffection, it could not of its own resources eject the English garrisons, and had to appeal to France. Help was given, on condition that Queen Mary, who had been destined to be the bride of the heir to the throne of England, should be sent to France in 1548 as the prospective bride of the Dauphin, the heir to the throne of France. But Scotland had escaped from an English occupation only to risk a French occupation. Especially after 1554, when Arran was superseded as governor by Mary of Guise, the queen mother, Frenchmen were appointed to offices of state and French soldiers were introduced to garrison Scottish fortresses. In 1558 Mary married the Dauphin, Francis, who in the following year became king of France. Contemporaries did not know, as we do, that Francis would die in less than three years, leaving Mary a childless widow. The likelihood was that Mary and he would have children and that their descendants would rule both France and Scotland. The prospect for Scotland was absorption into France.

The Scottish reaction was predictable. French troops had never been welcome in Scotland and the Scots were not going to risk their persons or their fortunes in an aggressive war against England. Thus patriotic resentment against French domination reinforced the other motives which, for a generation, had been leading to the growth of an anti-French and pro-English party. Even so, it is doubtful if a revolution could have been carried through had a situation not developed in which Scottish dissidents could again obtain English help. Mary Tudor, the English queen who had pursued a papalist policy, died in November 1558 and was succeeded by her sister Elizabeth. But Elizabeth, born to Anne Boleyn while Henry VIII's first wife, Catherine of Aragon, still lived, was, in the eyes of Roman Catholics, illegitimate, and Mary Stewart, as the next heir, assumed the style of Queen of England. It was clearly to Elizabeth's interest to have the French ejected from bases which could be used to launch a pretender on her realm.

Elizabeth's opportunity came in 1559. In the spring Mary of Guise suddenly turned fiercely on the Protestant preachers, but their lay friends, who styled themselves the 'Lords of the Congregation', prepared to support them, and John Knox arrived from Geneva in May to incite attacks on religious houses. The insurgents gathered enough strength to occupy Edinburgh. But their untrained and ill-paid forces could not keep the field, and the regent's French professionals were soon able to regain the capital and await reinforcements in Leith, which was turned into a fortress impregnable except to artillery such as the rebels did not possess. Twelve years earlier the Scots had called in the French to rid their country of the English: now they could liberate themselves from the French only with the help of England.

The rebels may have toyed with the idea of deposing their absent queen, but opinion was on the whole against this, and a kind of provisional government was formed, with a figurehead in the Duke of Châtelherault (formerly Earl of Arran), the heir presumptive. Elizabeth had even less taste than the Scots for deposing sovereigns, but was prepared to come to terms with an administration under such respectable leadership. She sent help, first by sea, then by land, and in July 1560, after the situation had been simplified by the death of Mary of Guise, peace was made by the Treaty of Edinburgh, between England and France. In 1548 the only escape from an English occupation had been a French occupation, but this time the forces of both countries were to withdraw, leaving the Scots to settle their own affairs. It is significant of the dependence of Scottish affairs on the international situation that at this crisis the settlement was made by an agreement between two foreign powers. The diplomatic revolution of 1560 was to prove permanent, for after it, although there were still vicissitudes in Anglo-Scottish relations, Scotland never again feared conquest by an English monarch or had to appeal to France for protection. A month after the Treaty of Edinburgh Parliament repudiated papal authority and adopted a reformed Confession of Faith.

It seemed possible that Mary, who had been in France for twelve years and whose husband was now king of France, might never return to a Scotland which had decisively rejected the French cause. But in December 1560 Francis II died. Mary's better prospects were now in Scotland, if only as a possible avenue to the throne of England on which her heart was set. She came back in August 1561, and showed considerable skill in conciliating the reformers in Scotland while at the same time reassuring Roman Catholics in England and on the continent. For a time it was hoped that Elizabeth and she would meet and that Mary, in return for recognising Elizabeth's right during her lifetime, would be acknowledged as her heir presumptive. But Elizabeth could not be brought either to a conference with Mary or to recognition of her right of succession, and this uncooperative attitude went far to render bankrupt the opportunist policy which Mary had until now been pursuing. Then in 1565 Mary married Henry Stewart, Lord Darnley. His father, the fourth Earl of Lennox, stood next to the Hamilton family in the Scottish succession and, by marrying the daughter of Margaret Tudor, widow of James IV, by her second husband, the Earl of Angus, he had put his family next after Mary in the English succession. The son of Mary and Darnley, born on

45

19 June 1566, thus had a double claim to be Elizabeth's heir. Darnley was murdered on 10 February 1567 and after Mary married the Earl of Bothwell, universally suspected of being his murderer, she was deposed in favour of her infant son and in 1568 fled to England, where she was kept a prisoner.

The faction which put James VI on the throne contained some of the leaders of the party which had carried through the revolution of 1560 with English assistance, and might have expected countenance from Elizabeth now. But the English queen was still no enthusiast for rebellion against a lawful sovereign; Mary's supporters, as well as James's, included many Protestants and old friends to the English alliance; and some of Elizabeth's advisers thought that England was best served by the strife of factions in Scotland. Not until 1573, therefore, did an English force intervene decisively and enable the king's party to capture Edinburgh Castle, Mary's last stronghold. But problems in Anglo-Scottish relations were still unsolved. Mary's claim to the English succession made her a potential agent of both English and continental Roman Catholics, and as long as she lived it was hard to make a conclusive case for James as Elizabeth's heir. Only in 1586 was Elizabeth persuaded to conclude a formal Anglo-Scottish league. It provided for mutual defence against papalist states, but its greater significance lay elsewhere. Mary's existence was ignored, though she was not executed until the following February; James became Elizabeth's pensioner, to the tune of £4,000 a year, though he was to learn that payments could be adjusted from year to year according to his behaviour; and Elizabeth undertook to do nothing to prejudice any claim he had to the English succession unless he provoked her.

There were still tortuous negotiations to be carried out with foreign powers and English politicians to woo them into acquiescence in James's claims. But doubts and hesitations dwindled, alternatives acceptable to English opinion were hard to see, and few can have been surprised when, on 25 March 1603, James VI of Scotland became James I of England. It was a purely personal union. There were still two kingdoms, each with its own parliament, administration, church and legal system. James himself would gladly have integrated the two, but, although he had the support of far-sighted men on both sides of the Border, his proposals were on the whole unwelcome. He did assume the title of King of Great Britain, but even this was distasteful to many, and after nearly four hundred years the people of England have not become accustomed to its use; a union flag was designed, but it offended the Scots, who complained that the English cross of St George was drawn through the Scottish cross of St Andrew, 'which is thereby obscurit'. However, by a Scottish statute of 1607 and an English judicial decision in 1608, all the king's subjects born after his accession to England shared a single nationality, and some laws which had restricted traffic between the countries were abrogated.

The fact was, of course, that dynastic accident, while it could join two states, could not unite two peoples or guarantee that a union of two kingdoms which had so long existed separately, even though in a single island, would be enduring. After all, continental history presents examples of the dissolution of unions which seemed equally inevitable—the Scandinavian kingdoms, Holland and Belgium, Spain and Portugal; in each of those instances union was achieved for a time, but the ultimate solution was separation. In Britain, however, there were subtle ways in which the two nations were being brought into partnership.

The linguistic link which had first been created with the English settlements in Lothian in the sixth century had grown ever stronger with the spread of Lowland Scots. Its earlier history can be traced, if traced at all, only in place-names, but, largely on their evidence, Professor Barrow has concluded that 'there is plenty of evidence that English-speaking people could be found in the thirteenth century in Dumfriesshire and Ayrshire, in Clydesdale and in many parts of Scotland north of Forth'. English was, after all, the language of business: the tongue of the burgesses, in the areas where there were burghs, ousted the French of the aristocrats and the Gaelic of the countryfolk. The late fourteenth century saw the composition of the first substantial verse in the Scottish vernacular, John Barbour's poem *The Bruce*, a spirited account of Robert I's doings in the struggle for independence.

Not long afterwards John Wyntoun, prior of Lochleven, composed an *Orygynal Cronicle* which began with the creation and came down to his own day; it is in Scots verse, more remarkable for its ingenuity and quaintness than for any poetical inspiration. Scottish poetry really begins with James I, who told the story of his captivity in England and his love for Joan Beaufort in *The Kingis Quair*, a work reaching high poetic quality. It was, too, about this time that Latin, which had hitherto been the all but invariable language for legal deeds (French made an occasional appearance) and which was not to be finally ousted until the nineteenth century, began to be displaced occasionally by Lowland Scots, for the earliest vernacular deeds belong to about 1380. There is a remark in the *Scotichronicon*, also belonging to this period, that the diocese of Argyll had been separated from that of Dunkeld in about 1200 because the Bishop of Dunkeld did not understand the language of the people of Argyll; this is not, of course, evidence that English prevailed in Perthshire by 1200, but it does prove that by about 1400 a Lowlander thought that the language barrier fell between Perthshire and Argyll.

By the sixteenth century Lowland Scots had hardly a rival except in the central and west Highlands. John Major, writing in about 1520, said that Gaelic was spoken by 'half Scotland', and it would be spread over half the area of the country, but the proportion of people who spoke it can have been little more than a quarter. By James IV's reign Gaelic was extinct in Ayrshire, and in Galloway it seems to have died out between that period and the Reformation. Reports that it survived in various parts of the Lowlands until later are the tales of travellers, who, even in the twentieth century, have been known to put down as 'Gaelic' some localised version of Scots which they found unintelligible. In the three northern counties, the Norn tongue became extinct in Caithness and was well on the way to extinction in Orkney, while even in Shetland the latest extant deed in the old language belongs to 1607. In the Highlands and the western isles, although they were broadly Gaelic-speaking areas, most men of substance were probably already bilingual, and the remarkable scarcity of deeds and records in Gaelic is so striking as to suggest that by the time Latin ceased to be the normal language for legal purposes there was no difficulty about the adoption of English.

Although the language spoken by the majority of the people of Scotland was a tongue which had diverged considerably from the English of England, most of those who were using it had called it 'English' and were prepared to concede the style 'Scots' to the Gaelic of the west—very properly from an historical point of view. However, in the sixteenth century the tendency was to dub Gaelic as 'Irish'—also appropriately enough from an historical point of view—and to claim patriotically that the language of the Lowlanders was 'Scots'. This happened most opportunely, to differentiate the speech of Lowlanders from the standard English which now began to penetrate into Scotland. Any chance there may ever have been that Lowland Scots would prevail as the language of the country vanished with the Reformation. It is one of the most important facts in their history that the Scottish people never had a printed Bible in their own tongue. And alongside an English version of the Bible there was an English *Book of Common Prayer*, an English *Book of Homilies*, an English *Book of Common Order* and even an English *Metrical Psalter*. The anglophile character of the Reformation came out very strongly in this field and there was an immediate effect on Scottish literature.

Already before 1603 the Scottish Lowland vernacular was in a fair way to being displaced as a literary language. Although there was a long and healthy tradition of Scottish verse, English was readily adopted in its place, for example by William Alexander (1567–1640) and William Drummond (1585–1649). With prose there was no such native tradition, and it may be said that Scots prose was extinguished before it had a chance fully to develop. Although one or two narratives of the first half of the sixteenth century, and passages in official records like the Acts of Council, show how effective and vigorous it could be, it was never adapted for use in the loftier subjects like theology and philosophy. In prose generally there was a change direct from Latin to English, without an intermediate phase of Scots.

Even without assimilation of the two languages, works written in southern English would be intelligible enough to Scots, and there is plenty of evidence of their familiarity with English poetry from that of Chaucer onwards. This meant that the rich heritage of Elizabethan and Jacobean England was the heritage of Scots as well as English. Indeed, the ready access of the Scots to works in English probably militated against the development of the Scottish printing press, which had a meagre output indeed until late in the seventeenth century. Because the Scots could read English, there was little Scots printing; because there was little Scots printing there were few works available in Scots.

The fact that the Scotland which counted politically was a country speaking a form of English meant that Scotland, viewed from the standpoint of English policy, presented a problem quite different from either Wales or Ireland. It was even seriously argued in English courts before 1603 whether Scots should be reckoned as aliens in England because, from the judicial point of view, the chief mark of an alien was that he spoke a different language.

At first after the Reformation there was no doubt in men's minds that Scotland and England shared one religion. In 1571 the king's party besought Elizabeth to 'take upon her the maintenance and protection of the true religion preached and established in both the realms', and in 1585 the articles for a treaty between England and Scotland began with a reference to 'the true, ancient Christian religion which they now profess'. By 1585 it was indeed apparent that there were differences, for Presbyterianism had become far stronger in Scotland than it was ever to be in England. But both ecclesiastical factions thought in terms of uniformity throughout Britain, whether on a Presbyterian or an Episcopalian foundation.

It was this last feature which, before half a century had passed, was to impose an intolerable strain on the personal union. It could endure only as long as the crown, the unifying factor, was stronger than the separate institutions of the two countries. James VI and Charles I had serious trouble from time to time with the English Parliament, but until 1640 they could if necessary carry on the government without it; the Scottish Parliament might be restive, but was relatively powerless against the crown.

Page 51 Interior of Leuchars Church—the Norman architecture of the twelfth century at its best

Page 52 (*above*) Bothwell Castle—the opulence of the thirteenth century;
(*below*) Borthwick Castle—the solid austerity of the fifteenth century

Thus the personal union endured. But in the later part of Charles I's reign the situation changed. The Scots, after banding together in the National Covenant (1638) against the king's ecclesiastical and constitutional innovations, took up arms against him. In England civil war began in 1642. For a time it seemed that in these novel circumstances union might be achieved on a new basis, for in 1643, by the Solemn League and Covenant, the Scots agreed to give military aid to the English Parliament on condition, so at least they understood, that the Presbyterian system would be imposed on England. This seemed logical, but power in England passed from Parliament, which on the whole favoured Presbyterianism, to the army, which upheld Congregationalism. There was soon a different constitutional emphasis as well, for the English Parliamentarians and the Scots, while they might fight against the king, believed in the monarchy, whereas the English army moved towards republicanism. Thus the two countries began to follow divergent courses in both religion and politics. In the end, the English executed Charles I and established a commonwealth, the Scots accepted Charles II as king on condition that he would adhere to the Covenants. The result of this breakdown of the personal union was the conquest of Scotland by English armies (1651).

This was union of a kind—a union by force such as had not been known since the days of Edward I. The Scottish government had collapsed in the face of the English invaders, who declined to recognise any authority not derived from their own commonwealth. Thus the Scottish representatives who were consulted were brought together at the behest of the English administration, and their consent, both to the principle of union and to its details, was a mere formality. It was remarked that the embodying of Scotland with England was 'as when the poor bird is embodied in the hawk that hath eaten it up'. The members who went from Scotland to the commonwealth and protectorate parliaments at Westminster were, almost by definition, collaborators, and a good many of them were actually officers of the English army. The truth, plain for all to see behind the façade, was that Scotland was an occupied country, with an authoritarian government in which

53

power lay mainly with the officers of garrisons at Leith, Inverness, Inverlochy, Perth and Ayr and a number of subsidiary posts. Almost as detestable as the military character of the administration, and its financial exactions, was its ecclesiastical policy: it dismissed the General Assembly, tolerated 'diverse ways of worshipping God', and encouraged sectarianism and schism. Most Scots believed that only Presbyterianism should be permitted, and many of them, devotees of the Solemn League, believed that it was Scotland's mission to presbyterianise England; as long as that obsession lasted harmonious Anglo-Scottish relations were impossible.

To many Scots union was not abhorrent in principle, and in 1648, when the moderate Covenanters came to terms with Charles I, they had recommended a closer union, or, failing that, the sharing of economic and commercial rights. But the Scots wanted union on negotiated terms, and there was on the whole a sense of relief when, with the restoration of Charles II in 1660, the existing union was dissolved. However, the conditions in which a personal union could operate successfully were not restored, for the English Parliament was much stronger than of old and even the Scottish Parliament was more assertive. Not only were the two countries at loggerheads in their commercial policies, but Scotland, dragged into England's wars with Holland, saw her traditional trading patterns disrupted by hostilities she had never sought. In 1670 the two parliaments did appoint commissioners to consider union, but the Scottish demands for equal representation in a united parliament were quite unrealistic and the English were not ready to concede the trading rights which the Scots demanded. Negotiations broke down. The later years of Charles II and the reign of James VII saw some recovery of royal authority, and the personal union continued under something approaching absolutism.

The Revolution of 1688–9, which replaced James by William of Orange, again created difficulties. The English Parliament had won a resounding victory over the crown by dictating terms to the new monarch; it now sat every year and played an ever larger part in shaping policy. The Scottish Parliament, too, now had a will of its own. The ability of the two parliaments to pursue conflicting policies threatened the fabric of the union. William's administration was unpopular in Scotland for many reasons, and Anglo-Scottish commercial friction came to a head with the establishment of a Company of Scotland designed to compete with the English East India Company and with the failure—for which William was blamed—of an attempt by the Scots to find an outlet for their trade by planting a colony at Darien near Panama. William found himself king over two countries with divergent economic policies and even divergent foreign policies, for the Darien venture involved a quarrel with Spain, a country with which William had special reasons for wanting to keep the peace. Shortly before his death he recommended an attempt to find a solution by a closer union.

It was becoming increasingly evident that Scotland was in danger of subjection not to a king of England who was also—though he sometimes seemed to forget the fact—king of Scots, but to the English ministry of the day which advised him. Yet no amount of Scottish agitation about economic grievances would have brought union nearer, for it did nothing to induce among the English a desire for union and a readiness to extend commercial privileges to the Scots. The opportunity of the Scots arose from novel circumstances. In 1689 Scotland and England had separately made identical settlements of the succession after William and Mary, but at the time it seemed unnecessary to go beyond their offspring and that of Mary's sister, Anne. However, William and Mary had no children, and the last of Anne's children died in 1700. In 1701 England designated Sophia, Electress Dowager of Hanover, the senior Protestant in the royal line, and her heirs, as future sovereigns of England. But no such act was passed in Scotland. Thus in 1702, with the death of William and the opening of the War of the Spanish Succession, England was faced with the possibility that during a life-and-death struggle against France and Spain, Anne might die and Scotland choose a different sovereign from England, to become once more a potential base for a hostile continental power.

There were three possibilities. Scotland might follow England's example and settle the crown on the Hanoverian line, under whom the personal union could continue as before; Scotland could make a different choice and bring the existing union to an end; or some closer form of union could be devised which would obviate a recurrence of such a crisis. The first course commended itself to few Scots, for they would thereby throw away their principal bargaining counter and would continue to be frustrated by English economic restrictions and humiliated by having to acquiesce in policies shaped by English ministers. The second course was utterly unacceptable to England. The third—closer union—offered opportunities for negotiation in which the Scots could hope for concessions in return for giving up their somewhat shadowy independence.

In 1703–4 the Scottish Parliament forcibly demonstrated the seriousness of the situation by passing an Act anent Peace and War and an Act of Security. The first in effect provided for an independent Scottish foreign policy even if the personal union continued; the second proclaimed that on Anne's death the Scottish estates were to nominate a successor, of the royal line of Scotland and a protestant, but not the successor to the crown of England unless the sovereignty of the Scottish kingdom, the power of its Parliament, its religion, liberty and trade, should be secured against English or any foreign interference. This brought retaliation from England in the Alien Act: Scots were to lose their English nationality, and certain traffic across the Border was to cease, unless the Scots either accepted the same heir as England or appointed commissioners to treat for union. The Scots were not likely to do the first and thereby throw away their main card, but the second course was what a good many men in both countries by this time really wanted.

When commissioners met to negotiate there can have been little doubt about the broad lines of the settlement they must reach. The idea of union was no novelty, and discussions, formal and informal, which had taken place intermittently during a century, as well as the lessons of the Cromwellian experiment, showed what would be acceptable. An outline agreement had actually been drawn up in 1703. England was bound to stipulate for an incorporating union, the Hanoverian succession and the substantial uniformity of fiscal policy. The Scots, in return, were bound to exact, besides security for their church and their legal system, not only freedom of trade with England and her colonies but also fiscal concessions which would ease the transition period before complete uniformity operated and compensate the Scots for shouldering part of the burden of England's national debt. Scotland's proportion of a taxation, based on an estimate of her relative poverty, was set at only one-fortieth of the English proportion, and her representation in the British Parliament, based on a compromise between her relative poverty and her population (which was probably a fifth that of England), was set at about one tenth of the English—45 members of the House of Commons and 16 representative peers in the House of Lords.

The Articles of Union embodying these conditions had to be debated in the Scottish Parliament. There was much strong feeling against them: the remnant of Covenanters objected to the final extinction of the policy of the Solemn League, and more moderate Presbyterians found it hard to swallow the subjection of Scotland to a Parliament predominantly Anglican in its membership; Episcopalians objected to a settlement which made the maintenance of Presbyterianism a 'fundamental and essential' condition of union; and Jacobites saw in the Hanoverian succession a blow to their hopes. But all this did not constitute a united opposition. On the other hand, the commercial concessions had a wide appeal, most Protestants welcomed the Hanoverian succession, the legal profession and those who valued Scots law were satisfied. It is no mystery why the terms were accepted. The opposition proved extraordinarily irresolute in parliament and the simplest explanation of their antics is their uncomfortable awareness that the union might after all be the best thing for their country. Besides, what was the alternative? England was not going to permit a disruption of the existing union, and the scanty and ill-trained Scottish regiments could not have resisted Marlborough's veterans.

If patriotic Scots concluded that rejection of union might bring civil war and armed conquest it is to their credit. There is certainly no need to postulate bribery to explain what happened. Admittedly, the prospective abolition of Scottish offices, some of them highly lucrative, was going to weigh against the uncertain prospects of promotion in the south, and it was reasonable for leading politicians to expect compensation. Besides, in those days and long after, MPs had to be 'managed' by the executive, and patronage was an essential instrument in carrying on the government. In the passing of the union, therefore, certain tactics were employed which had no novelty about them and which were to persist for another century and more in British politics. A certain amount of actual cash did change hands, but much of it consisted of sums already owing, most of it went to men already committed to the union, some of it to men who continued to oppose the union, and some of it consisted of amounts far too trifling to affect the attitude of even the most impecunious Scots peer. Dr P.W.J. Riley, in *The Union of England and Scotland*, made a full examination of the membership of the last Scottish parliament — not only the nobles, on whom attention has focussed, but the burgh and shire commissioners as well — to elucidate the background of each member, to discover their earlier political attitudes and to determine whether their opinions changed. His conclusion was that money had an effect on the voting pattern.

Yet the Scots made a grave miscalculation. They thought of the treaty as a written constitution, and, even with all the concessions they had obtained, they would not have accepted that an omnicompetent parliament had power to abrogate provisions which they fondly imagined to be 'fundamental and essential'. Defoe, a contemporary observer, thought that if the terms of the union were violated it would be ipso facto dissolved, and in 1776, when John Wilkes moved a bill to improve parliamentary representation, he said that even to alter the proportion of MPs laid down in 1707 'would be a breach of public faith and a violation of a solemn treaty between two independent states'. But the theories of English constitutional lawyers prevailed, and the union has proved to have no more sanctity than any other statute. From time to time attempts have been made to appeal to the terms of union, but always without success. The list of violations of the treaty is already a long one, and always growing longer. The abolition of the Scottish mint, the abolition of the heritable jurisdictions, the withdrawal of the privileges of the royal burghs, the successive increases in the number of Scottish members of the House of Commons, the abolition of the election of Scottish representative peers (1963), the abolition of the Scottish privy seal, the freeing of university teachers from the need to be members of the Church of Scotland—all these have been violations of the union. So was decimalisation, and so indeed is metrication. The fact is that, contrary to the beliefs and hopes of those who framed it, the treaty of union has proved to be a mere scrap of paper, to be torn up at the whim of any British government.

The union of the two peoples had, though with many vicissitudes, been in the making in the course of many centuries before the union of the crowns and the union of the parliaments. The events of 1603 and 1707 were only two incidents in a long process, a process of which it is not easy to discern the beginning and a process of which we have not yet seen the end.

CHAPTER 3

The Monarchy

For many centuries central government meant the king in person rather than any impersonal crown in the shape of institutions which could maintain rule irrespective of the capacity and attention of the monarch. We are not without information about early dynasties, for 'lists of kings' so abound that they have perhaps been more of an embarrassment than a help to those who have thought it worth while to study them. It seems that the Pictish royal family had matrilineal succession, so that a king was succeeded not by his son but by his brother, as his mother's son, or his nephew, as his sister's son, or by a cousin. A Pictish king could be fathered by a foreign prince, and so inherit another kingdom through his male ancestry.

In the united kingdom of the Picts and Scots the succession is said to have been affected by Irish practice, whereby any member of what was called the *derbfine* was eligible to succeed; *derbfine* meant 'certain kindred', and anyone whose father, grandfather or great-grandfather had been king—which was as far as most men know their ancestry—could advance a claim. The 'eldest and worthiest' of such claimants was supposed to become king, so that a brother might be preferred to a young son or a cousin to a younger brother. There was a constant temptation for a trial of strength to determine who was worthiest, and although a reigning king could try to obviate trouble by designating a successor or 'tanist', the tanist himself might be challenged. In practice there was more often than not a bloody conflict, ending in the accession not of the eldest and worthiest but of the strongest and least scrupulous. Out of the fourteen kings who reigned between 943 and 1097, ten were killed in feuds, usually in favour of a successor: the fourteenth of the line was merely blinded and mutilated.

Attempts have been made to rationalise these sanguinary on-goings, but this kind of 'free for all' among the members of a family was common among primitive peoples, Germanic as well as Celtic. The Vandals had a law that a king should be succeeded not by his next of kin but by his eldest relative. In Denmark, over a period of a century, not one king was the son of his predecessor, and in England, during the ten reigns in the hundred years before the Norman Conquest, there was hardly a succession that was not disputed and only twice did a son succeed a father. Primogeniture did not arrive in England even with the Normans. William I was followed by his second son; Matilda, the daughter of Henry I, was set aside in favour of her cousin, Stephen; Stephen's son was set aside in favour of his cousin, Matilda's son, Henry II. Henry II's eldest son, Richard, was succeeded by his brother, John, who murdered their nephew, Arthur, who had a better claim by primogeniture. Indefeasible right by primogeniture was not finally established until Tudor times, for the Wars of the Roses in the fifteenth century bear some resemblance to what had been happening in Scotland in the eleventh.

On the death of Malcolm II in 1034, Scotland was faced with a succession problem not unlike the more celebrated one which was to occur after the deaths of Alexander III and the Maid of Norway. Malcolm had no son, and all the male lines in his immediate kindred had been liquidated. He was succeeded by Duncan I, the son of one of his daughters, but there were competitors in Thorfinn, Earl of Orkney, son of another daughter of Malcolm II, and Macbeth, who may have been the son of a daughter of either Malcolm or Malcolm's father, Kenneth II. Macbeth must himself have been in the royal line, for his marriage to Gruoch, a grand-daughter of Kenneth II or Kenneth III, gave him no claim. At any rate, Duncan was defeated and killed, and Thorfinn and Macbeth possibly partitioned the kingdom between them. In short, Macbeth, far from being the usurper of legend, proved his worthiness in the customary manner and was acceptable to most of his subjects. It was only with the help of a southern army that the elder son of Duncan was able to establish himself as Malcolm III, after killing first Macbeth and then Macbeth's stepson, Lulach. When Malcolm III died in 1093 his brother Donald, the eldest male of the house, asserted his worthiness by seizing the throne and killing Malcolm's eldest son by his first wife, who, like his father before him, had obtained southern help and reigned briefly as Duncan II. Donald was next confronted by Edgar, Malcolm's eldest surviving son by his second marriage. Edgar had a poor claim, since his uncle Donald was the eldest male of the house and the heir by primogeniture was the son of his late half-brother Duncan, but, as with his father and his half-brother before him, English might supplemented his feeble right. It was Edgar and the other descendants of Malcolm III and his English wife Margaret, best thought of as 'the Margaretsons', who kept the throne. But the descendants of Duncan II troubled them for over a century.

Within the Margaretson line, the succession went on without a break, yet less by design than because within their kindred there was hardly ever a serious alternative to the heir by primogeniture. Edgar, who was unmarried, was followed by his next brother, Alexander I, and to the childless Alexander succeeded the next brother, David. David had only one son, Henry, who reached adult years, and when Henry predeceased his father the next in line was Henry's elder son, the twelve-year-old Malcolm IV. Then William, a younger brother, was the only possible heir to the childless Malcolm. When William died, his son, Alexander, was already sixteen and therefore not a minor. On the death of Alexander II there was no alternative to the eight-year-old Alexander III.

But primogeniture was not regarded as a foregone conclusion. David I, to ensure that his son Henry would succeed, caused him to be styled 'king-designate'. Then, when Henry died before his father, Henry's son Malcolm was conducted round the land to be seen by his future subjects. William the Lion did not marry until 1186, when he was about forty-three—the early Margaretsons showed little enthusiasm for matrimony—and his heir was not born until twelve years later. It must have looked for a time as if William was not going to have a son, and it is said that in 1195 he proposed to designate one of his daughters as his successor, but that the Scottish magnates opposed this suggestion, arguing that his brother David and his nephew, John the Scot, should be preferred to a daughter.

Alexander II married when he was twenty-three but had no children by his first marriage, which lasted for seventeen years, and when his first wife died, in 1238, there must once again have been despair about a direct heir. To make matters worse, John the Scot, Alexander's cousin, had died childless in the previous year. Therefore, in 1238, so it was alleged, a Scottish council declared that if Alexander II did die without a son he should be succeeded by Robert Bruce, Lord of Annandale, the nearest male of the royal line (though inheriting through a female), to the exclusion of females. The crisis came to an end with the second marriage of Alexander II in 1239 and the birth of his son, the future Alexander III, in 1241.

Reviewing these events one can see, all too clearly, that the Scots had been very lucky to have preserved a regular succession. One can see, too, that when Alexander III's two sons and his daughter died in his lifetime he could not take it for granted that his grand-daughter, the infant Maid of Norway, would succeed him. He therefore, in 1284, obtained from the magnates of the realm a formal undertaking to accept the child as his successor.

Even so, Margaret's accession on her grandfather's death was contested by Robert Bruce, who brought forward the 1238 declaration in his favour. Bruce had put his name to the under-taking in 1284 to accept the Maid, but he may have argued that he had then envisaged the succession of a woman of marriageable age, possibly a woman already married, whose husband would be king, and that he had not bargained for the accession of a child of three. However, Bruce seems to have withdrawn his opposition, for in 1289 he assented to a treaty by which Scotland, England and Norway made plans for the acceptance of the Maid in Scotland.

When the Maid died, and the momentous competition for the throne was submitted to the adjudication of Edward I, Bruce again put forward his claim. But the settlement of 1238 had been made under circumstances which no longer obtained. Bruce was the son of the second daughter of David, Earl of Huntingdon, younger brother of William the Lion, and in 1238 it had been logical to prefer him to the line of the eldest daughter, then represented only by a female. But by 1290 the line of the eldest daughter also had a male representative, in the person of John Balliol. On the principle of primogeniture, which the Scottish succession had now so long followed in practice and on which Edward I's own tenure of the English throne was based, Balliol now had the best right. Bruce's contention that his claim was superior because he belonged to an older generation and so was nearer the common royal ancestor seems a weak one, though he could with truth have asserted that, at the age of eighty, he was older, if not worthier, than his rival.

When Edward's choice, Balliol, abdicated after his four years' reign, Scotland was again without a king, though there was a lingering loyalty to Balliol. But the significant thing is that the concept of the identity, the integrity, of the kingdom had become too strong to depend on the presence, or even the existence, of a king in person. The first visible symbol of this had been the seal made for the 'guardians' who were appointed to govern the realm when Alexander III was succeeded by his little grand-daughter in Norway. The seals of the kings had depicted the monarch enthroned on one side and mounted on the other, but the seal of the guardians bore the figure of St Andrew, Scotland's patron saint, on one side, and a lion rampant, the badge of the Scottish kings, on the other. 'The Lion', it became evident from two slightly later incidents, symbolised the lawful government of the realm. Thus, in 1304, when Scotland was once more without a king, the defenders of Stirling Castle declared that their allegiance was to 'the Lion'. And in 1336, with the boy-king David II absent in France, there were Scots who asserted that they were subjects 'of the Lion and none other'.

Besides, in the years when Scotland was kingless, another concept emerged besides that of the impersonal crown: ultimate power or sovereignty was seen to lie with what was called 'the community of the realm'. This community, so it was declared, chose the guardians after the death of Alexander III; Wallace and

Moray, as well as the guardians who carried on resistance later, claimed to be acting in the name of the community of the realm; and Robert Bruce's propagandists asserted that he had been chosen as king by 'the whole community of the realm'. There can be little doubt that the ph--se was synonymous with the *bone gent*, *probi homines*, 'good men' and *haut hommes* who protested in 1291 when Edward insisted on Scottish acknowledgement of his overlordship. The words were to change their meanings later, when any free man, it may be assumed, was technically a *probus vir*. But in the days of Bruce there was no question of the 'community' meaning all free men or all citizens. In practice, a handful of notables, lay and clerical, were usually the active force, but claimed to be acting on behalf of what might be called the significant men or politically conscious citizens. There is no mystery about the term 'community', which was then in common currency. In contemporary England the coronation oath referred to laws which 'the community of the realm shall determine', and parliamentary proceedings referred to the 'community' apparently as something wider than the prelates, earls and barons. There were also 'communities' below the national level. The 'communities' of the burghs of Scotland are mentioned in 1296; in 1309, when Bruce was laying the foundations of his kingship, the 'communities' of several earldoms were said to support him; on the other side of the Border, an English shire was well understood to constitute a 'community'. The significance of the phrase can be exaggerated, but it does indicate a notion of cohesion, of a corporate entity, almost of a 'corporation' in a quasi-legal sense, and this was to make a valuable contribution to constitutional development.

The statement in the Declaration of Arbroath in 1320 that the magnates and the community had it in their power to 'make' a king was no mere verbiage, for the community, embodied in parliament, had already defined the succession by statute. There might have been no need for a statutory definition had there been a direct line of lawful male heirs, but there was not. After Bannockburn, King Robert still had no legitimate son, and in 1315 a statute declared that the king's daughter, Marjory, agreed to give way to the king's brother, Edward, on the ground that he was a man skilled in war for the defence of the realm: this echoed the preference for the worthiest member of the royal house. The statute added that, failing heirs of Edward and Marjory, the leaders of the community were to take counsel for the choice of another king. Three years later, Edward Bruce was dead and Marjory also was dead, but by her marriage to Walter, the High Steward of Scotland, she had a son, Robert. In 1318 a fresh statute therefore acknowledged this infant as heir presumptive. When, in 1324, a son was at last born to King Robert's queen, there was evidently yet another statute affirming the right of this boy to succeed, and he became king as David II in 1329. But when all these definitions were being made, Edward Balliol, son of King John, was still the active representative of a senior line, and it is worth stressing that the Bruce, and subsequently the Stewart, tenure of the throne depended on statute, so that on what were later to become Jacobite principles neither would have been on the throne at all. Besides, when Edward Balliol challenged David II he found much support, perhaps because some thought he had as good a claim, against the child David, as Edward Bruce had had against the girl Marjory in 1315.

David II died childless in 1371 and was succeeded by his nephew, Robert the Steward, first of the Stewart kings. Robert had had several children by Elizabeth Mure long before he married her, and he was so closely related to her that canon law forbade their marriage. True, they had later obtained a dispensation authorising them to marry and legitimating issue already born or to be born, but this was one of many instances when no dispensation could wholly remove doubts about the legitimacy of children who, according to canon law, had been born in incest. After Elizabeth's death he had married Euphemia Ross, by whom he had children whose legitimacy was above reproach. In the hope of avoiding disputes, a statute of 1373 defined the succession as passing to each of the king's sons in turn, first those by his first wife and then those by his second, and the heirs male of each of them; female lines were explicitly excluded, though a final clause stated that, should all male lines fail, then 'the true and lawful heirs of the royal blood and kin' should succeed, which may mean that parliament could define the succession afresh.

The eldest son of Robert II by Elizabeth Mure did succeed as Robert III, and the crown remained with his descendants. But the family of Euphemia Ross from time to time disputed their claim. Her only surviving son was the figurehead of the conspiracy for the murder of James I in 1437. The vengeance taken on the murderers eliminated the male line of descent from Euphemia Ross, but there were descendants through females. True, they were excluded in terms of the statute of 1373, but another statute could have redefined the succession, and their existence was a kind of skeleton in the cupboard which caused uneasiness even so late as the reign of Charles I, when a descendant of Euphemia Ross recklessly declared that he had the best blood in the kingdom.

The succession became tenuous in the extreme—James I had only one surviving son, James II had only two sons who reached an age to marry, James III only one who married, and James IV only one who survived infancy—but it did go on, in a fashion which must have seemed almost miraculous. Then, when James V died in 1542, he was the last heir under the statute of 1373, but his daughter, at the age of one week, was unhesitatingly accepted as his successor. The contrast between what happened then and the uncertainty when the Maid of Norway succeeded shows how completely hereditary succession had come to be accepted.

In England, Plantagenet, Lancastrian, Yorkist and Tudor contested the throne, and no less than five kings—Edward II, Richard II, Henry VI, Edward V and Richard III—were done to death by subjects or rivals. In Scotland the score in such fatalities was only two—James I and James III—and the crown passed undeviatingly from father to son. There was never a wholly convincing rival to the ruling line, there were no wars of succession, no king was dethroned in favour of a competitor. Unquestionably this gave a certain stability, but, while strict adherence to heredity obviated disputes, it involved the acceptance as kings of minors, absentees or invalids. Robert II was fifty-five when he succeeded and he lived for another nineteen years, making him an uncommonly old man by the standards of the time. Then, after nineteen years of the increasingly senile Robert II, Scotland had

67

sixteen years of his invalid son, Robert III. As a direct outcome of
Anglo-Scottish warfare, two kings, David II and James I, were
prisoners in England, one for eleven, the other for eighteen years.
Anglo-Scottish warfare likewise led to the premature deaths of
James II and James IV, one at the siege of Roxburgh in 1460 and
the other at the battle of Flodden in 1513. The chief trouble was
minorities: every sovereign from James I to James VI, with the
solitary exception of James IV, succeeded as children, three of
them as infants; from the death of Robert I to the death of James
VI (1329–1625) there were seven minorities in ten reigns. All in
all, for two thirds of that long period Scotland did not have a
king able to exercise effective personal rule.

Besides, the early Stewarts can have enjoyed hardly any pre-
eminence. Three baronial families—Balliol, Bruce and Stewart—
had in turn been raised to the throne; would the third prove more
lasting than the first and second? A succession repeatedly defined
by statute might be altered by statute in favour of yet another
dynasty. The situation almost invited the putting forward of rival
claims, and it is surprising that there were not more of them. This
apart, the tenuous nature of the royal succession, when so often
only the king's own life stood between some noble and a royal
inheritance, meant that another actor was always waiting in the
wings. Thus, two Dukes of Albany and an Earl of Atholl were
successively heirs presumptive to James I; two Dukes of Albany
were heirs presumptive to James III, James IV and James V; and
an Earl of Arran was heir presumptive to Mary. If there is any
validity in Elizabeth Tudor's remark that to acknowledge a
successor was to set her winding-sheet before her eyes, then
assuredly those Scottish kings were not likely to forget their
winding sheets.

Not infrequently it fell to one of those heirs presumptive to act
as guardian, governor or regent during the minority or captivity
of a king, and the office brought both opportunities and tempta-
tions, if only to curry favour by easy-going rule. For some thirty
years—the end of Robert II's reign, most of Robert III's and the
captivity of James I—authority was vested in Robert, Duke of
Albany, who from 1406 carried on the government in his own

Page 69 St Mary's Church, Haddington, with the transepts and choir recently restored after being roofless since English invasions in the 1540s

Page 70 West Highland grave-slabs: (*left*) Cristinus MacGillescoil, Prior of Iona, c 1450; (*right*) Murchardus MacDuffie of Colonsay, died 1539

name, not in that of the absent king, and on his death in 1420 his authority passed to his son Murdoch. At this point Scotland was threatened with something like a line of 'mayors of the palace' who were not even competent rulers.

The whole period from the fourteenth century to the sixteenth is often seen as a melancholy repetition of the same pattern. Out of the strife and disturbance of a minority one family or another emerged with the powers of kingship as its prize: in the minority of James II it was the Livingstons, in that of James III it was the Boyds, in that of James V it was the Angus Douglases. The king, on attaining maturity, would deal firmly, even brutally, with those who had governed during his minority, he would endeavour to restore the resources of the crown and respect for the law, and would be making real headway when he was cut off while still in his prime—James II and James V were only thirty, James III was thirty-six and James IV was forty—and the whole miserable cycle would start all over again. The period is also seen as one of strife between the crown and 'the barons' or 'the magnates', and nineteenth- and twentieth-century historians have come down heavily on the side of the crown against 'the barons'. But historians, in this as in other matters, like to be on the winning side. The issue was never so clear-cut, if only because 'the barons' never united against the king and the king never, or hardly ever, pursued a policy opposed generally to 'the barons'. Besides, if it is true that nobles helped to keep the crown weak, would the alternative, the rule of a strong and absolute king, have been an unmixed blessing under vicious or tyrannical rulers? If there was to be a check on the crown, the nobles alone could supply it. Nor is it by any means clear that the king was always right and the nobles always wrong.

Any attempt to assess the situation meets with the difficulty that we know far more about the kings and their policies than we do about the nobles and theirs. Emphasis is placed on the weakness of the monarchy, and it is not difficult to see how the theoretical authority of the king bore little relationship to the practice of government. For example, all justice derived from the king and legal proceedings were conducted in his name. But jurisdiction had been alienated in one way or another, and the competence of royal courts was much curtailed by subjects who were judges in their courts of barony or regality. A regality possessed a system of legal administration reproducing in miniature that of the kingdom; its courts had power to deal with all cases except treason; the fines exacted went into the pockets of the lord of the regality; and when a tenant in a regality was summoned before a royal sheriff or justiciar his landlord could demand his return for trial in the court of the regality. Besides, the office of sheriff was itself usually held in heritage by a local magnate. The whole scope of lay courts, whether royal or baronial, was in any event much restricted by the wide competence of the courts of the church, which dealt with many matters now regarded as secular.

Little was visible throughout the country to keep the lieges aware of the authority of the central government. The only lay officials normally seen were local magnates, in the shape of barons and lords of regality, and even when local magnates were disguised as sheriffs it was not at once obvious that they were delegates of the king. Nor were there the 'government buildings' which meet the eye everywhere today: the nearest approach to them, the royal castles, were usually in the custody of local magnates, now disguised as keepers or captains.

The Scottish monarchy, whether or not it can be called a constitutional monarchy in the modern sense, was assuredly a limited monarchy. The king never had at his command a standing army or even the equivalent of a modern police force. At the worst— and this happened too often—the only tactics he could employ were to play on the rivalries and feuds of different families and to commission one magnate to act against another. This was little better than setting a thief to catch a thief, and was apt to create as many problems as it solved.

Yet the crown had resources which an active king could exploit to make his rule effective. His residual rights as the ultimate source of law had never been effaced, and men would still bring their complaints to parliament or council. He could respond by providing regular 'sessions' for the administration of civil justice and gradually draw more business to his courts. As criminal justice was always largely dependent on 'ayres' when justices deputed by him went on circuit, he could use this machinery both to punish wrongdoers and to increase his revenues by imposing financial penalties. It was indeed something of a convention, in England as well as in Scotland, to make high-sounding declarations that 'the king's peace shall firmly be kept throughout the realm'. There are traces of legislation for law and order under Robert I, and both David II and James I proclaimed that 'firm peace shall be observed and kept everywhere throughout the realm'. Another statute of James I, to the effect that the same laws should prevail throughout the whole kingdom, was repeated in much the same terms by James IV. No doubt such statutes could be no more than ineffective expressions of pious aspirations, but the point is that men continued to look to the king for the maintenance of law and order, and in the end, as royal power increased, this was to bear fruit. Royal justice, as a remedy for lawlessness, was welcome to the lieges.

It was also true that the central government possessed extensive patronage which made it the dispenser of things that ambitious men wanted—lands, pensions, offices and titles, as well as the feudal casualties which accrued from its tenants. During a minority, or the rule of a weak king, such patronage was not used for the statesmanlike end of winning support for royal authority, but it gave an active king opportunities to buy or to reward service. Moreover, if the crown could confer lands and titles it could also take them away by revocation or by forfeiture.

Not the least important action that a vigorous king could take was the simple one of moving about the country, showing his face to his people to make them aware of the central government. The far-flung travels of James IV and James V from Whithorn in the south to Orkney in the north and from Aberdeen in the east to the Hebrides in the west, must have impressed on their subjects the reality of kingship in a way that would have been unthinkable in the days of aged and infirm kings like Robert II and Robert III. We get glimpses of James IV going on his way, accompanied by 'five loud minstrels' and scattering largesse to 'a wife that brocht

73

strawberreis to the king' or to 'a wife that brocht cherreis to the king and criit on him for silver'. Yet such sporadic appeals to personal loyalty could not wholly counter the claims of local magnates to a permanent allegiance.

By exploiting the various reserves of power, a forceful king could be astonishingly successful in even a few years of active rule. James I, returning after eighteen years of captivity to a country which he had not seen since he was twelve, was nevertheless able not only to pass within weeks a whole code of statutes intended to secure the observance of the law and the extension of justice, but also, within months, to execute the leaders of the Albany family which had misgoverned in his absence, and to forfeit their land. Though some of his legislation may not have been novel, he seems to have had a real solicitude for order. In many ways the first James charted the course for his successors, and some of his aims, embodied again and again in later legislation, were finally attained by the sixth James. Yet James I had defects. Personal vindictiveness, an angry temper and sheer cupidity led him, for example, to execute the aged Earl of Lennox, Albany's father-in-law, along with the Albany kin. It was reaction against the king's unstatesmanlike ruthlessness and acquisitiveness, as well as the dynastic claims of the Euphemia Ross line, which led to his murder. His fate was a lesson lost on James V and Charles I, each of whom, at intervals of about a century, pursued courses not unlike his, and met with disaster. Wiser monarchs adopted other methods.

When James II emerged from tutelage at the end of his minority, the Livingston family had gained ascendancy. It is true that they were hardly of noble, let alone royal, birth, but even so it is indicative of the crown's reserves of power that an eighteen-year-old king could overthrow them with apparent ease. In this reign, interest centres on the struggle with the Douglases. The possession of lands stretching from Roxburghshire through all the southern counties to Ayrshire made the Earl of Douglas a marcher lord on the grandest scale. He could be, and often was, a bulwark of Scotland, but he was under the temptation to intrigue with his other neighbour, the king of England. The Douglases acquired lands in Banffshire, Moray and Ross as well. Besides the wealth and following which their territories gave them, they also had immense prestige, beginning with 'the Good Sir James' during Bruce's war of independence and continuing with captains like the second earl, the 'dead man who won a fight' at Otterburn in 1388, and the fourth earl, who died as lieutenant-general of the French army and Duke of Touraine.

They also, generation by generation, intermarried with the royal family, including the younger, and unquestionably lawful, descendants of Robert II. Any Earl of Douglas in the fifteenth century could have made a claim should parliament once more have had to determine the succession. If the Douglas holdings were tantamount to a principality in the south of Scotland, the Lord of the Isles, who was also Earl of Ross, had a principality in the north which, if not comparable in wealth to that of Douglas, had resources of warlike manpower. When the eighth Earl of Douglas made a 'bond' or alliance with this northern potentate, James II murdered him with his own hand, and in 1455 the royal forces drove the ninth earl across the Border and brought about the downfall of his house. To all appearances it was only after the crown had taken the initiative that Douglas renounced his allegiance and, by referring to 'him who calls himself king of Scots', challenged James II's right to the crown. This may be an illusion arising from the fact that our sources tell us more about royal policy than about Douglas policy, but on the whole it is hard to escape the conclusion that James II could be as ruthless and acquisitive as his father had been. On the other hand, James II, perhaps more skilful in this particular than his father, used his patronage to good effect. There was a distribution of earldoms, lordships and lands which created something like a new peerage and looks like a bid for support by rewarding services rendered, procuring promises of future service or detaching some of Douglas's allies.

James III, on taking over the government at the age of eighteen, was able at once to dispossess the Boyds in much the same way as James II had dispossessed the Livingstons. He took equally resolute action against his younger brothers, the Duke of Albany and the Earl of Mar; Mar died or was put to death in prison, Albany escaped, to join the exiled Earl of Douglas as an English agent. The 'opposition' to this king, if it can be so called, showed more intelligence and initiative than the opponents—or perhaps one should say the victims—of James I and James II. They made capital out of the king's alleged dependence on men not drawn from the ranks of the nobility, and, when a Scottish army was assembled at Lauder to resist an English invasion, they seized the opportunity to arrest and hang several of the king's 'favourites'. But James III, like his father, used his patronage to build up a royal party. As a second crisis approached, in 1488, he created four lordships and earldoms and even Scotland's first non-royal dukedom—this for the Earl of Crawford, son of an earl who had caused a good deal of trouble to James II. In the final trial of strength, which led to the king's death after an engagement at Sauchieburn, nearly all the leading men from north of the Tay were on the king's side—possibly the first, but certainly not the last, occasion when the loyal or conservative north supported the house of Stewart. The opposition might not have carried the day had they not been able to use the heir apparent as a figurehead, and it may be significant that they made a kind of appeal to opinion by securing a vindication in parliament.

James IV had the advantage of being nearly sixteen when he became king, and he seems to have had the better qualities, without the defects, of the first three Jameses. After the first years of his reign there was little or no disaffection anywhere in the Lowlands, and he was able to concentrate on the Highlands. It was something like a united nation that he led to defeat at Flodden in 1513.

James V's minority—a very long one, as he was only seventeen months old when his father was killed—followed the same pattern as those of James II and James III, and this time its final phase was the control of the king by the Earl of Angus. As Angus had antagonised most of the other nobles, it is easier this time to understand why, as soon as the king escaped from Angus and assumed personal rule, he was able to act so resolutely and drive Angus out of the country. James V was guilty of the same reckless acquisitiveness and severity as James I; he divided the nation and, although he escaped assassination, it was disaffection among his subjects which led to the disastrous defeat of Solway Moss and his death in despair.

There were still to be two more long minorities after James V's, for his daughter Mary was only a week old when he died and Mary's son, James VI, was only a year old when his mother was deposed. But even James V's reign, and still more those of Mary and James VI, were affected by novel complications arising from the Reformation and from changed circumstances in the relations of Scotland with England and France. These complications produced stresses which led to more violence in the relations between sovereign and subjects than ever before. Hitherto, during the active reigns of monarchs—it might be different during minorities when one party of magnates confronted another—there had seldom been anything violent enough to be dignified by the name of civil war. In the fifteenth century there was only twice a campaign in which the forces of an adult king encountered rebels in arms: the campaign against the Black Douglases in 1455, which James II won; and the Sauchieburn affair, which James III lost. James IV and James V never had to meet a rebellious army at all. Nor did the Reformation in Scotland involve massacres or wars of religion as in France, mass executions and popular uprisings cruelly suppressed as in England, or brutalities like those in Germany and the Low Countries. The whole of Mary's long minority passed with few confrontations between Scots except when they were acting as auxiliaries to French or English, and even in the crisis of 1559–60 little Scottish blood was shed.

Mary's personal reign, however, though brief, was marked by an unprecedented instability. She returned in 1561 at the age of eighteen, after a childhood spent in France, to find power in the hands not of a baronial family but of a revolutionary party which had made an alliance with England and set up a reformed church. Although she herself continued to attend Mass, she was no fanatic: when it suited her private ends, she could make concessions to the reformers, she could hint at her readiness to accept the *Prayer Book*, she could even enter into a Protestant marriage.

The young queen of 1561 was not already cast for the part of the Roman Catholic martyr of 1587. Yet, despite the highly intelligent policy of conciliation which she was prepared to adopt, her six years of rule saw three rebellions. In 1562 the Earl of Huntly headed a rising which has been seen as an attempt to bring about a Roman Catholic reaction but which probably owed as much to the earl's personal feud with Lord James Stewart, Mary's half-brother. Lord James had indeed been her adviser in her tolerant policy, but he had also been recently endowed with the earldom of Moray, which Huntly had been administering. The queen, taking the field in person, made short work of Huntly. In 1565, when Moray lost influence after the queen's marriage to Darnley and her reversal of the pro-English policy which she had pursued, Moray in turn raised a rebellion which was routed, again by a force under the queen in person, in a campaign called the Chase-about Raid. In 1567, after Mary had alienated so many of her subjects by her marriage to Bothwell, two armies did meet, but the queen surrendered without fighting.

Yet, while there was a general revulsion of feeling against Mary, it was only a minority of her opponents who agreed to her deposition and her supersession by her infant son, James VI. Thus the country was divided as hardly ever before, because, perhaps for the only time between the Bruce–Balliol episode and the Jacobite rebellions, the two contending parties each claimed to be fighting for the rightful sovereign. When the 'king's men' and the 'queen's men' first met, at Langside in 1568, there was little bloodshed, for a contemporary reported that only one man was killed on the king's side and there is some reason to believe that the total number was in fact no more than four. Recent military operations had been mainly campaigns of movement, not of sieges, but Mary's supporters were able to hold out in Edinburgh Castle, until an English siege train was brought up, because the castle garrison had the principal Scottish artillery at its command.

After the fall of Edinburgh Castle in 1573 the Earl of Morton was regent for James VI, and, in the words of an official record, he 'pacified the seditions and civil war by which the realm was miserably afflicted, wherethrough our sovereign's lieges enjoyed a reasonable quietness and rest'. When Morton's ascendancy came to an end in 1580 there were dissensions between the Protestant and pro-English party and a more conservative faction which had hankerings after Catholicism and France or Spain. Now one, now the other, prevailed, but the changes of government, as we should now call them, were not brought about by fighting. In what had become something of a Scottish tradition, two forces might indeed face each other, but the weaker decided that it was prudent to withdraw rather than fight. It has been said, apparently without much exaggeration, that they were content to count heads, whereupon the weaker party dispersed. The point is that in the absence of a standing army a resolute band of men could assert themselves by the simple device of surprise. A demonstration in force usually sufficed to bring about a bloodless coup d'état. Thus political decisions, the outcome of a contest between two parties, were not indeed always made as a result of debate in parliament or council, but they were made, in the ultimate analysis, as a result of the choice by individuals of one policy or another, or of adherence to this party or that. The decision was, in short, the result of something like a democratic process.

Although James VI's minority did not end, any more than Mary's had done, with a single family in control of affairs, he started his personal rule with a divided nation and hardly any resources in administrative machinery or money, so that he had to rely very largely on his own skill in tactics and diplomacy. In the end, but only after a long struggle, he was remarkably success-ful. Even when he was weakest, however, he found that there was what looks like almost a superstitious reluctance to fight against the royal standard, and rebellions were apt to be half-hearted affairs which almost petered out when the sovereign appeared. The fact that anyone defeated in an encounter with the king could not escape the dreaded penalty of forfeiture was no doubt a deterrent to rebellion, but, just as loss of life and limb as a result of the strife of factions was rare, so also was the permanent loss of property and status. After any coup d'état or other encounter which changed the government, pardon of the vanquished generally followed within a relatively brief space of time and much of the turnover of heritable property proved to be only transient. The permanent dispossession of a family was far from common and executions for treason extremely rare.

James VI, though perhaps not the ablest of the Stewart dynasty, was the most successful of his line in governing Scotland, not only in the sense that he made his will prevail in policy but also in the sense that his administration made unique contributions to the growth of order, extensively and intensively. He was a peacemaker who detested feuds, duelling and the carrying of firearms. He was eager to teach his Scottish subjects better ways and to raise their standards to those of 'other well governed commonwealths'. By the end of the century even half-hearted rebellions and demonstrations in force were things of the past. After the 1590s nobles never of themselves challenged the crown: when rebellion came again, under Charles I, it came from a different and more complex marshalling of forces. James succeeded in isolating ecclesiastical disaffection from the baronial support which would have made it dangerous: Charles I drove the two into combination. But from a riot in Edinburgh on 17 December 1596 to another riot in Edinburgh on 23 July 1637 there stretched forty years of unprecedented tranquillity. And by dying in his bed, at peace alike with his subjects and with foreign powers, James did something few of his predecessors had managed to achieve.

James VI had certain fortuitous advantages. The union of the crowns enhanced his prestige; in England he had personal security and was immune from coups d'état, and he was surrounded by flattering courtiers and obsequious prelates such as he had not always known in Scotland. Besides, the ultimate effect of the Reformation was to strengthen the monarchy. The Scottish Reformers were as determined as any others to assert the divine right of kings against papal claims; and while emphasis on the responsibility of kings to God could lead to the claims of a theocratic clergy to dictate to the crown, it could lead equally to the king's conviction that he was answerable to God alone and not to any of his subjects as intermediaries. Already before the Reformation the king had had influence in the church, if only by the part he took in appointing prelates. But hitherto there had been no mistaking the independence of church and clergy. James V had complained that churchmen and their followers fought on the slightest provocation, relying on their privileges and immunities to escape punishment; and, as long as the church courts had independent jurisdiction, the royal courts were not sovereign. With the Reformation, civil courts largely ousted ecclesiastical courts, the churchmen's immunities came to an end, and the crown took into its own hands the disposal of ecclesiastical property. Thus the patronage—in the wide sense of the term—at the crown's disposal was enormously increased, and the place of the crown in the conveyancing of lands was extended, since all transfers of church lands now required royal confirmation. James VI made capital out of both this extension of his patronage and the Reformers' claim of divine right for the king.

One of the most important and enduring achievements of the seventeenth century was the transformation of Scotland from a country in which the law had often been ill-enforced into one in which the law was generally obeyed. The explanation is not a single or simple one. Much was done by James VI, who directed the administration with a passion for order. After the wars with Charles I, Scotland was subjected to a period of severe disciplining at the hands of the Cromwellian army of occupation, which introduced conditions more orderly than had ever been known before and brought a novel impartiality and efficiency to the administration of justice. Throughout the whole century the Privy Council was assiduous in its attention to breaches of the law; and in 1672 Scotland at last got a permanent central court for criminal justice—the High Court of Justiciary. All this extension of law and order was achieved without anything like modern police and with only occasional recourse to military force. Very likely some of the credit is due to the bishops, ministers and kirk sessions and their persistent work, in alliance with central and local authorities, to uphold certain standards of conduct. The sessions exerted unremitting pressure against assault, drunkenness, witchcraft, slander and petty theft and acted as general 'watchdogs' in the parish. Where they had the weight of public opinion behind them and were backed by the local magistracy their constant vigilance was rewarded. But the great change was partly one of outlook on the part of the people, who gradually became more interested in trade, manufactures and the extension of education and culture, and more satisfied with the slowly but steadily improving economic conditions.

In the seventeenth century there was an institutional cohesion which had been lacking previously; unity no longer depended on the person of the king, for the organs of government operated in the absence of the king; and the nation in fact developed an institutional as well as an emotional unity when it made war on the king, in the person of Charles I. All parts of the country now shared many things in addition to the monarchy, and a uniform system of government existed. Perhaps the most striking thing is that when revolution came in 1689 it came not by violence but by vote in a convention.

Until the seventeenth century the power of the central government had been limited by recurrent financial weakness: the phrase 'chronic financial anaemia' has been used, but this over-simplifies, for royal finance, like royal authority, was not inadequate when there was a strong king in control. Something of the pattern which was long to persist had been established in the twelfth century, when stray references show that, besides traditional dues, the kings drew customs, profits of justice, the produce of lands in the royal demesne, rents from lands which were let, rents or 'ferms' from the royal burghs, and feudal casualties. From the fact that William I was able to raise 10,000 merks to secure his release from his undertaking to do homage for his kingdom in 1189 and 15,000 to pay to King John in 1209, apparently as part of an arrangement whereby the English king undertook to arrange royal marriages for William's daughters, it seems a safe inference that there was an efficient machinery for taxation; indeed, it may be that William was in a stronger financial position than Alexander III, who arranged to pay 4,000 merks to Norway for the western isles only in four annual instalments, and who died heavily in debt.

Robert I added his own lordship of Annandale and the earldom of Carrick to the royal demesne, and a good many properties were at his disposal through the forfeiture of those who had taken the English side. But the war had been costly, much land had been wasted and the king's supporters had to be rewarded. Thus the old Bruce property of Annandale, as well as the recently acquired Isle of Man, went to Edward, the king's brother; the earldom of Moray, which had apparently been a royal possession since the 1130s, went to Thomas Randolph, the king's nephew; properties forfeited by the Comyns in Aberdeenshire went to Hays and Keiths; and so on, to the comparative impoverishment of the king. In 1326 Bruce had to explain to a parliament the depleted state of his coffers and ask his subjects for a tenth of their incomes.

The next crisis arose with the need to pay the ransom of David II. Besides increases in the rate of customs, exceptional measures, including direct taxation, were resorted to, with marked success, and by the end of the reign the royal income had risen to a level not to be equalled again until after 1500. With the much less vigorous rule of Robert II and Robert III, direct taxation as a regular instrument of fiscal policy was allowed to lapse. James I, like David II, had a ransom as a reason, or pretext, for direct taxation, but it had become so unfamiliar that it was thought burdensome. Moreover, after David II's reign it seems not to have been considered practicable to raise the rate of the customs, so that the yield could increase, if it increased at all, only as trade expanded. From the reign of Robert I the burghs began to enjoy a tenure which meant that the revenues from them were mostly fixed in perpetuity. The feudal casualties which fell to the crown were often given away gratis or for small compositions. The proceeds from fines in local courts were negligible as a source of royal income, since only small compositions were handed over, but the administration of criminal justice could be profitable when a king had the time and energy to concentrate on it.

One thing which could be done was the recovery of property and revenues which had been alienated. In 1357, when David II returned after his captivity, there was an act that the king should call back all lands, rents, possessions and customs which had been given away. There was a similar act when James I returned from his captivity: pensions and allowances paid direct to individuals from the customs and from burgh ferms were to stop; all income was first to come to the exchequer, where claimants could submit proof of their claims; the titles of all who were in possession of lands which had once belonged to the crown were to be subjected to scrutiny. Action could also be taken to try to prevent the renewed alienation of crown property. David II declared that the lands pertaining to the crown should remain with the crown for ever. There was a similar act under James I and one in 1455 which is better known but which in fact contained nothing new in principle. It came, however, at a significant point, after the forfeiture of the vast possessions of the Black Douglases; it laid stress on the need to retain in royal hands the chief fortresses of the realm, and it emphatically included the great customs among the patrimony of the crown.

Land, whether kept as demesne or let in return for rent, was still the main source of wealth, and the most useful action a king could take was to acquire more of it. The early Stewarts had little in their hands except their own patrimony and remnants of the Bruce patrimony, lying mainly in Carrick, Bute, Arran, the Cumbraes, Renfrew, Roseneath and Cardross, and it was to their disadvantage that Robert II had a numerous progeny who had to be provided for by the earldoms of Fife, Menteith, Strathearn and Atholl and the lordship of Badenoch. James I's ruthless action against his immediate kinsmen, the Albanies, recovered Fife and Menteith and brought the new acquisition of Lennox; later, by devious methods, he gained Strathearn, March and Mar. Strathearn and part of Menteith were soon granted out again, but the conviction of the murderers of James I recovered Strathearn and brought in Atholl and the lordship of Brechin (which had belonged to Atholl's wife). The chief gain during James II's reign was the great Douglas heritage. Under James III the lordship of Kilmarnock, formerly the property of the Boyds, was acquired; the earldom of Orkney and lordship of Shetland were annexed to the crown in 1472, the earldom of Ross and the southern teritories of the lordship of the Isles in 1476. The residue of the lordship of the Isles was added under James IV (1493). It is true that minorities were always apt to provide opportunities for the diversion of revenues into private hands, and not all of those properties were retained by the king, but many were, and substantial progress was made. It was an advantage that fifteenth-century kings, unlike Robert II, had few offspring clamouring for earldoms and lordships; in the whole century not a single king's son founded a new comital family which endured.

Wealth was the key to power, if only because, in simple terms, it solved a military problem. If the noble in his stone castle was not to continue to defy the king, the king needed artillery to batter down its walls. The significance of the new weapon was possibly appreciated by James I, who imported 'a huge bombard of brass', and certainly by James II, for the guns which he imported, including the famous Mons Meg still to be seen in Edinburgh Castle, were the instruments by which he overcame a baronial coalition which might have reduced him to impotence. It was, indeed, an excessive interest in artillery which led to James II's death, for he was killed by the bursting of a cannon. But guns were expensive, as were skilled gunners and the mustering of the manpower and oxen necessary to drag the cannon over roadless country. Here was one excellent reason for the royal desire to acquire wealth, which meant land.

It is nevertheless true that some of the kings, beginning with James I, may have been acquisitive by nature as well as by policy. James III, who was described as 'wondrous covetous', hoarded a vast fortune in a 'black box' in Stirling Castle, the fate of which, after his death at Sauchieburn, led to much speculation but was never ascertained. James IV, despite his enormous expenditure on artillery and on ships, left a sound financial position. The events of James V's minority, however, were not conducive to sound finance, and by the time he began his personal reign the financial officials were carrying a large deficit and the country was in effect bankrupt. But James, of whom it was said that he 'inclineth daily more and more to covetousness', was outstandingly successful in exploiting both foreign and domestic policies to improve the financial situation. Perhaps the one justification of his harsh and vindictive proceedings is that fines and forfeitures were profitable.

The revenues derived from lands, thanks partly to the additions made by forfeitures and revocations, partly to increased rents and duties, rose from £5,300 in 1535–6 to over £15,000 in 1542, and the total revenues from ordinary sources rose to some £46,000 in 1539–40. Besides, the dowries of James's two successive French brides brought him the equivalent of about £300,000. The pope permitted him to exact heavy sums directly from the church, while he profited indirectly from the rich abbeys to which his bastard sons were provided. James was a great spender, with ambitious building programmes at Linlithgow, Stirling, Holyrood and Falkland, a taste for luxuries and the maintenance of a lavishly staffed household, but even so his personal fortune when he died was rumoured to amount to 300,000 livres and certainly ran into tens of thousands of pounds. There need be little mystery as to what became of it. The Earl of Arran, who was governor for twelve years after his death, was careful to insist that no questions should be asked about his financial dealings, and the presumption must be that most of James V's accumulation was dispersed by the Hamiltons.

Thus, when Mary began her personal rule in 1561, the financial position was again desperate. As in her father's day, the ecclesiastical situation came to the rescue. By an arrangement made in 1561 nearly all ecclesiastical revenues became subject to the deduction of a third, which went partly to pay the ministers of the reformed church but partly—and for a time increasingly—to augment crown finances. Besides, the comprehensive powers which the crown assumed over the disposal of church benefices gave it greater opportunities than before to use ecclesiastical revenues to reward service. However, Mary's rule was brief, and the early years of James VI's long minority were marked by tumult and civil war in which the ordinary revenues could not be properly ingathered. In the early 1580s the treasurer had a deficit of £45,000. By this time the ordinary revenues had become so stereotyped that any increase in rates was hardly to be thought of, and when James achieved maturity his cautious policy deterred him from either financial exactions or proceedings which would have brought in property by forfeiture. Even the immediate necessities of the

Page 87 Earl's Palace, Kirkwall, built by Patrick Stewart c 1600: the finest domestic building in Scotland of its period

Page 88 Craigievar Castle, the finest of the early seventeenth-century tower-houses

court could not be met. In 1594 the chapel royal was not water-tight; in 1599 'his hienes palaceis and castellis ar altogidder ruynous and at the point of decay, his munitioun and ordinance unmountit, without provisioun of pulder and bullet, his majesteis movabillis waistit, worne and consumit'; and guests summoned to royal banquets found that they were expected to provide the food, so that the invitation was one 'to tak pairt of your awne guid cheir'.

It was out of those desperate circumstances that, thanks to the skill and tenacity of James VI in accustoming his subjects to a respect for law and order, the inevitable solution was at last found in taxation, imposed almost annually and widening in its scope. There was much grumbling under James, and the con-tinuance and increase of regular taxation under Charles I was one of the causes of the rebellion against that monarch, but taxation had come to stay. Indeed—and it is more than a little ironical—the Covenanters who rebelled against Charles I found that war against him was far more expensive than his government had been, and had to impose taxation on a scale he had never dreamed of. After that came the harsh and systematic levies of the Crom-wellian period. From the Restoration onwards it became generally accepted that the government of the country must be financed from taxes.

But while much was novel in the seventeenth century, much that was antique remained and even intensified. The Declaration of Arbroath had claimed specifically that the Scottish kings had numbered a hundred and thirteen. As about half of them were purely fictitious, it is not surprising that there was some uncer-tainty about the precise number, but the Scots never had any difficulty in claiming upwards of a hundred, and this article of faith continued into the seventeenth century, to become a belief in indefeasible hereditary right. Although the Scots rose in rebel-lion against Charles I, any idea of superseding the monarchy or even of superseding the person of Charles was quite outside their imaginings. Men spoke about the 'unparalleled lineal descents of an hundred and seven kings' or pleaded the cause of 'a race of kings who have governed you for two thousand years with peace and justice and have preserved your liberties'. The supposed royal line, stretching back to Fergus I in 330 BC, was depicted in the long gallery at Holyroodhouse by command of Charles II. Indefeasible hereditary succession almost implied absolute monarchy, for if subjects had not the ultimate sanction of deposition, it was hard to see what restrictions they could place on the monarch's power. This idea, too, became explicit. An act of 1681 declared succession by blood to be one of the 'fundamental and unalterable laws of the realm'. An act of 1685, quite logically, went further:

> this nation hath continued now upwards of two thousand years in the unaltered form of our monarchical government, under the uninterrupted line of one hundred and eleven kings. ... We and our ancestors have enjoyed those securities and tranquillities which the greater and more flourishing kingdoms have frequently wanted: those great blessings we owe ... to the sacred race of our glorious kings and to the solid, absolute authority wherewith they were invested by the first and fundamental law of our monarchy.

That remarkable statement bore no relation to what was to happen within four years, when a king was declared to have forfeited the crown and the throne declared to have become vacant.

CHAPTER 4

Parliament, Council and Courts of Law

The central executive was first formed by the king's household and its officers, most of whom appear on record early in the twelfth century. Some offices became hereditary and more or less honorific: the Breton family who acquired the office of steward became the Stewart kings; the office of constable has been in the Hay family since Robert I's time and is held by the Earl of Erroll; the office of marshal went to the Keiths in Bruce's time and remained with them, as Earls Marischal, until they died out in the eighteenth century. But the chamberlain, initially responsible for the royal *camera* or chamber (where the king, like his prudent subjects, kept his money), long remained the principal financial officer, for only in the reign of James I were most financial functions transferred to the treasurer and comptroller. The chancellor, as keeper of the seal with which kings, from the late eleventh century, authenticated their charters, became the head of the Chancery, where professional scribes drew up legal documents, many of these concerning the conveyance and inheritance of land.

Besides his immediate 'familiars', the king had his court or *curia*, in which his own tenants were commonly obliged, in terms of their charters, to render 'suit' or presence. But the king could be approached by any of his subjects who sought justice. He could hear their pleas in person, but he might seek advice, and it was a small step when he delegated the hearing of cases to his court, in which professional legal experience developed. Thus the King's Court became a court of appeal from other courts. Equally, in taking decisions on domestic or foreign policy, the king might seek advice from important men besides his immediate *entourage*.

Their advice was given in a council: 'counsel' and 'council' are sometimes hard to differentiate.

The expansion of the selective council into something more like a parliament seems to have been associated with the concept of the *communitas*, which indicated an awareness that the people of the realm, or some of them, had a corporate identity. Besides the community of the whole realm there were territorial communities, but the realm could also be thought of as divided into what one might call vocational communities. Thus the self-styled *communitas*, which professed to act on behalf of the nation, developed into a parliament which consisted not indeed of a single *communitas* but of *tres communitates* or three estates, for to the lay tenants of the crown and the great churchmen there were added burgesses. In 1295, when John Balliol made a treaty with France, the *universitates et communitates* of the towns of Scotland were participants, and the seals of the communities of six burghs were appended to the confirmation of the treaty. *Universitas*, even more clearly than *communitas*, has the meaning of a corporate body, and it is difficult to believe that the consent of the burghs could be given to the treaty unless burgh representatives had been present at a parliament along with nobles and prelates. It was, however, as a result of financial pressure that the burghs attained integration in Parliament. In 1326, when Robert Bruce had to ask his people for a tenth of their incomes, burgesses from certain burghs were present at a Parliament at Cambuskenneth to consent to their share. When the need to ransom David II from his English captivity produced another financial crisis, again the burghs had to help to provide the money. By the second half of the century a burghal element was a recognised constituent of a Parliament, though few burghs were regularly represented. In the main it was royal burghs which sent commissioners to Parliament, but it seems to have been importance—and tax capacity—rather than status, which determined the selection, for some of the important ecclesiastical burghs were represented almost, if not quite, from the outset.

Parliament, associated as it was in origin with the king's *curia*, was invested with some of the formalities and powers of a court of law. It met on a summons of forty days, and even when other courts developed it retained jurisdiction, notably in cases of treason. But Parliament's non-judicial functions could be exercised by a less formal body, known in earlier times as a General Council and later as a Convention. This probably evolved by occasionally enlarging the king's ordinary council (which itself became known as the Privy Council), by the presence of invited barons, prelates and burgesses—perhaps, in a moment of emergency, those who were within easy reach. There was no prescribed period of notice for the calling of such a body, nor had anyone a right to be invited, at least before the seventeenth century.

Attendance at either Parliament or General Council was probably thought of as a duty rather than a right. Certainly some found it irksome to attend, and this was one reason for the beginning of a practice whereby Parliament delegated its powers to a commission consisting of some of its members, while the others went home to get on with what they thought more important matters, such as—in a predominantly rural society—taking in the harvest: in 1367 and again in 1369 'certain persons were chosen by the three estates to hold the Parliament, and leave was given to the others to return home on account of the harvest' or 'on account of the importunity and dearth of the season'. As late as 1543, but not thereafter, Parliament thus delegated its full powers.

Parliament could also delegate certain specific functions to committees. Powers of justice in the first instance could go to the Committee for Causes and Complaints; powers of appeal to a committee for 'the falsing of dooms', that is, the reversing of the decisions of lower courts. Equally, a committee could be delegated to frame legislation for subsequent approval by the whole Parliament, and such a committee developed into the 'Committee of Articles' which expedited parliamentary business and in time controlled it. It has indeed been said that the Scottish Parliament had hardly taken shape when it went a long way towards abdicating its powers by appointing commissions and committees to do its work. The Committee of Articles, or something like it, certainly existed under James I, and a 'Committee to Frame Articles' was formalised under James III.

When James I returned in 1424 from a captivity of eighteen years during which he had seen the workings of the English Parliament, he attempted innovations. He first passed an act reminding all who held land of the crown that as suitors of the king's court they were under an obligation to attend his Parliament. It would have been unrealistic to expect them all to come, and, while the intention may have been to raise money by fining absentees, it may be that what the king had in mind was to prevail on the general body of his tenants to send representatives. An act of 1428 therefore provided for the election of commissioners to come from each shire. Another of James's acts provided for the choice of a 'common speaker of the Parliament' who, though chosen by only the commissioners of shires, was to 'propose all and sundry needs and causes pertaining to the commons', and it has been suggested that the king was aiming at something like a two-chamber parliament on the English model. Shire commissioners, however, were not elected, the Scottish Parliament remained unicameral and the predominance of the higher social classes continued, for prelates and nobles were not likely to pay much attention to the burgesses, whom they greatly outnumbered and who had no shire representatives as allies. Indeed, rather than any increase in the representatives of the middle classes, there was instead an increase in the number of nobles. Certain of the more important tenants of the crown began to receive individual summonses to Parliament and attained a new dignity as 'lords of Parliament', forming a peerage of a lower grade than the earls. About fourteen such lords had made their appearance by 1449, and between then and 1460 another eight lairds had been raised to this dignity.

As time went on, the composition of Parliament was modified in various ways, though without any change of principle. The spiritual estate, consisting primarily of bishops, abbots and priors, was not immediately affected by the Reformation. The holders of abbacies—whether genuine abbots or commendators—retained their seats, and this element, though increasingly consisting of lay commendators, lasted until the transformation of abbeys into heritable lordships removed their holders from the spiritual estate into that of the nobility. The bishops likewise retained their places. Those who held office in 1560 were succeeded usually by clergy of the reformed church, occasionally by lay titulars, and such holders of bishoprics continued to sit as part of the spiritual estate. There was more than once talk after the Reformation of adding to the representation of the church, but nothing came of it, and by the time the office of bishop was first abolished, in 1638, the General Assembly had lost its taste for parliamentary representation, so the clerical estate disappeared, to be restored in 1661 and abolished again in 1689.

The estate of nobles increased with new creations, especially after the beginning of the seventeenth century, though some of them, arising from the erection of religious houses into temporal lordships, represented transfers from the spiritual estate. The number of royal burghs likewise increased, from about 40 in 1500 to 66 in 1700, and more burgesses than before actually came to Parliament: about 1500 there might be only 10 or 12, in 1560 there were 22, in the seventeenth century there were sometimes 50.

The most important change was the admission of shire commissioners, to form in effect a fourth estate. An act of 1587 revived James I's act of 1428: two commissioners were to be elected annually by the freeholders of each shire except Clackmannan and Kinross, which were to elect one each. The voting qualification was the tenure of land of the crown of a yearly value of 40s according to the 'old extent', a traditional valuation.

The broadening membership, while it may have increased the weight which Parliament carried and may indicate an extension of the involvement of the subjects in the government of the country, did not add to Parliament's initiative or independence. There was too much scope for the influence of the administration. The bishops and commendators were, quite simply, royal nominees, and the bishops remained peculiarly the creatures of the crown. Nobles in the first generation—and there were many of these in the fifteenth and seventeenth centuries, though fewer in the sixteenth—were, equally, crown nominees. In the shires, the crown had means of making its wishes known to ensure that those elected were such as 'to give his majesty satisfaction'. So far as the burghs were concerned, crown control over the town councils, who chose the parliamentary commissioners, was reflected in burgess representation in Parliament. From time to time steps were taken to ensure that town councillors in general were well-affected to the government of the day, and the crown could also interfere in the affairs of particular burghs. If it could, as it sometimes did, nominate the provost of Edinburgh, it could also when it chose nominate the provosts of lesser burghs.

By the seventeenth century the burgesses and the shire commissioners could have outvoted the clergy and the nobility. Thus in 1633 there were 12 bishops and 66 peers, 9 officers of state, 46 shire commissioners and 52 burgh commissioners; in 1661, when there were no bishops, there were 74 peers, 55 shire commissioners and 61 burgh commissioners. But the numerical preponderance of shire and burgh commissioners was nullified by the fact that in the Committee of Articles, where alone members might hope to shape legislation, each estate was equally represented. As early as 1469 there were five members from each estate 'for the articles' and in the seventeenth century each estate usually contributed eight members. Thus a dozen or fewer bishops had equal weight with either the burgesses or the shire commissioners. Besides, the Committee of Articles included officers of state, who were on the whole likely to align with the nobles and clergy and were almost inevitably agents of the administration.

It is not clear if the members of the Committee of Articles had ever been freely elected, and under James VI a method of appointment operated which ensured that royal influence would prevail: the bishops selected eight nobles, who in turn chose eight bishops, and those sixteen then chose the barons and burgesses. Now, as the bishops were the king's creatures, they necessarily chose nobles whom the king recommended, and those nobles, in choosing bishops, had only royal nominees to choose from. In 1621 James VI's secretary wrote that 'the lords of the articles were chosen with such dexterity that no man was elected (one only excepted) but those who by a private roll were selected as best affected to Your Majesty's service'. The same method of selection was revived in Charles II's reign, and in 1669 the king's representative wrote of the articles: 'If they be amiss, blame me, for I wrote the lists and not a man was altered.'

The procedure was for Parliament to meet, appoint the Committee of Articles to prepare the legislative programme and reassemble later to give its approval. But the committee itself must have been little more than an agent of the king or council, who had gone far towards framing legislation before Parliament met. Time-tables show that this was so: the Parliament of 1633 met on 20 June to elect the committee, and when it met again on 28 June it passed 168 statutes *en bloc*. The Committee of Articles can have done little more than approve measures already prepared. This procedure gave little, if any, opportunity for debate, and the brevity of sessions of Parliament also meant that there was little time to organise an opposition.

All in all, the relations between Parliament, Committee of Articles and Privy Council had some parallels to the way in which parliamentary government functions today, when a cabinet very largely controls the legislative programme and determines in advance what measures will pass. Some might even conclude that the old Scottish method of simply passing the government's measures without discussion was more sensible than the elaborate procedure of conducting long debates the outcome of which is wholly predictable. However, before the modern charade developed, the English Parliament did go through a phase of real independence, and it is this which is hard to parallel in Scotland. The reason for the difference lies largely in the fact that, although the consent of the Scottish Parliament to the government's financial requests was necessary from the fourteenth century, Parliament was never thereafter able, until its last days, to use 'the power of the purse' to put pressure on the crown. One reason for this was, of course, the degree of crown control over the membership; but a second was that between the fourteenth century and the seventeenth taxations were rare and usually so modest that the opportunity of using finance as a lever hardly occurred; and a third was that taxations could be granted by Conventions which were called, if not for that specific purpose alone, at any rate on terms which precluded them from proceeding to general discussion.

Yet with all the crown's powers, Parliament was not entirely useless for expressing public opinion. When James VI's controversial proposals for changes in church worship, the Five Articles of Perth, came up for parliamentary ratification in 1621, there was opposition in the Committee of Articles, and, when the house divided, 11 clergy, 35 nobles, 20 shire commissioners and 20 burgesses voted in favour, while 15 nobles, 19 shire commissioners and 25 burgesses voted against. No government could ignore such figures, and the obnoxious articles were not enforced. In the 1630s the phrase 'a free parliament' began to be heard. When Charles I was in Edinburgh in 1633, he was present in person in the parliament house to note how members voted, and it was even claimed that the voting figures were falsified. A petition prepared soon afterwards suggested that such proceedings 'may seem against the constitution of a free parliament'; and the National Covenant of 1638, which was concerned with constitutional as well as ecclesiastical grievances, appealed for 'free assemblies and parliaments'. No doubt to many a 'free' parliament meant one which would be dominated by their own faction, but the aim was at least to reduce royal control. When Charles's administration collapsed, and his opponents were in the saddle, they showed this clearly enough. A Triennial Act laid down that Parliament should meet at least every three years, even if the king declined to summon it. The king was also forced to agree that he must not appoint councillors, officers of state or even judges without Parliament's consent.

After 1660, when the king came back, his nominees the bishops again sat in Parliament, and the Committee of Articles was selected as of old. But the practice of approving the articles without discussion was not restored; something of a tradition of free speech survived, and although there was still inadequate opportunity for full debates, longer parliamentary sessions gave time for an opposition to emerge. In 1673 a disgruntled faction arranged a series of speeches designed to operate the practice of 'no supply without redress of grievances'. We are told that 'warm debates arose in the house' and that members spoke 'with abundance of freedom and plainness'. The administration was startled, but the main result was that Parliament was not called again for eight years.

Yet it was evident that the so-called 'restoration' of 1660 had been a restoration of only the externals of government, while many underlying realities were different. The nobles recovered influence which they had lost to the clergy in Charles I's time, and, besides, real authority lay as never before with the crown's ministers in Scotland rather than with the king personally and his advisers in London. And there were other features making for a potentially revolutionary situation. Not only was the cry for 'free parliaments' revived, but there were also many appeals to 'fundamental laws'. The political opposition appealed to 'the fundamental laws of the nation', the ecclesiastical opposition suggested that real 'authority' lay with those who had 'the fundamental laws of the land' on their side. On the other hand, 'the fundamental laws of the kingdom' were cited in support of the prerogative, and it was contended that the imposition of the Covenant had been contrary to 'the fundamental laws and liberties of the subjects'. While all might thus appeal to 'fundamental laws' for their own ends, the concept could represent a belief in something above either crown or parliament. In 1686, when James VII offered free trade with England in return for the relief of Roman Catholics from the laws against them, there was unprecedented opposition. The Committee of Articles accepted the government's proposal by a majority of only 18 : 14, the bishops voting 4 : 2 against and the burgesses 7 : 1 against, and on this issue the usually subservient Parliament defeated the crown. The Revolution of 1689 was in a sense a triumph for the 'fundamental laws' and an assertion of a right superior to the king's, a right which enabled a Convention to declare that a king had 'forfeited the crown' and to accept a new monarch on conditions which almost implied a contract.

After the Revolution, Parliament, fortified by having passed judgment on a king, found itself in a novel situation. The Committee of Articles was abolished and for a few years use was made of a standing committee, genuinely representative and freely elected, as the channel by which 'overtures' or proposals for legislation were transmitted for open debate in the house. Gradually, however, the practice developed of submitting overtures right away to the full house, but causing them to 'lie on the table' after a first reading to give time for consideration. In 1700 committees were denuded of the power of initiating measures, and could discuss only matters first remitted to them by Parliament, and in the last Scottish Parliament (1703–7) committees were dispensed with altogether, so that measures were conducted through all their stages in the full house. Moreover, the bishops, those traditional crown agents, had disappeared, and, far from thinking in terms of providing the crown with other agents, Parliament instead made arrangements for the larger shires to have one or two additional members. This more independent and self-assertive Parliament also at last made use of the power of the purse. In 1689–90, when King William showed reluctance to establish Presbyterian government, pressure was put on him by withholding supply, and it was similar tactics which compelled Queen Anne to give her assent to the Act of Security of 1703–4, which threatened that Scotland would adopt a different sovereign from England.

The Scottish Parliament was never the sole legislative organ in the land. The estates were from time to time summoned to meet as a convention, with powers in legislation and taxation equal to those of a Parliament, though without judicial functions. In the seventeenth century the composition of a Convention approximated to that of a Parliament, and it now met after due notice of twenty days. It was, however, usually called for certain specific purposes, defined in the royal letters of summons, and it could not proceed to other business. After the revolution no more Conventions were called, and Parliament was free of this competitor.

The Privy Council was another legislative body. It undoubtedly had special importance for temporary or provisional legislation in the intervals between sessions of Parliament, but the line of demarcation between its powers and those of a Parliament or Convention is hard to find. For example, the first measure to give effect to the demand for a school in every parish was an act of council in 1616, anticipating parliamentary action by seventeen years.

The royal burghs had their monopoly of foreign trade, which was convenient to the crown in that it facilitated the collection of customs and which was regarded as a fair compensation for the burden of taxation borne by the burghs; and they also had certain exclusive rights in crafts. The regulation of commerce and manufactures was therefore to some extent a matter for the annual convention of royal burghs. In early times there had been a Court of the Four Burghs, evidently Edinburgh, Berwick, Roxburgh and Stirling. Berwick and Roxburgh were lost by Scotland in the fourteenth century, and in 1369 Lanark and Linlithgow took their places. The Court of the Four Burghs is referred to as late as 1507, but representation had widened and already by 1487 Parliament had ordained that commissioners of all burghs should meet once a year to treat of matters of common concern.

Other legislative competitors of Parliament were the Provincial Council of the pre-reformation church and the General Assembly after the reformation. Whether, as the Presbyterians claimed, the assembly was sovereign in ecclesiastical affairs was debatable, but its powers certainly encroached, as did those of Convention, Privy Council and Convention of Burghs, on the powers of parliament. And there was yet another legislative body of a sectional nature, for the Court of Session, by its acts of sederunt, made laws on court procedure and on matters connected with the legal profession. All in all, the concept of the unchallenged sway of an omnicompetent parliament must not be taken to apply in Scotland.

Parliament, General Council and Privy Council had all evolved from the King's Council of the early Middle Ages. But the King's Council had also been a court of law, and judicial, as well as legislative, deliberative and executive functions stemmed from the council, in a process of differentiation. Parliament itself was a court of law, and one purpose for its meetings had been 'that the lieges should be servit of the law'. But in the fifteenth century it became plain that Parliament was not enough. The judicial committees of Parliament, whether for causes and complaints or for falsing of dooms, operated only when Parliament was in session and evidently could not meet the exceptional demand when, after a long period of weak rule, the vigorous James I returned from captivity in 1424. In 1426, therefore, Parliament decided that the chancellor and certain discreet persons to be chosen by the king from the three estates should hold three sessions yearly to hear cases. In 1439, however, provision was made for two sessions yearly by 'the king's chosen council'. The need for 'sessions' was clearly coming to be recognised, but uncertainty as to whether they should stem from Parliament or from Council continued. The nine 'lords of the session' referred to in 1458 were selected three from each estate in parliament, but in 1491 the chancellor 'with certain lords of council or else the lords of session' should sit three times in the year 'so that justice may be put to due execution to all parties complaining'. In the end it was the Council that produced the permanent civil court. James IV's reign (1488–1513) saw a marked stage in development. In 1504 a special council was ordained to sit 'continually in Edinburgh or where the king makes residence', with a jurisdiction concurrent with that of the lords of session. This was a temporary measure to overtake arrears; but there is ample evidence from records that the Council was consistently active in the hearing of civil causes, and before James IV's death something very like the Court of Session had taken shape.

Development was arrested in the troubled minority of James V, but it resumed in the 1520s. In 1526 eight persons, four spiritual and four temporal, whose only function was 'to sit continually upon the sessions', were appointed to join with the lords of the Privy Council and the 'ministers of court' to deal with civil causes. Among the persons named were Alexander Myln, Abbot of Cambuskenneth and a future lord president of the Court of Session, three professional canon lawyers, one of the lairds who were beginning to make the law a profession and two other lairds who held heritable sheriffdoms. The ecclesiastical element was strong, because there was far more professionalism among churchmen, and the procedure of the civil judicature was shaped largely by the legal knowledge and experience which churchmen brought to the judicial committees of Parliament and Council and then to the Court of Session. The years from 1526 to 1528 appear to have seen a rapid differentiation of the 'Session' from the Council. Out of fifteen judges who were to be named as members of the Court of Session when it was endowed in 1532, no less than eleven had already been acting as judges on 'the Session' in 1527. And in 1528 councillors who were not specially appointed for the Sessions were excluded from attendance.

There was, then, a body of professional and semi-professional judges, holding regular sessions and perhaps well on the way to becoming full-timers. It remained to provide endowment to pay judicial salaries, and this was forthcoming in circumstances arising from the onset of the Reformation. It was equitable enough that finance should come from the church. For one thing, as already mentioned, many of the judges were churchmen, in effect paid by being appointed to ecclesiastical benefices. For another, at a time when laymen were beginning to challenge clerical pretensions, it was in the interests of churchmen that there should be a strong civil court whose sentences might be more effective than the process of 'cursing' or excommunication by which the church courts had hitherto enforced the payment of ecclesiastical revenues. However, the events which produced the endowment of the Court of Session were fortuitous. Henry VIII's proceedings in having himself acknowledged as supreme head on earth of the Church of England alarmed the papacy, which was willing to make almost any concession to prevent Scotland, too, from slipping from its grasp. Therefore on 13 September 1531 the pope issued a bull relating that James V desired to establish a college of justice for civil causes with half of its members churchmen, and ordaining that the Scottish prelates should contribute annually 10,000 ducats (about £10,000 Scots) for its endowment. A year later the pope conceded that no Scottish case falling under ecclesiastical jurisdiction was to be called to Rome in the first instance but was to be judged by ecclesiastics appointed by the king. The Scottish Parliament, remarking with truth that, while earlier popes had been generous, 'Pape Clement, now pape of Rome, has bene mair gracius and benevolent till his grace than to all his forbears', recorded the king's resolution to remain faithful to 'the seat of Rome and hali kirk', related the king's intention to institute 'ane college of cunning and wise men ... for the adminis-

103

tration of justice in all civil actions' and nominated the Abbot of Cambuskenneth as president, with seven clerics and seven laymen as judges.

Because of these transactions James V is apt to be remembered as 'the founder of the Court of Session', but all that happened was the endowment—the inadequate endowment as it turned out—of a court which already existed. Of the fifteen judges nominated to the College of Justice in 1532, all but one had been active in the Court of Session in the previous year. The fact that the 'lords of session' now became 'senators of the College of Justice' was a change in nomenclature to impress Italian ears, a mere piece of window-dressing. Everyone knew that the king was not going to spend £10,000 a year, or anything like it, on the salaries of fifteen judges, and the Scottish prelates, on their part, did not relish a permanent imposition of this amount. They agreed instead to pay £72,000 in four years, to be pocketed by the king, and assign certain benefices, amounting to £1,400 yearly in value, to pay judicial salaries, while the crown was to assign benefices in its patronage to provide another £200. Since the clergy on the bench had previously been paid by being appointed to benefices, even the change in endowment was not very significant.

The court thus formalised, with its 'Auld Fifteen' judges, underwent little change in organisation until the early nineteenth century. Even the provision that eight of the judges should be drawn from the 'spiritual estate' survived the Reformation, though the reformed church set its face against the appointment of its bishops or ministers as judges and the 'spiritual men' on the bench were usually laymen masquerading as 'parsons' and so forth because they drew the revenues of specific benefices. In addition to the 'Fifteen', certain 'extraordinary lords', who served without salaries, were from time to time appointed to the bench, sometimes apparently as an honour, sometimes as a step towards appointment to an 'ordinary' seat as a vacancy arose, but this practice ended in 1723.

The Reformation extended the scope of the court. Previously the ecclesiastical courts had dealt not only with executry and matrimonial cases but with a wide range of other business, much

Page 105 Church interiors old and new: *(above)* 'The Stool of Repentance', painted by David Allan (1744-96); *(below)* Craigsbank Church, Edinburgh

Page 106 (above) Slateford Aqueduct, carrying the Union Canal (1822) over the Water of Leith; *(below)* Clyde steamers racing in the days before 1914 when there was no need to count the cost of coal

of it arising from failure to fulfil obligations or contracts, and a very substantial part, almost certainly the major part, of Scottish litigation had been transacted in the church courts. Besides, not only were secular judges excluded from a wide range of business while clerics who were pursued in the secular courts could plead that they were 'spiritual men' and exempt from secular jurisdiction, but if, for example, the lords of Council gave a sentence in favour of one competitor for a benefice, the defeated party could appeal to the court of Rome. At the Reformation there was a period of confusion before it was determined which tribunals should inherit the jurisdiction of the ecclesiastical courts. The bishops were not in 1560 deprived of their judicial powers, and continued to act at least in some matrimonial cases; the courts of the reformed church, under the new superintendents, advanced some claims to the old ecclesiastical jurisdiction; and in the prevailing uncertainty some litigants had recourse to the Court of Session. In 1564 Queen Mary established the Commissary Court of Edinburgh, with jurisdiction over the whole country in divorce suits and in executorial matters involving testaments above a certain value, while local commissary courts, based on the old episcopal courts, continued or were revived, with a subordinate jurisdiction. However, the Court of Session, besides having an appellate jurisdiction from the Commissary Court of Edinburgh, gradually drew to it the bulk of the actions for nonfulfilment of bonds and contracts which had previously gone through the church courts.

There were many complaints, throughout most of the history of the Court of Session, of inefficiency and delay. Some Scots, swallowing their patriotism, had to admit that the commissioners for justice appointed by the Commonwealth put the lords of session to shame. In the early eighteenth century there were reforms to accelerate procedure, and Duncan Forbes of Culloden, as Lord President, was congratulated on converting the courts of law into the courts of justice. By the late eighteenth century, partly because of the increasing bulk and complexity of business arising from economic changes, the court was again unable to cope expeditiously with the cases brought before it, and it underwent reconstruction soon after 1800. Hitherto each of the fifteen judges had taken it in turn to sit alone for a week in the Outer House to hear cases in the first instance, while 'the haill Fifteen' sat together in the Inner House to hear appeals. Now the number of judges was reduced from fifteen to thirteen and the court was reorganised into an Outer House in which five judges operated concurrently, each hearing cases alone, and appeals went to an Inner House of two divisions, each consisting of four judges, the first division presided over by the lord president, the second presided over by the lord justice clerk. The commissary courts came to an end in the 1820s and their functions in divorce were transferred to the Court of Session; a civil jury court was established in 1815 but it was abolished in 1830 and its work too went to the Court of Session; the court also took over the functions previously pertaining to the Exchequer Court, the Teind Court and the Admiralty Court. In the twentieth century, with the growth of business in an increasingly complex economy and society, it has again been necessary to increase the number of judges, and by 1992 the total had grown to twenty-four.

'The High Court of Parliament' had always been the supreme court, if there was such a thing, and after the union with England the question arose whether appeal should now lie to the British Parliament. The Articles of Union, while emphatic that no jurisdiction, either in first instance or by way of appeal, should be exercised by certain specified English courts 'or any other court in Westminster Hall', said nothing about the House of Lords, and the question was probably not discussed. But appeals from the Court of Session to the House of Lords—now, of course, a British and not an English court—were allowed. It has long been the practice to appoint some Scottish judges as lords of appeal to sit on the judicial committees of the House of Lords.

In becoming senators of the College of Justice, Scotland's civil judges had not ceased to be 'lords': they have always been so styled, and since 1905 their wives have been 'ladies'. They were 'lords *of Council* and Session', and this is a constant reminder of the conciliar origin of the court. The Privy Council indeed retained judicial functions which overlapped with those of the Court of

Session in civil cases as well as with those of the Court of Justiciary in criminal cases. In short, whatever functions might be delegated, the residual powers of the king, as the fount of justice, remained with his Council.

While the nominal membership of the Privy Council might be very large—fifty or more in the early seventeenth century—the number who attended regularly was small, with a quorum of only seven. Peers of old families played a less active part after about 1600 and the effective work was done by a handful of officials and lawyers; prelates, too, who were often canon lawyers, were important until the late sixteenth century and then, after a partial eclipse, the bishops returned in force for a short space under Charles I. The Council was, it must be remembered, in almost constant session to deal with the day-to-day executive business of the government, and therefore readily available. Its response to the many cases brought before it seems to have been prompt, and it probably had a flexibility in procedure which gave it certain advantages over other courts. It is not altogether easy to see why some cases went to the Council rather than to the Court of Session or the Court of Justiciary, any more than it is to see why some legislation emanated from the Council rather than from Parliament, but the fact remains that, while institutions had come to be differentiated with the passage of time—Parliament, Privy Council, Court of Session—functions in legislation, administration and justice were never completely differentiated as long as Scotland was an independent kingdom.

Although the Council exercised residual powers in criminal as in civil justice, the central criminal courts had not originated, as the Court of Session had, in the Council. They evidently derived from the justiciars who in the twelfth and thirteenth centuries shared responsibility for justice on a territorial basis—one for Scotia, one for Lothian and one for Galloway. It is not clear how far Celtic society had a place for the punishment of crime by king's judges, since crimes were seen as offences merely against the family, but from Anglo-Saxon and then Norman England there came (with the office of justiciar) clear concepts of royal rights of justice and of crimes as offences against society and against the state. The king, though omnicompetent as the ultimate source of justice, had certain pre-eminent rights. His regalian rights, his *regalitas* or regality, included in early definitions treasure-trove, murder, premeditated assault, rape, fire-raising and robbery with violence. From such definitions developed the concept of 'pleas of the crown', which came to be murder, robbery with violence, rape and fire-raising—as well, of course, as treason against the king's own person. Competence to try such serious crimes was often reserved when the king granted jurisdiction to barons, and the justiciars became essentially the king's judges for these crimes.

In the fifteenth century there was a justice general, usually a peer, and the office became hereditary in the house of Argyll from 1514 to 1628. Under him were justices depute, often also peers, and they, like the earlier justiciars, were supposed to conduct circuits or 'ayres' (*anglicé* eyres) throughout the country. Proceedings long continued to be somewhat spasmodic. As the court held by the justice general and his deputies in Edinburgh could not serve the whole realm, and as justice-ayres were only intermittent, much reliance was placed on special commissions of justiciary, often granted to magnates with their own interests to serve. Various plans for reorganisation were made in the last years of the sixteenth century, but little came of them. The real difficulty may well have been financial, and the device which in the end solved the problem was to use, as commissioners of justiciary, the senators of the College of Justice, who were already salaried judges. This had been foreshadowed earlier, and in the later 1620s eight senators were appointed as itinerant justices and a pair of them made responsible for each quarter of the country. When, in 1671–2, the Court of Justiciary, in very much its modern form, was finally organised, the principle of utilising senators was followed. The lord justice general remained head of the court, with the lord justice clerk as his lieutenant; but the old-style deputies were replaced by five senators as commissioners of justiciary. The judges were to sit in Edinburgh during the 'session' and to go on circuit annually to certain specified towns. In 1830 the office of lord justice general was merged with that of lord president, and in 1887 all senators became commissioners of justiciary, so that the two central courts, for civil and criminal justice, came to have the same personnel. Yet each judge holds two offices, and wears distinct robes to show in which capacity he is acting. The court, which still sits in other centres besides Edinburgh, is a court of first instance for treason, murder and rape and a court of appeal from the sheriff courts in other criminal cases. A commissioner of justiciary (like a sheriff trying serious crimes) sits with a jury of fifteen, who decide by majority and may give the verdict 'Not Proven'. A Criminal Appeal Court, set up in 1926, is in effect an augmented session of the high court of justiciary.

The origins of local courts are to be found in the delegation by the king of judicial powers which he could not exercise in person or in his own court. Such delegation could take place in association with the tenure of land. Already in the twelfth century those who held land of the king—religious houses, lords of wide territories, barons with relatively small holdings and possibly even anyone holding a piece of land for knight service—had the right to hold courts for their tenants. It was almost inherent in the whole concept of the 'feudal pyramid' that the relation between the king and his tenants, who rendered 'suit' in his court, was repeated at lower levels. In general, every crown tenant, or at least every substantial crown tenant, had the right to punish his dependants by imprisonment or death, but the precise scope of his jurisdiction varied. Exception was normally made of the 'pleas of the crown', and as definition developed the jurisdiction of an ordinary baron's court never extended to such cases. But some greater tenants, lay and ecclesiastical, were endowed with regalian rights: they could deal even with the pleas of the crown—except, of course, treason—and their jurisdiction constituted a 'regality'. A regality court, presided over by the lord's steward, gave judgements in cases elsewhere dealt with in royal courts, and within a regality the steward operated much of the machinery which was operated elsewhere by the sheriffs—for example the issue of brieves and precepts and the holding of inquests in connection with succession to heritable property. As long as regality courts existed, they had

111

criminal jurisdiction equal to that of the High Court of Justiciary and civil jurisdiction equal to that of a sheriff.

But delegated justice could be dissociated from landholding and exercised by justiciars and sheriffs. The sheriff was at first an administrative and financial, rather than judicial, officer, but he acquired judicial functions as the king's representative, though it is likely that initially he acted only on the royal estates, holding a court for royal tenants, just as barons acted as judges on their estates. His seat, the headquarters of the sheriffdom, was at first in the king's castle, later in the king's burgh. As time went on, the sheriff accumulated more and more judicial functions and concurrently shed his executive and financial functions, until he became primarily a judge. In early times appeal lay from him to the justiciar. The office of sheriff usually became hereditary and the professional functions could be carried out by deputies.

In 1747, an act abolishing heritable jurisdictions affected nearly all local courts. Baron courts were not abolished, but their competence was restricted to very minor cases and, with the passing out of existence of the old agricultural system, in which they had played an important part, and with the increasing efficiency and availability of sheriff courts, they fell into desuetude. Regality courts were abolished, and so were hereditary sheriffships. Subsequently the shrieval system was reorganised, with a two-tier arrangement of sheriffs principal and sheriffs substitute. Until 1975 there were twelve sheriffs principal, each responsible for a county or group of counties; they were full-time judges only in Edinburgh (Midlothian and Peebles) and Glasgow (Lanarkshire) and elsewhere were advocates practising in Edinburgh and giving only limited time to their sheriffdoms but were able to hear appeals from sheriffs substitute. Since 1975 there have been only six sheriffs principal, all full-time judges. In general, therefore, 'the sheriff' is effectively the sheriff substitute, of whom there are about eighty, a judge in a court with competence to try nearly all crimes except treason, murder and rape and nearly all civil cases except divorce.

CHAPTER 5

Politics since the Union

It would be totally misleading to represent modern Scottish politics as having been determined by relations with England, yet changing attitudes to the union have done a good deal to shape the context of political life. There have been three phases. First there was about half a century of considerable discontent; then came roughly a century, 1750–1850, when the union was all but invariably accepted as part of the established order; thirdly, since the 1850s the union has been subject to recurrent criticism.

Some irritation in the years immediately following the union was almost inevitable, for not all the implications of the treaty could have been foreseen, and it had to be worked out in practice. After those initial years there still had to be a period of somewhat painful adjustment, while the Scots learned what it meant to be governed as part of a larger whole. Scott makes one of his characters in *The Heart of Midlothian* say, 'When we had a king and a chancellor and parliament-men o' oor ain, we could aye peeble them wi' stanes when they werena guid bairns. But naebody's nails can reach the length o' Lunnon'. The economic effects of the union were at first disappointing, mainly because in that sphere too there had to be a period of adjustment, and it was the middle of the century before the resultant expansion of Scottish commerce and manufacture became convincingly evident. It seemed in general that Scotland's interests were persistently ignored. The alien character of the government was illustrated by the prevalence of, and the sympathy with, smuggling—a consequence of the higher duties introduced at the union and their collection by English excise officers who operated with unprecedented efficiency. The 'free trader', as the smuggler was euphemistically called, was always the hero, and 'to jink the gauger' [evade the excise officer] was an honourable exploit. There were the Malt Tax Riots in Glasgow in 1725 and the Porteous Riot in Edinburgh eleven years later. In each case public opinion was with the law-breakers, and an officer who fired on the mob was tried and condemned; in Glasgow he was saved by a royal pardon, but in Edinburgh not even a royal pardon availed to save Captain Porteous from lynching.

Some have seen in the Jacobite rebellions further evidence of Scottish dissatisfaction. But the efforts of the Pretenders to make capital out of what they called 'the late unhappy union' and their promises to restore Scotland to its 'ancient, free and independent state' brought them small returns even in the 'Fifteen, while it has been shown that in the 'Forty-Five more Scots were in arms on the government side than on the Jacobite side. To most Scots, the Duke of Cumberland's forces were 'our army'. The welcome given to Cumberland, after his victory at Culloden, as 'the deliverer of this church and nation' and 'the happy restorer of our peace', rather suggests that by the middle of the century Scottish adjustment to union was complete. By that time a generation had grown up which had never known an independent Scotland.

What happened in the second phase, after about 1750, was the creation of a Scottish political consciousness which shared in British politics. The period before this adjustment in outlook began has been described as one of political torpor. It is certainly true that, however popular feeling might be stirred when vital Scottish interests were involved, there was no steady concern with the doings of the Westminster Parliament.

This was partly due to the restricted parliamentary franchise, for there were less than 4,000 voters in the whole country and even fewer had an effective voice. Of the 45 Scottish MPs, 30 represented the counties, one for each county except the six smallest, which were arranged in pairs, one of the pair taking it in turn to elect a member. The handful of voters in each county might be swayed by the interest of one or two magnates. Of the 66 royal burghs, Edinburgh sent a member and the others were arranged in fourteen groups of four or five. The member for a group was chosen by only four or five delegates, who had themselves been appointed by their town councils. Over-all, the government and its agents, by judicious use of patronage, exercised wide and often decisive influence. When the system of Henry Dundas, 1st Viscount Melville, had been perfected, at the end of the eighteenth century, this 'uncrowned king of Scotland' could boast that he controlled the results of the elections in at least 36 constituencies. The issue at elections was usually personal rather than political.

As the nominations of the Scottish MPs had been managed by the government of the day, they were not in a position to deny their maker when they reached Westminster. Their allegiance was not to political principles, but to the 'manager' for Scotland. At one point, it is said, one of them complained that the government's Scottish minister, the lord advocate, was not tall enough. 'The Scotch members', he explained, 'always vote with the Lord Advocate, and we therefore require to see him in a division. Now, I can see Mr. Pitt, and I can see Mr. Addington, but I cannot see the Lord Advocate'.

The first indications of a change came at the time of the American War of Independence (1776–83). Signs of awakening are not indeed to be found among the Scots at Westminster. During the unpopular administration of Lord North, and even towards its disastrous close, when the American colonies were lost and Britain involved in grave peril through war with France and Spain, the Scottish MPs did not depart from their tradition of subservience. In 1782 only six of them supported the motion of no-confidence which led finally to North's downfall. But the record of the Scottish MPs was not the record of the people of Scotland. The correspondence columns of newspapers, the records of debating societies, the pamphlets and the printed sermons, the addresses drawn up by various bodies, all disclose eager discussion of the rights and wrongs of the American dispute and of the conduct of British policy. The number of periodicals produced rose from about nine in 1770 to twice that number ten years later. It was significant of a changing emphasis that in 1775 the printer of the *Caledonian Mercury* felt it necessary to explain that 'the multiplicity of articles concerning American affairs ... obliges us to delay the debates in the General Assembly'. While there were loyal addresses to the king, some opinion was from the outset favourable to the colonists, and it strengthened as time passed.

Already before the war there had been agitation in Edinburgh for a broadening of the city constitution, and criticism of the maladministration of burgh finances. There had also been the first demands for the extension of the county franchise. With the stirring of public opinion towards the end of the war, interest turned more eagerly to the reform of the burgh constitutions and of the franchise, which was obviously far too restricted to reflect the new political consciousness. Six years after the end of the American Revolution came the French Revolution. Initially it stimulated political discussion and the reform movement; but later, especially after war began with revolutionary France in 1793, there was severe repression of liberal tendencies, which were deemed unpatriotic, and all talk of reform was suspect.

After the war ended, in 1815, agitation revived and was followed by reforms in administration in the 1820s, then reform of parliamentary representation and of the burgh constitutions in the 1830s. Subsequently the parliamentary franchise was extended by successive stages until adult suffrage was attained, and genuine representation was introduced in local government as well. There were also repeated increases in the number of Scottish members of the House of Commons. Scotland thus possessed the means to play a full part in British politics.

But any number of changes in electoral machinery would not of themselves have prevailed on the Scots to make British politics their own. There were other factors at work, leading to the fusing of the political consciousness of the two nations. It is true that there were some intrusive episodes, like the agitation in 1826, in which Sir Walter Scott took part, against the proposed abolition of the Scottish £1 note. But the general picture was one of the assimilation of Scottish life and thought to those of England.

One factor in this process, which has been going on ever since, has been the acceptance in Scotland of English literature and English history. The two countries have shared, as their common heritage, an ever-growing body of English literature: much of it, it is true, written by Scots, and some of it by Irishmen, but still English literature. To assimilate the spoken tongue to the literary language, some Scots in the late eighteenth century—and more in later times—assiduously cultivated English accent and idiom. Equally, the study of English history and the comparative neglect of Scottish history led to the acceptance of the false idea that the two countries share the same historic background. How far this can go was illustrated in 1965, when it was proposed that the seven hundredth anniversary of Simon de Montfort's parliament and the seven hundred and fiftieth anniversary of Magna Carta— both events which took place in what was at the time a foreign country—should be commemorated in Scotland. The Scottish Education Department was so insensitive as to suggest a school holiday to mark the occasion. The English would like to repeat the success which the Irish 'Scots' had in early centuries in foisting their own history on their partners in a united kingdom. The victory has not been complete, for Scotland has not yet taken over and made her own such heroes of English history as Ralegh and Drake, for instance. Yet the process continues, as we can see from the recent addition to the Scottish Calendar of the alien figure of Guy Fawkes, the anniversary of whose attempt to blow up the English Parliament—admittedly with a Scottish king in it— passed unnoticed in Scotland until a generation ago. Scotland's past tends to be viewed through the eyes of English historians, who regard anything not English as quaint, backward or even downright barbarous.

Industrial changes made a further contribution to assimilation, by speeding up travel and bringing about co-operation in various business ventures. The accompanying social changes intensified class divisions. Not only could the Scottish employee be persuaded that the English employee's interest and his own were one, but the unity of some industries throughout Britain increased the sense of solidarity. It is true to this day that Scotland is a more egalitarian country than England, but as a result of class-consciousness, horizontal division into classes became once more, as it was in the twelfth century, more important than vertical division into nations.

Again, there was the penetration into Scotland of a sense of sharing in British foreign policy. During the many wars of the eighteenth century, at least before the American War, days of thanksgiving for victories and of fasting for defeats were indeed observed, but they aroused little enthusiasm. Besides, throughout most of the country there was an inveterate prejudice against service in the regular army. If a son enlisted it was a family disgrace, and to get him out a matter of family honour. A minister remarked that in nineteen years only one person in his parish had been banished for theft and only one had enlisted as a soldier: and he added that 'having been got out of the army, he has ever since lived an industrious labouring man'. But during the long French wars of 1793–1815 the real danger of invasion and defeat, added to the economic ramifications of the war, went far towards consolidating national feeling as British. There was no difficulty about finding recruits for the volunteers, who had the enthusiasm, if they did not have the skill, to give an account of themselves against Boney's regulars. It is noticeable, too, that while it is rare to find in street-names or in monuments any commemoration of earlier wars, they still keep alive the memory of Wellington and Nelson, Trafalgar and Waterloo. In later times the acceleration of news services further contributed to a sense of sharing in the wars. And, of course, the old hostility to the army gave way to pride in the achievements of Scottish regiments.

Yet another feature was the part played by individual Scotsmen in British affairs. The union opened up careers south of the Border on a scale hitherto undreamed of—in medicine, in literature, in the diplomatic service, as well as in humbler capacities. It was a Scots gardener who made the discovery that 'although God had not given the English overmuch wit or sense, yet they were braw bodies to live with'. The ambitious carved a place for themselves in British culture and government, especially after the political awakening in the late eighteenth century. In the 82 years from 1707 until 1789 Scotland provided only three cabinet ministers; but between 1789 and 1832—only 43 years—she provided ten. The process was to accelerate. In the late nineteenth century and the early twentieth, to mention only the two highest positions in church and state, out of ten successive prime ministers six were Scots and out of five successive archbishops of Canterbury three were Scots. In a similar context, Scotland's share in populating and administering the British Empire increased the sense of unity with England. Behind the opportunities for careers in England and in the Empire lay the attractions of an English education—English public schools for some, Oxford and Cambridge as the avenue to success even for men who had already taken a degree in Scotland.

Scottish political history, then, merged in the nineteenth century into British political history. But still with a difference—a difference in the record of the political representation of the two countries. After the first extension of the franchise in 1832, a general election usually saw the majority in the House of Commons change from Conservative to Liberal or vice versa. But this was the result of a swing of the pendulum in England. In Scotland, only once between 1832 and 1918 did a general election fail to produce a majority of Liberal members. It happened more than once that a Conservative majority in England was outweighed by an overwhelming Liberal majority in Scotland, so that Scottish voters determined the complexion of the British government.

The first thing to shake the Liberal predominance was the split in the party over Irish Home Rule in 1886, when the Unionist section commanded a certain amount of Scottish support. It was the amalgamation of those Liberal Unionists with the Conservative party which gave that party real prospects in Scotland, and it is significant that the term 'Unionist' has been used in Scotland in preference to 'Conservative'. Yet, even though deprived of its Unionist wing, the Liberal party again commanded majorities in Scotland after 1900.

The reasons for the Scottish attachment to Liberalism are not obvious. It is true that radicalism can be found in Scotland as early as the 1790s, when some extreme reformers went to the point of treasonable correspondence with the French revolutionaries. It reappeared after 1815, and, when the parliamentary reform which came in 1832 benefited only the middle classes,

119

agitation for further extension of the franchise went on. But to see Scottish Liberalism as the expression of Scottish radicalism would be a great oversimplification. The Liberal party in the nineteenth century was far from radical, and Scotland's essential radicalism found its outlet rather in deviations from the major parties: there was, for example, the support for Chartism in Scotland, just as, later on, when the Labour party superseded Liberalism as the alternative to Conservatism, there was Scottish support for the more extreme Independent Labour party. However, the more radical line taken by the Liberal party in the early years of this century in national insurance, reform of the House of Lords, Irish Home Rule and Scottish Home Rule, may well have attracted wider support in Scotland than in England.

The whole situation changed after World War I. The first disaster for the Liberals was in 1924, when their Scottish representation fell to nine. In 1945 not a single Liberal was returned in Scotland and in the next two or three elections there was only one—Mr Grimond in Orkney and Shetland. Subsequently there was a certain recovery, for in one general election the four most northerly constituencies were all won by Liberals and a fifth, in the Borders, was captured shortly afterwards.

In 1922 there were 29 Socialist members in Scotland; there were 35 in 1923 and 38 in 1929. In 1931 the Socialist landslide was as marked in Scotland as elsewhere, for the National Government won no less than 67 of the 74 Scottish seats. In 1935 Socialists won 24 Scottish seats and it was again plain that they provided the alternative to Conservatism. At the same time, while Socialism built up its position on the ruins of Liberalism, a very large number of former Liberals preferred to vote for the Conservative party, which gained a position it had never held in the days of Liberal ascendancy.

For a time the swing of the pendulum operated almost as much in Scotland as elsewhere. Between 1918 and 1950, the Conservatives had a majority on four occasions; Labour, equally, had the largest number of seats on four occasions, though without an over-all majority. It is probably only a coincidence that inconstancy started after women got the vote in 1918. This period of oscillation was followed by one almost of equilibrium. In 1945 the Socialists had 41 seats, the Conservatives only 32, and this was in line with the general swing to the left in Britain as a whole. But in 1950 Labour had 37, Conservatives 32, and in 1951 Scotland followed the general swing to the right only to the extent of giving each party 35 seats. In 1955 only a single seat changed hands, passing from Labour to Conservative. But this phase of stability did not last. In 1959 Labour increased their seats to 38 and Conservatives dropped again to 32. This trend has continued, and all the more recent elections have shown a considerable Labour preponderance.

It would be tempting to see the Scottish preference for Socialism as a repetition of the Scottish preference for Liberalism. But such a comparison is superficial. In the nineteenth century neither major party was a class party; society was divided from top to bottom between the two. It was not in the programme of the Liberal party to further the interests of merely one section of the community. It could reasonably be characterised—and this is undoubtedly where part of its appeal lay—as a party pledged to social justice, especially in its more radical days after 1900, but it was not pledged to serve the selfish interests of its supporters or to set up a new privileged class in place of an old. Besides, the Liberal party had had no monopoly of social justice, and the Conservatives made quite a lot of capital out of some of their social legislation. In fact, as the electorate was enlarged and Scottish working men started to use their votes, some looked at the peers and big business men who were Liberals and said, 'That's no party for us'. The whole situation was much more complex than it seems to be when viewed from the standpoint of the class-dominated politics of the twentieth century.

Although the Labour movement had some Scots as leaders almost from the outset, their work was done mainly in England and it took the party so long to become rooted in Scotland that it can hardly be regarded as indigenous. Keir Hardie (1856–1915), a Lanarkshire miner, left the Liberal party in 1888 to form a Scottish Labour party, with R. B. Cunninghame Grahame as chairman and himself as secretary. But when Hardie reached

Parliament as a Labour member in 1892 it was for a London seat, and it was not until 1906 that Scotland first acquired Labour MPs—two of them; a third was added in 1910.

Minor parties had various fortunes. The Communist party was founded in 1920, initially with a view to revolution. However, William Gallacher, who declared that his party had 'something better to do than waste time over parliamentary elections', subsequently sat for many years as member for West Fife and Scotland's sole Communist MP. In 1929 Communist candidates polled 24,000 votes and in 1931, although it was a year of disaster for the left, they polled 31,000. Although Communists are so often voted into controlling positions in Trade Unions, their fellows have never given them more than meagre support at parliamentary elections. Extremists used to find what seemed a more respectable and less unpatriotic outlet in the Independent Labour Party, for two or three of its handful of members held seats steadily in the west. Clydeside had a reputation for being 'Red' from at least 1918, when there was a 'Red Friday' riot, and it remained preponderantly left-wing in its representation, though it was noticeable that even in 1945, when a massive swing swept Labour into power, five out of the fifteen Glasgow MPs were Conservatives. After World War II minor parties continued to play an almost insignificant role. The Communists have not held a seat and have lessened their poll: in 1955 they totalled only 13,000 votes. The ILP disappeared after 1951, and the only small party to make an impression was the Scottish National Party.

After the century during which there had been almost universal acquiescence in the union, there came a third phase, during which the union has repeatedly been questioned. In 1850 it was complained that Scotland had only 'the fag-end of a single man's time and the fag-end of the time of the parliament of England' and in 1851 the Convention of Royal Burghs drew up a memorial on the neglect of Scottish affairs. In 1853 there was founded a National Association for the Vindication of Scottish Rights. Among its leaders were William Edmondstoun Aytoun, Professor of Rhetoric in Edinburgh, best known for his romantic *Lays of the Scottish Cavaliers*, and James Grant, a prolific writer of historical novels.

Page *123* (*above*) A nineteenth-century coastal steamer, the *St Clair* (1868–1937), which carried passengers, mail and general cargo from Leith to Aberdeen, Caithness, Stornoway, Orkney and Shetland; (*below*) the first of the inshore fishing boats provided under the Highlands and Islands Development Board scheme

Page 124 (above) West coast vegetation: the gardens at Inverewe; (below) diesel train on the West Highland line to Fort William and Mallaig

In other words, the movement was inspired partly at least by middle class romanticism, which has played a conspicuous part in nationalist movements ever since. This is not surprising, for the urban proletariat was apt to regard itself as part of a British 'working class' and the upper and middle classes were more open to influences which did something to counteract anglicisation.

Although the Scottish vernacular, as a spoken tongue, gradually gave way to English, it had been revived as a literary language in the eighteenth century by Allan Ramsay, Fergusson and Burns and has been kept alive ever since. Although not one person in a hundred may ever read the verses of Scottish poets, the fact that they exist has helped to maintain a sense of national identity. Early in the nineteenth century there was the romantic movement in historical writing, associated mainly with Sir Walter Scott, and this spread widely, if sometimes inaccurately, an acquaintance with Scotland's past as something of marked individuality. In the same period the classical age of Scottish historical scholarship had begun, and those who read its output could be in no doubt that Scotland had a distinctive past in which there was much room for pride. On a very different plane there was the lively cultivation, most of it deplorably unhistorical, of clans and tartans, kilts and bagpipes. This too was restricted socially, for in the Highlands the kilt is almost confined to the landed gentry and their imitators. The beginning of the cult is often attributed to the romantic movement of the early nineteenth century and it is true that the first visit of a Hanoverian king to Scotland—George IV in 1822—was a 'tartan occasion'. But it was actually as early as 1789, a year after the death of Bonnie Prince Charlie, that George, then Prince of Wales, first made his appearance in 'Highland dress'. One wonders what his great uncle, the Duke of Cumberland, would have thought of it.

Romanticism is a slender foundation for a political movement. The Association for the Vindication of Scottish Rights seemed to have much support: the committee included the lord provosts of Edinburgh and Perth, a public meeting in the capital was attended by 2,000 people and one in Glasgow attracted 5,000. Resolutions demanded a secretary of state for Scotland and more Scottish

MPs. The association was critical of the use of the title 'Queen of England', of the small proportion of public money spent in Scotland and of the absence of naval and military establishments there—all points which were to be repeated time and time again. But it all amounted to little more than aimless agitation and the association dissolved in 1856.

The next period of activity came in the 1880s. The main issue was the demand for a Scottish secretary, which had never been quite lost sight of during the previous thirty years. In 1881, when the matter was raised in the House of Lords, it was supported by the Earl of Rosebery, a gifted young politician and a close friend of Gladstone, the prime minister. Rosebery himself was a staunch adherent of legislative union, but he was aware that others were prepared to go further than he was, for he remarked that 'the words "Home Rule" have begun to be distinctly and loudly mentioned in Scotland'. Gladstone began to toy with the idea of all-round devolution within the British Isles to assist an 'over-weighted parliament'. Presently he was converted to the cause of Home Rule for Ireland, which absorbed his energies for the remainder of his career. Thus, while all-round devolution became secondary, Irish Home Rule was adopted as part of the Liberal programme, though at the cost of a split, and as the Liberal-Unionists and their conservative allies, in reaction against Irish Home Rule, became in effect 'unionists all round', opinion crystallised against Scottish Home Rule. On the other hand, 1886 saw the foundation of the Scottish Home Rule Association. The agitation of the 1880s did not produce Home Rule, but it did produce a secretary for Scotland in 1885, an indication that, although a separate legislature might not be conceded, there could be a separate administration.

To Scottish Liberals the idea of a separate parliament made a very special appeal, for, on Scotland's voting record, it could be expected to give them uninterrupted control. The English Liberals, however, who knew that the Scottish vote could put them into power when they did not have a majority in England, did not share the Scottish enthusiasm. It is not surprising, therefore, that although Scottish Home Rule became officially part of the Liberal programme, to be made much of when the party was in opposition, yet when it was in power no effective action was taken. During the Liberal governments from 1906 onwards, a Government of Scotland Bill was almost an annual event, and the Liberals could unquestionably have carried such a bill through if they had really meant business, but the matter was not regarded as one of urgency. Yet, if World War I had not come when it did, if Irish Home Rule had been put into effect in 1914 as intended, and if the Liberals had remained in office, it is hard to see how they could have continued to evade the fulfilment of their undertakings.

Once more a period of activity led not to Home Rule but to other measures of appeasement. The Scottish Grand Committee for the consideration of Scottish bills, set up originally by the Liberals in 1894 but lapsing under a Conservative administration, was revived in 1907; Redford Barracks were built near Edinburgh, to obviate the threatened removal to England of Scotland's last cavalry regiment, the Scots Greys, and accommodating an infantry regiment as well; a new military camp was established at Stobs, near Hawick; and a large naval base created at Rosyth.

After World War I the Socialists were in the same position with regard to Home Rule as the Liberals had been. Ramsay Macdonald, the first Labour prime minister, had been secretary of the Scottish Home Rule Association formed in 1886; Keir Hardie had sponsored a Home Rule Bill in 1906; Tom Johnston—who was later to be an outstanding Scottish Secretary—was an office-bearer in a new Home Rule Association formed in 1917. However, while the Labour party paid lip-service to Home Rule while out of office, its promises were forgotten when it was in office. Many of the Labour men were not only internationalists in principle, but had so fallen under the spell of England as to have little sympathy with Scotland. There was also the same practical consideration as there had been with the Liberals. The British Labour Party has been bound to look with disfavour on a Scottish parliament if it would lose them the Scottish Labour vote, which at general elections in 1964 and on other occasions, put them into office when they did not have a majority in England. It was perfectly safe for the Socialists to support Home Rule Bills during the Conservative government of 1924–9, knowing that there was not the faintest chance of their becoming law. After 1928, however, the stream of abortive Home Rule Bills dried up; there was not another until 1966.

The agitation between the wars had produced other concessions. The secretary for Scotland was upgraded to a secretary of state in 1926, and in 1928 the boards hitherto responsible for a good deal of Scottish administration were for the most part replaced by departments under him. It was the logical consequence of this policy that in 1939, with the opening of St Andrew's House, the headquarters of Scottish administration were moved from Whitehall to Edinburgh. Just after the war, in 1948, the powers of the Scottish Grand Committee were enlarged.

But those who cared seriously about Home Rule were frustrated. The one party which had come anywhere near to taking effective action—the Liberal party—was now an almost negligible political force. Even had the Labour party been serious, its administrations of 1924 and 1929–31 were weak and short-lived and when it attained real power in 1945 other issues predominated. Frustration had led in 1928 to the formation of the National Party of Scotland. With its left-wing bias and its tendency to aim at complete separation from England, it made a very poor showing at the general elections of 1929 and 1931. A separate 'Scottish Party', founded in 1932, with a more moderate tone and the support of the Duke of Montrose, Professor Dewar Gibb and Sir Alexander McEwen, polled 6,000 votes at a by-election in 1933. In 1934 the two parties amalgamated, to form the Scottish National Party, but tensions between moderate and extreme elements persisted and in 1942 the moderates withdrew to form a body called 'Scottish Convention'.

After World War II there was again a period of intense activity. There was a 'Covenant', to which about 2,000,000 names were ultimately appended, pledging its signatories to work for legislative devolution within the framework of the United Kingdom. Then came a stirring incident in 1950, when the ancient Scottish coronation stone, removed to Westminster Abbey by Edward I in

1296, was recovered by a group of young Scots and deposited in the abbey of Arbroath; there was agitation against the numeral II in the Queen's title after her accession in 1952; there was a somewhat dubious plot to blow up St Andrew's House; and there was the actual blowing up of one or two pillar boxes bearing the obnoxious numeral in the royal monogram. As a sop to the Scottish sentiment which was so obviously stirred, in 1953 the Queen, after her coronation in London, came to the High Kirk of St Giles in Edinburgh to receive into her hands—but not to wear —the crown, sceptre and sword of state of Scotland. Not all Scots approved of the surreptitious recovery of the coronation stone; but it was universally felt to be an affront when this ancient relic of the Scottish monarchy was ignominiously hustled back to London in the boot of a police car. Fewer Scots approved of the dangerous pastime of blowing up pillar-boxes; but Scotland's highest legal luminary gave a solemn ruling against the propriety of the numeral II. And the effect of the pageantry in St Giles' was rather spoiled by the fact that the Queen had been advised to turn up for the occasion in everyday walking-out dress, with a handbag slung over her arm, exactly as if she had been out on a shopping expedition and had just strolled in casually.

But Scottish Nationalist candidates continued to lose elections and in the main to lose their deposits. There had been only one exception: in 1945, at a by-election, Dr Robert McIntyre became MP for Motherwell, only to be unseated at the general election a few weeks later. It was another twenty-two years before Mrs Ewing had a similar victory in a by-election at Hamilton; and as some had foreseen, she shared Dr McIntyre's fate at the next general election. The Scottish National Party was much encouraged by the 1966 general election, when their total vote was the highest ever, by Mrs Ewing's feat and by the very successful performance of their candidates at local government elections in 1968. But it became evident that once more the steam had gone out of the nationalist movement for the time being. Far from the local government gains being repeated, many seats were lost in 1969 and 1970. At the general election of 1970, those who said that they would not be surprised if the SNP won no seats at all were very nearly right: the last result to be declared, that for the Western Isles, proved to be the first victory of a nationalist candidate at a general election. A second seat was won at a by-election in 1973. One element in the occasional successes of the nationalists had been a sense of disillusion with the two major parties and a feeling that they would not do much for Scotland, especially its outlying areas; it was this attitude of 'a plague on both your houses' that had led to the remarkable success of the Liberals in 1964–5 in capturing all the northern seats and one Border seat.

In 1973 a Royal Commission on the constitution, under Lord Kilbrandon, recommended a Scottish legislature with wide powers, combined with a reduced number of Scottish MPs at Westminster. Whether anything like this would be implemented seemed to depend on the attitude of the two major parties. Up to this point it had been clear that, however strong sentiment might be in favour of some kind of Home Rule, when Scottish voters went to the polling booths they tended to vote on British political issues and support the programme of a British political party. They would have been in a position to demand Home Rule only if their concern for Scottish issues was so strong as to cause them to return a substantial number of Nationalists to Westminster, but there had been little sign that they would put Scottish interests before the interests of their class or what they thought best for Britain as a whole. The other way in which Home Rule could come about would be for one of the two major parties to adopt it as part of its programme—and, for a change, keep its word. But it was barely conceivable that the Conservative party, the Unionist party, could repudiate what had always been a central item of its policy. Even a somewhat innocuous plan for a 'Scottish Assembly', proposed by Conservative headquarters, was bitterly criticised by Scottish Conservatives. It was even harder to believe that the Labour party would decide to further Home Rule—even apart from the practical advantages to it of Scottish support at Westminster. The party's philosophy was based on the division of men into social classes rather than into nations, and the whole structure of organised 'Labour' stands for the negation of nationalism. Despite Kilbrandon, it seemed likely that previous patterns would recur and that Scotland, instead of Home Rule, could expect no more than further instalments of appeasement. The effect of the startling results of the 1974 elections, which gave the SNP seven seats at Westminster in February and eleven in October, will be explained in chapter 11.

Already before 1974, however, the situation was changed by Britain's entry into the European Economic Community and the discovery of oil under the North Sea. When Britain joined the Common Market on 1 January 1973, Scotland was for the second time joining a larger union. The economic prospects were extensively, but inconclusively, debated, and one cogent point seemed that as Scotland's trade with the Common Market countries formed a much smaller proportion of Scotland's total trade than was true of the United Kingdom as a whole, economic advantages might well be slow to reach Scotland and perhaps intensify the preponderance of a prosperous south-east England. It was soon apparent that direct trade, at least, between Scotland and the continent was dwindling, for traffic came to be mainly by vast lorries operating via some port in the south of England. But economic considerations were not the whole story. Scotland's occasional restiveness under rule from London suggested that the country might not take kindly to a situation in which decisions were made in Brussels. Scots saw, too, that countries comparable to their own in size—and even little Luxembourg—were separate members of the community, each with a direct voice in its policy; they noted, too, that Norway, many of whose problems resemble their own, rejected membership. The fact that so many of the British people as a whole were lukewarm to the EEC and that many left-wing politicians denounced it hardly contributed to give it a favourable reception in Scotland.

North Sea oil, it seemed, was presenting Scotland with an unprecedented economic asset, the value of which was likely to increase as other supplies of fuel became more unreliable and more costly. The fear that the exploitation of this asset would have little regard for Scottish interests, and that it might be directed from London, or even from Brussels, strengthened the nationalist cause, which made much of the slogan 'Scotland's Oil'. On the other hand, it was obvious that only very forceful action indeed would persuade London to stand aside and see the control of the oil pass to an independent Scotland which might not be in the EEC. However, if 'Britain's Oil' was going to be fragmented by the concept of 'Scotland's Oil', it soon became evident that fragmentation could go further. Far and away the bulk of the North Sea oil was situated in the far north and was going to be brought ashore in Shetland, so 'Shetland's Oil' in turn appealed to islanders who had no enthusiasm at all for the SNP and for rule from Edinburgh.

Discussion of the Kilbrandon proposals or any other scheme for legislative devolution encountered a fresh complication with the reorganisation of local government in 1974-5. When half of the population of Scotland formed a single region of Strathclyde, with its own elected council, many thought it absurd to insert a further elected assembly, for the whole of Scotland, between such a body and Westminster. It was regretted that the local government changes had been undertaken in advance of plans for devolution, because the government of the country and the government of its parts could more usefully have been considered in a single exercise.

CHAPTER 6

Central and Local Administration

In the present situation, when separate Scottish departments perform many functions, there is a tendency to read into the treaty of 1707 the idea that the union, though legislative, was not administrative. But it was only with the great extension of governmental activity in the nineteenth century that separate Scottish departments emerged. The present state of affairs was not in the minds of those who framed the union treaty.

Precisely what was in their minds is not easy to determine. The inference to be drawn from the treaty's general tenor seems to be that the union was to be administrative as well as legislative. Yet certain provisions made a unitary administration not quite practicable, whether the framers of the treaty realised it or not. Scots law was to remain; the Scottish courts, with their judges and officials, were to continue; there were to be separate seals for Scotland; the Scottish registers and records were still to be kept 'in that part of the united kingdom now called Scotland'. Then there was the provision about the Privy Council: 'The queen and her successors may continue a privy council in Scotland, for preserving of public peace and order, until the parliament of Great Britain shall think fit to alter it or establish any other effectual method for that end.' The Privy Council was abolished in the very next year, but no substitute was then explicitly provided 'for that end', that is, for preserving public peace and order in Scotland.

Appointments had to be made to Scottish offices, and were bound to be made on the advice of someone who could speak for Scottish interests. The judicial system, the seals and the registers, required either separate administration or administration on Scottish advice. Emergency decisions had to be taken at times of riot and rebellion. The abolition of the Privy Council left a kind of vacuum: who was to take over its wide residuary powers in the day-to-day maintenance of order? There was, all in all, bound to be some kind of minister with a degree of responsibility for Scottish affairs.

As the administrative implications of the union were worked out in practice, the years from 1707 to 1746 were a period of experiments and expedients. At times there was a secretary for Scotland; at times there was none and Scottish affairs were handled by one of the two English secretaries—known at that time as the secretaries for the northern and southern departments —who shared responsibility for home and foreign affairs. The vacillation between those two arrangements was due more to the personal or party considerations of the moment than to any reasoned policy or principle. However, the amount of Scottish business was too small for the job of a third secretary to be a full-time one, and those who supported the idea of a unified administration could ask: why should Scotland require a separate secretary any more than, say, Yorkshire?

After 1746 Scottish affairs were managed, nominally, by one of the two existing secretaries; and after 1782, when the secretariat was reorganised, by the home secretary. But the formal position hardly corresponded with reality. That there were difficulties in the way of a completely unified administration had already been demonstrated in the periods between 1707 and 1746 when there had not been a third secretary. Between 1725 and 1742, for example, effective control of Scottish administration was in the hands of the Duke of Argyll and a good deal of authority lay with Duncan Forbes, first as lord advocate, later as lord president. And so it continued. There was always a Scottish administrator, whatever his title or office; and many of the functions of a Scottish secretary were discharged by the lord advocate; who was in practice little less than minister for Scotland. Through his hands passed applications for appointments; bills relating to Scotland were framed in consultation with him; and the details of policy, if not its broad lines, must often have been shaped in his office.

This role of the lord advocate served well enough for a time.

But the scope of government business began to expand, the extension of the franchise increased interest in how affairs were conducted, and MPs became—for a time—more independent. Restiveness appeared. Even before the first Reform Act, it had been waggishly reported, 'Arrived at Edinburgh the Lord Chancellor of Scotland, the Lord Justice-General, the Lord Privy Seal, the Privy Council and the Lord Advocate—all in one post-chaise, containing a single person.' After a generation of agitation, a secretary for Scotland was at length appointed in 1885. Especially at first, the new office had the weakness of lack of continuity: there were five secretaries for Scotland within the first two years. Too often it was a mere stepping-stone towards higher office, and it did not always command the whole-hearted attention of its nomadic holders.

As the scope of governmental activity extended in the nineteenth century, the needs of central administration were met largely by ad hoc boards. The Board of Supervision, erected under the Poor Law Act of 1845, supervised the work of the parochial boards; as its functions were extended, it became the Local Government Board in 1894 and the Board of Health in 1919. The Board of Commissioners in Lunacy, dating from 1857, supervised local boards and reported on establishments for the care of the insane. Its title was changed in 1913, rather curiously, to the General Board of Control for Scotland. For prisons a board of directors had existed from 1839, and in 1877 they were replaced by the Prison Commission. The Fishery Board appeared in 1882. The Board of Agriculture, as organised in 1911, took over the functions of the Fisheries Board and the Congested Districts Board (set up in 1897 to deal with specific Highland problems). In addition to the Boards, there was the Scotch Education Department, established in 1872 to supervise and co-ordinate the work of the School Boards, provide inspectors and control examination standards.

The general concept lying behind the earlier boards was that administration should be directed by bodies composed partly of specialist and professional members who were usually paid—for example, medical or legal practitioners or individuals with know-

135

ledge of fisheries—and partly of eminent laymen representing the public, for example lord provosts or sheriffs, who were unpaid. The existence of the boards meant that there was something of a ready-made empire for the secretary for Scotland to take over in 1885. From that point the independent or specialised character of the boards became less conspicuous, and they tended more and more to consist of nominees of the secretary and to work under his direction. When the Board of Supervision was reconstituted as the Local Government Board, the lord provosts and sheriffs who had previously been members disappeared; in the Board of Agriculture of 1911 there were three members, none of them there ex officio or required to have special qualifications, but all of them appointed on the recommendation of the secretary and required to comply with his instructions. Besides, the secretary was ex officio 'vice-president' of the fictitious committee of the privy council which, with the lord president of the council as its figurehead, constituted the Education Department.

Clearly the boards were going to become a mere façade for the secretary. Before 1914 there was a good deal of discussion about the position. On the one hand, it was argued that the concentration of so many functions in the hands of the secretary had the result of increasing the power of the permanent officials, who were not adequately supervised and made to feel their responsibility, through a minister, to the public, so that administration had a more bureaucratic tinge in Scotland than it had in England. It was urged that the boards should be maintained, against the encroachments of the secretary, because they provided for control by persons with technical knowledge and experience of public affairs. On the other hand, it was argued that the boards were not responsible to parliament, that they did not preserve the distinction between persons selected for political offices and for permanent offices and that they were staffed through patronage rather than by the competitive examinations now necessary for civil servants. The Royal Commission on the Civil Service, in 1914, condemned the board system.

Owing to the war, the victory of the civil service and the secretary was deferred. The first change was the appointment, in

1919, of a parliamentary under-secretary for Scotland, with specific responsibility for health. Then in 1926 the secretary himself was upgraded to a secretary of state. As a result of changes made in 1928 and 1939, departments under the secretary superseded the boards—the departments of Agriculture, Education, Health and Prisons. This meant that the office of the secretary was discharged through four departments of equal status, each under a permanent secretary responsible to the secretary of state. The Board of Control retained its separate existence; on the other hand, some of the older and residual functions of the secretary came into the hands of a Scottish Home Department. Up to the beginning of 1935 nearly all the work of the Scottish Office was done at Dover House in Whitehall, but at that point an office was opened in Edinburgh, and in 1939 St Andrew's House became the headquarters of Scottish departments. A second under-secretary was added to the establishment in 1940, a minister of state in 1951 and a third under-secretary shortly afterwards. As a result of the findings of the Balfour Commission of 1952–4, responsibility in Scotland for roads and bridges, animal health and the appointment of justices of the peace was transferred to the secretary of state. The distribution of functions among departments has several times been modified: in 1992 there were five departments — Agriculture and Fisheries, Education, Home and Health, Environment, and Industry. A number of United Kingdom ministries still operate north of the Border, especially in fields where there is no separate code of law, no distinctive Scottish tradition or no peculiar Scottish needs.

Local government in anything like the sense in which we understand it today is in the main a recent creation. Until at least the seventeenth century the most familiar kind of local government was the government of landowners. In the days when tenants' strips lay intermingled with each other, the cattle and sheep of several tenants grazed together, and agricultural operations required joint action, regulations for 'good neighbourhood' were made in the baron court, which did a good deal of the work done nowadays by the Land Court, and also encouraged good husbandry by rules for the care of the cultivated and pasture land.

137

The parishes and the burghs, however, were also units of local government. From the early thirteenth century every part of Scotland and every inhabitant of Scotland was within a parish, which was thus a unit of which everyone in the rural areas was conscious. Primarily it was a worshipping community, but it was also, in modern terms, something of a rate-paying community to the extent that all its inhabitants contributed to the upkeep of the church and the priest, and the church, as the only public building in the parish, was used for secular as well as religious purposes. There was a curious element of something like democracy, for the appointment of the parish clerk lay formally with the parishioners: in practice he was often nominated, but the people had at least to give their approval, and the franchise in such 'elections' extended to women. The Reformation laid a fresh emphasis on the parish and introduced the kirk session of elders. The parish has perhaps the longest history of any organisation in the country and over the centuries has been significant for secular as well as ecclesiastical purposes.

Some burghs perhaps originated before parishes, but they vanished as units of local government in 1975. While towns could grow by natural process, a burgh, as a legal institution, had to be created by a definite act and only the king could erect, or authorise the erection of, a burgh. It is true that we have no evidence of the creation of quite a number of burghs and know only when their burghal status is first mentioned. Stirling, Roxburgh, Berwick and others were already going concerns as burghs in the 1120s, and when David I authorised his new abbey of Holyrood to create its burgh of Canongate he referred to 'my burgh of Edinburgh' as something already in existence. The creation of many burghs can be assigned to later twelfth-century kings; examples of ecclesiastical burghs, founded by royal licence in the same period, are St Andrews and Glasgow; and, rather later and more slowly, lay magnates followed the example of the churchmen.

From the outset, burghs were demarcated socially and economically in a predominantly rural scene, and institutional demarcation soon arose. Initially a burgh, like any other estate, was in the charge of an officer of the owner of the land on which it stood: the term *prepositus*, which gives us the 'provost' of the Scottish burgh, was used in the twelfth century of any officer appointed to have charge of an estate. But the burgesses, at least in royal burghs, achieved a cohesion which made them legally a corporate body and they acquired the right, probably not later than 1300, to elect the provost and also the subsidiary officers or bailies. By about the same time there would be a gild or council which made regulations for the burgh's affairs. Another important step was the introduction of 'feu-ferm' tenure. At first the rents of the tofts, or plots of ground, in a royal burgh, were paid to the Treasury by the individual burgesses, but from the fourteenth century the burgh authorities compounded by making over to the crown a specified sum, fixed in perpetuity, as the 'burgh ferm'. Hitherto each burgess had stood in a direct relationship to the king; now it was the community which stood in such a relationship. And one can speculate whether this facilitated the representation of the burghs in Parliament, which started in the same period.

For a time, burghs erected directly by the king on his own lands far outnumbered those erected, under licence from the king, on the lands of the church or of barons: in 1286 there were at least 37 royal burghs but only 7 ecclesiastical burghs and 7 baronial burghs. At that stage the king's burghs and the others were alike 'free burghs', and some at least of the non-royal burghs had privileges identical with those of royal burghs. Foreign trade was always restricted to burghs (partly for convenience in collecting customs), but not at first to royal burghs, and each burgh had its monopoly of trade within a certain area, its 'trade precinct'. Only within a burgh could articles be manufactured for sale, and only burghs were normally authorised to have markets and fairs. It is true that a royal burgh was usually associated with a royal castle and would be the head place of a sheriffdom, but this did not give it a distinct status. Some burghs initially royal could be granted to barons along with the land on which they stood; on the other hand, a burgh not initially royal could be transferred to the crown.

Later, though perhaps not completely until the seventeenth century, a 'free burgh' was equated with a 'royal burgh', and there were many disputes between royal burghs, which claimed a monopoly of foreign trade, and non-royal burghs which, they held, were encroaching on the monopoly. The term *burgus regalis* first appears in 1401 and, by a curious coincidence, the term *burgus baronie* appears in another document of the same year. Such a burgh of barony was not a new thing in substance, and it is not clear if even at this point a different status was implied, but by 1450 a clear concept of a 'burgh of barony' had emerged, and from that point there was a stream of creations of such burghs. They were regularly granted authority to have craftsmen to manufacture articles, markets (usually each week) and fairs (perhaps once or twice a year). Such burghs could be erected without affecting the free burghs' rights in foreign trade. A burgh of barony, on the lands of a baron, differed only in name from a burgh of regality, on the lands of a magnate, lay or ecclesiastical, whose lands had been erected into a regality.

If the burghs had ever been democratic in anything like the modern sense, they had long ceased to be so by the eighteenth century. In Edinburgh, for example, the town council consisted of 33 members, 19 of them chosen by their predecessors and themselves choosing their successors, and 14 of them being deacons of the incorporated trades, which had a total membership of under 700. Yet by 1800 the population was over 100,000 and there were over 10,000 householders paying rents of £5 or more, for whose representation the oligarchy made no provision. In some burghs of regality and barony the superior simply appointed the magistrates, while in others there was no corporate organisation at all, no provision for assessment, no possibility of organising police or of furnishing amenities. In hardly any burgh was there any control over the actions of the councillors, who could do very much what they liked with the burgh's revenues, for their fellow townsmen had no power to vote them out of office. Because of this weakness, in some burghs there were set up, alongside the burgh councils, 'police commissioners', elected bodies with power to impose rates and with such functions as cleansing, lighting and watching.

In 1833 came three reforms in burgh organisation. The Burgh

Page 141 Dunstaffnage Bay and Ben Cruachan, 1954. The pier has since been demolished. The cantilever bridge on the left was built in 1903 to carry the Ballachulish branch railway across the mouth of Loch Etive

Page 142 West Lothian landscape at Broxburn: on left, the Union Canal passes between shale bings and is crossed by the 'Refinery Bridge', to the right of which are rows of shale-miners' cottages; at top right is the viaduct of thirty-six arches carrying the Edinburgh-Glasgow railway over the River Almond

Reform Act provided that in royal burghs the councils should be chosen by the persons qualified to vote in parliamentary elections, that is, householders whose property was valued at £10 or more. Twelve 'populous places' which had become parliamentary constituencies in 1832 became 'parliamentary burghs', with councils and constitutions like those of royal burghs. Thirdly, the General Police Act permitted the adoption by any burgh of provisions for watching, lighting and cleansing which would involve the election of police commissioners such as already existed in some places. In 1850 the Police and Improvement (Scotland) Act made arrangements for the erection of populous places into burghs and by 1892 there were over 100 such 'Police Burghs'. In some older burghs the police commissioners and the town council had already amalgamated by special acts, and in 1892 the Burgh Police (Scotland) Act merged them all. One important feature of the nineteenth century was the extension of the functions of town councils to, for example, the provision of gas, electricity and local transport.

The extension of something like local government beyond the parishes and the burghs and into the county, was the work of the seventeenth century. Justices of the peace, first appointed by James VI, acquired certain administrative duties after the Restoration, not least in connection with roads. The more important office of commissioners of supply was an offshoot of the growth of taxation. The taxes raised by the Covenanters for their war against the king required new valuations of property, and those valuations, at first made—in default of suitable secular organs of local government—by presbyteries, were later made by commissioners specially appointed in each shire. There was no release from taxation during the Cromwellian occupation and although 1660 brought a 'restoration' it proved impossible to do without taxation based on regular assessment, so that what had begun as a revolutionary expedient became part of regular administration. Commissioners were initially proprietors, superiors or life-renters of land to the annual value of £100 Scots—later raised to £100 sterling; but in time sheriffs and magistrates of burghs were added. Almost as soon as the commissioners appeared, their

143

possible value for other purposes besides assessment was realised, and in 1668 they were associated with justices of the peace for road administration. They became responsible for financing the militia, maintaining court-houses, raising money for the apprehension of criminals and their detention in prison. The commissioners remained the most important officers in local government until 1889, when most of their functions, as well as the administrative functions of JPs, were transferred to county councils.

Very much as commissioners of supply acted in the shire, so 'heritors' acted in the parish. Under a system stemming indirectly from the medieval obligation on the inhabitants to maintain the parish priest and the church, the proprietors of land were responsible for the minister's stipend and the maintenance of church and manse. To this duty was added responsibility for schools and schoolmasters, and by acts of 1663 and 1672 the heritors were brought into poor law administration. In education and poor relief they worked closely with the kirk session, and the membership of the two bodies not infrequently overlapped.

The parochial boards, set up in 1845, consisted, broadly speaking, of proprietors of heritage above a certain value, along with the kirk session, and, in a burgh, the magistrates. They were large and unwieldy, having often over 100 members and in one case over 2,000. From 1854, when compulsory registration of births, marriages and deaths was introduced, they were empowered to appoint the registrars, and in 1867 they received powers in connection with public health. The parish councils, which took their place in 1895, had only from five to thirty-one members, elected by the county or burgh electors, with responsibility for poor law, the appointment of the registrar, recreation grounds and the administration of property held in trust for the parish. They did not have public health duties, which had gone to the county councils in 1889.

The vast increase in administrative activity in the nineteenth century led to a transformation of local government. The trend was to multiply authorities at local level, each with a specific function, just as boards proliferated at central level. Thus, as just mentioned, parochial boards were set up for poor law. In 1872 school boards, elected by rate-payers, were constituted in each parish and burgh. In 1857 boards of lunacy were established, twenty-seven in all, appointed by the county and burgh authorities. Road trustees had previously existed under Turnpike Acts, but under the Roads and Bridges Act of 1878 new road trustees were constituted in counties, while in burghs (except the smallest) town councils and police commissioners acted as road trustees. The county did not acquire a real organ of government until 1889, when county councils appeared, to take over some of the functions previously exercised by commissioners of supply and those of the road trustees. They were to be elected triennially, at first by all occupiers of land or premises within the county, but the franchise was later widened along with the parliamentary franchise. In addition to a number of constituencies, each returning one member, a member was to be chosen by the town council of each burgh with a population over 7,000. The commissioners of supply were not entirely superseded in their traditional sphere of finance, for they still appointed half the members of a standing joint committee—the other half being appointed by the county council —which had powers to control capital expenditure or works involving loans and also to act as the county police committee. There were also from 1889 district committees, consisting of the councillors for the constituencies in a district along with representatives of the parish councils in that district.

It became evident early in the twentieth century that the system which had developed in the nineteenth had defects. The multiplication of elected bodies led to a decline in the interest of voters and candidates alike. At the first school board election in Glasgow, in 1873, 39 candidates stood for 15 seats and more than half the electorate voted. But as time went on and apathy grew, it was difficult to persuade the public to vote and candidates to stand: in 1911, out of 960 elections, 540 were not contested. Much the same became true of parish councils, and the board of supervision had to be allowed to nominate members. Besides, for some purposes the parish was too small a unit. This was certainly true in education, for larger units would make it easier to arrange for itinerant teachers for special subjects, easier for teachers to change

145

from one school to another, and easier to equalise standards and costs. Moreover, it was obvious that secondary education could never be satisfactorily organised on a parochial basis.

Modifications were therefore made. Secondary education committees were set up in 1893, one in each county and one in each of the six largest towns; and in 1908 parishes were allowed to amalgamate for school board purposes. It was logical therefore that the Education Act of 1918, which replaced the school boards by education authorities, still separately elected, made the education authority areas coterminous with the county, except that the five largest towns had their own authorities.

A revolution came in 1929. There were by that time no less than nine bodies in local government—town councils, county coun ils, district committees, commissioners of supply, standing joint committees, parish councils, education authorities, district boards of control (which had been boards of lunacy until 1913) and distress committees (appointed under the Unemployed Workmen Act of 1905). Seven of these were abolished, the ad hoc bodies disappeared, and only the town and county councils were retained, but one new body was added—the district council, consisting of the county councillors for a district plus members elected at the same time as the county councillors. The number of units was reduced from 1,340 to 461, including 226 district councils (subsequently reduced by amalgamation to 196).

The 1929 Act produced in effect a two-tier structure. The generally competent body was the county council, and the four chief cities were raised to county status so that they became all-purpose authorities. The lower tier was formed by the burghs and the districts, though the district councils had very limited powers and burghs were differentiated into 20 large burghs (later increased to 21), with populations of 20,000 or over, which controlled most public services except education, and 178 small burghs (later reduced to 176) which retained control of only such matters as lighting and cleansing. The county councils were enlarged to include delegates from town councils, with power to vote on matters for which the county had responsibility within burghs.

146

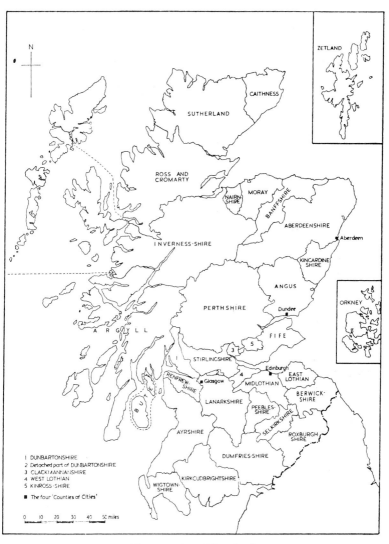

The counties of Scotland

Especially after World War II, modifications were made piece-meal to the 1929 scheme. There was a certain amount of voluntary amalgamation. The counties of Perth and Kinross, and of Moray and Nairn, agreed to combine for most purposes, and some other counties combined either with each other or with burghs for water supplies or for police forces. Later, amalgamation went much further, under dictation from the central government. Water was reorganised with thirteen water boards. The voluntary mergers for police purposes, which had already reduced the number from 49 to 33, were carried further with the result that there were by 1969 only 20 police forces. The fire service was also reorganised on a regional basis, with eleven fire brigades. In addition to such amalgamation of existing units, some extensions of governmental activity were carried out through completely new regional units: five hospital boards, nine river purification boards and eight planning regions. There was also the Highlands and Islands Development Board, whose sphere of operations was roughly the crofting counties. Gas undertakings were nationalised, and for them a single gas board was created for Scotland. Electricity, too, was nationalised, but for it there are two boards—the North of Scotland Hydro-Electric Board and the South of Scotland Electricity Board. All in all, therefore, in 1969 Scotland had one gas board, 2 electricity boards, 5 hospital boards, 8 planning regions, 9 river purification boards, 11 fire committees, 13 water boards and 20 police authorities, in addition to the 1929 structure of 4 cities, 21 large burghs, 176 small burghs, 33 counties and 196 districts.

Clearly, what had happened since 1929 had been along two lines. One was the creation of units larger than the counties and burghs, but the other was the creation of a number of ad hoc authorities. It seemed familiar to the historian who remembered what had happened in the nineteenth century, and we seemed to have returned to the confusion from which the 1929 Act rescued us, indeed the confusion seemed if anything to be worse, for before 1929 there were only 9 bodies active in local government, while in 1969 there were 11, if not 12. The concept of the all-purpose authority had been completely lost sight of, the principles of the

1929 reorganisation had been wholly discarded. Local government had certainly become a terrible mess, but it was not so clear that the mess resulted from the structure set up in 1929 rather than from the tinkering with that structure in subsequent years.

In 1969 a royal commission under the chairmanship of Lord Wheatley produced its Report on Local Government in Scotland, recommending the establishment of a rigid two-tier system, with 7 regions and 37 districts. As the report itself admitted that the public were 'on the whole satisfied' with the existing structure, it is not surprising that the proposals came in for severe criticism. History and tradition were coolly disregarded. The burghs were to vanish, although all through the centuries a distinction had been drawn between a burgh and a rural area. It was pointed out— though people should have learned long ago that it is futile to appeal to the treaty of union—that the Scottish institutions expressly safeguarded in the treaty were the law, the church, the universities, the Register House and the royal burghs. The counties also were to vanish, and although county councils were of recent origin, the sheriffdom, from which the county derived, had an antiquity comparable to that of the burghs. The people of Scotland have been thinking in terms of burghs and sheriffdoms as long, one might almost say, as they have been thinking at all, certainly for as long as we have evidence to show what they were thinking.

And, even granted the Wheatley view that the old institutions should be sacrificed, there was much scope for criticism in the suggested boundaries. The report said much about the critieria to define communities, but showed little appreciation of what a community means, and it was demonstrable that most of the regions and districts were in no sense communities. There was an obsession with size, and when it was pointed out that some small education authorities, for example, had produced better results than large ones had, it was blandly retorted that this was 'in spite of the handicap imposed by their small size'. Critics suggested that regions and districts not founded in communities would be likely to be bureaucratic and unable to resist the central government with the backing of public opinion. Among the regions, the

The regions and districts of Scotland

main target of attack was the proposed Highlands and Islands Region, extending from Kintyre to Shetland and centred at Inverness. The people of Argyll and the people of Shetland had never been accustomed to look to Inverness for anything, and councillors from Kintyre and from Unst knew nothing and cared less about each other's problems. Defence of small units did, however, meet the argument that much local authority finance had for some time come from the central government, and in the poorest Scottish counties the proportion of the expenditure so borne amounted to nearly ninety per cent.

Insufficient attention was paid to patterns of communication and to the fact that public transport throughout many parts of Scotland has deteriorated. There were some glaring inconsistencies. The South-West was constituted a region partly because it lay 75 miles from Glasgow and in some respects looked away from Glasgow rather than towards it; but on the other hand the Highland Region, with its headquarters at Inverness, was to include Lerwick, which lies more than 200 miles from Inverness and looks towards Aberdeen, and Campbeltown, which lies 150 miles from Inverness and looks towards Glasgow. Criticism was all the stronger because some areas had already experienced the results of amalgamation into large regions for water, fire and police. Every amalgamation had resulted in vastly increased expenditure, sometimes in return for no improvement at all in services, and this made people dubious about the claims that larger units would produce economies. Some felt that even small burghs might reasonably continue their existence to deal with purely local matters like cleansing, street-lighting and parks. It was pointed out, too, that the merging of towns with districts and regions would increase urbanisation: the cities and burghs, with their greater populations, would predominate, and their representatives outvote those from landward areas.

Some of the criticisms did make an impression, and the White Paper on the Reform of Local Government in Scotland, issued by the government in 1971, differed in some not insignificant ways from Wheatley. A new region was added for the eastern Borders, and Wheatley's Highlands and Islands Region was truncated by the transference of Argyll to the Strathclyde region and by the recognition of special 'island authorities' for the Outer Hebrides, Orkney and Shetland, which were to have nearly all the functions of the regions. When the proposals took shape in a bill, the outcome of the debates was to make Fife a ninth mainland region. The heaviest but unavailing criticism was directed against Strathclyde, centred on Glasgow and containing approximately half the population of the whole country.

The main principles of Wheatley stood, and the new arrangements produced much simplification. Police, fire and water became functions of the regions, with no separate authorities, though river boards remained. But the new regions and districts required vastly increased staffs, the salaries of top officials were startling, the financial burdens imposed on rural areas rose sharply, and discontent was not diminished by the fact that this happened at a time of inflation. Provision had all along been made for the election of 'community councils', which might conceivably perform some of the functions previously performed by small burghs, but they were to have no statutory functions and no statutory finance. And little was heard of the undertaking given in the White Paper that the government would consider how best to preserve 'charter rights and privileges, traditional and ceremonial usage'. Irritation at the loss by most burghs of their historic offices was not alleviated by the fact that the chairmen of the district councils of the four large cities were privileged to retain the title of Lord Provost. The abolition of the burghs involved the disappearance of the burgh courts, in which bailies had competence to deal with assault, breach of the peace and petty theft, but a non-professional magistracy continued in new district courts. The ancient Convention of Royal Burghs was in effect superseded by a Council of Scottish Local Authorities.

CHAPTER 7

The Highlands

The Lowlands are identifiable geographically with a coastal plain which begins in the most northerly mainland county, Caithness, perhaps vanishes briefly in Sutherland but beyond that stretches down the whole east side of the country, extending up various river valleys and finally merging in the central plain which straddles the Forth and Clyde estuaries. The Highlands, which lie to the west, not to the north, of the Lowlands, include the mountainous centre and the west coast down to Kintyre—so that there is a Highland town, Campbeltown, south of Berwick. But geography was not the only factor which shaped the division. Of the languages once spoken in Scotland, the Pictish tongue, the Welsh of the Britons, the French of the Normans and the Norse of the Scandinavians in time died out, leaving as rivals Gaelic, introduced by the Irish, and English, introduced by the Angles. By the later Middle Ages the Gaelic-speakers were confined to the centre and west, while the remainder of the country had become Teutonic in language if not in race. Thus, on the one hand, the Southern Uplands, south of the central plain, while not 'low land', are linguistically part of the Lowlands, while pockets of low-lying ground on the west coast and in the western isles are parts of the Highlands. The two regions also represented two different ways of life—a predominantly pastoral economy based on cattle, in the Highlands, and in the Lowlands a greater proportion of arable farming, though with extensive pasturage for sheep as well as for cattle. That the difference was radical is at once apparent if medieval burghs, royal castles, monasteries, cathedrals and sheriffs' seats are plotted on a map, for the Highland area is almost blank. In later times a new distinction arose, for it was in the Lowlands that industries principally developed.

Geographical and climatic differences had psychological as well as economic effects. From the east coast an open horizon beckoned the Lowlander to traffic on Scotland's ready-made highway to continental countries. In the west the sea runs far in among the roots of the mountains, but even on the outer shores of the mainland the prospect is not of a horizon but of island upon island, and until the end of the Middle Ages the far-away lands beyond the islands were out of reach. The climate is equally contrasted. The east has a fairly low rainfall, and, although in summer it attains higher temperatures than the west, it has much cool weather, brought by bracing east winds—some call them harsh—especially in the spring. These conditions fostered a temperament which was, to use a Scots word, somewhat dour, but ready for enterprise. The centre and west are quite different. Although inland and high-lying areas have severe winters, the west coast has mild ones as well as warm summers, kind to both plant life and animal life, and the luxuriant vegetation can rival what is found five hundred miles further south. But western Scotland is one of the world's wet regions, and much of the rain falls in the autumn —including August, when English tourists are most apt to arrive. In almost any month winds of hurricane force can lash the country with torrential rain, and from the coast they carry salt spray over the land to blast plant life. Few activities are more dispiriting than trying to win a harvest under such conditions, and climatic adversity is apt to breed apathy. Indeed, there are so many days when outdoor work of any kind is impossible that the inhabitants gained a reputation for indolence. It is not surprising that, even in fertile patches, the emphasis was on cattle-raising rather than on crops. And tending cattle, it was observed by visitors, was hardly a full-time occupation for an able-bodied man.

Everything seemed to conspire to differentiate Highlander from Lowlander, and to breed mutual suspicion. There were sound material reasons for the Lowlander's distrust. The fact is that the economy of the Highlands has probably never been self-sufficient. Nowadays the subventions needed to keep it going come from government grants, and in the last century they took the form of lavish spending by landowners who had no thought of financial gain. But in earlier days the subventions were forcibly collected by raids on the Lowlands. A fable with some point to it was that after the Creator had made the Highlander (out of horse-droppings),

Quoth God to the Highlander, 'What will you now?'
'I will down to the Lowland, Lord, and there steal a cow.'

This merely expressed succinctly what was said at greater length by contemporary observers. One, in the late fourteenth century, remarked that the Lowlanders were 'domesticated and cultured, trustworthy, patient and urbane, decent in their attire, lawabiding and peaceful, devout in religious observance', while the Highlanders were 'a savage and untamed people, rough and unbending, given to rapine, ease-loving, of artful and impressionable temperament, comely in form but unsightly in dress'. More than a century later John Major made a similar distinction between 'Wild Scots' who spoke 'Irish' and 'householding Scots', with whom 'the government and direction of the kingdom is to be found'. Some of the 'Wild Scots,' he went on, 'delight in the chase and a life of indolence; . . . taking no pains to earn their own livelihood, they live upon others, and follow their own worthless and savage chiefs in all evil courses sooner than they will pursue an honest industry. They are full of mutual dissensions'. He added that they hated the householding Scots, on account of their differing speech, as much as they did the English.

These writers express the prejudice arising from the conflict of two different ways of life, and the same prejudice lay behind formal documents. In 1414 some revenues were annexed to the abbey of Lindores, on the Firth of Tay, because its buildings were ruined and its rents diminished by reason of the proximity of the 'Wild Scots'; and ten years later a statute explained that certain provisions could not be applied in the Highlands because the Highlanders commonly robbed and slew each other. Both of the writers quoted above admitted the claim of Highlanders to be Scots, but to most Lowlanders the Highlanders were 'Irish' in race as well as language. By an oddly topsy-turvy process, the

Lowlanders had earlier adopted the history of the Irish 'Scots' as their own, but now they deemed the descendants of the Irish 'Scots' to be foreigners.

The monarchy, springing from the ancient Irish kings of Dalriada, was one of the few institutions which over-rode the geographical, racial and linguistic divisions of the country—or would have overridden them if the Highlanders had always remembered their allegiance. But, after centuries of Norse ascendancy, it was only in 1266 that the western isles were ceded to Scotland, and the thirty years that passed between that event and the beginning of the wars of independence were too brief for the growth of a new loyalty, far less the extension to the west of the institutions which were providing cohesion elsewhere. One of the few known acts of King John Balliol (1292–6) was to establish sheriffdoms for Skye, Lorne and Kintyre, but development was soon arrested by war. It is not surprising that in Robert Bruce's day, not for the last time, local feuds were more important than patriotism. There were three leading families in the west, descended from the twelfth-century chief Somerled: one of them— the MacDougals of Lorne—supported Balliol, the others were divided; in one case an eldest son supported Balliol and his two brothers were on Bruce's side.

In the next generation, even the son of one of Robert Bruce's supporters joined Edward Balliol, and neither David II nor the earlier Stewarts gained anything like the confidence of their western subjects. It was at this stage, in the mid-fourteenth century, that the 'lordship of the Isles' emerged. Down to 1266 there had been a kingdom of the Isles, nominally subordinate to Norway and with its headquarters in Man. Man was finally lost to the English in 1333, and it was Islay, probably the most valuable of the isles after Man, which became the base of a family descended from the kings of the Isles and styling themselves Lords of the Isles. Their property included some territories on the west mainland and, early in the fifteenth century, they acquired by marriage the earldom of Ross, which extended across to the Cromarty Firth. In 1411, in pursuance of his claim to that earldom, the Lord of the Isles led an army across Scotland, with a view, so it was thought, of mastering all Scotland north of the Tay. The battle which ensued, at Harlaw, was in one aspect a family quarrel between cousins—and that in itself was characteristic—but the burgesses of Aberdeen and the farmers of the eastern plains who resisted the Highlanders may well have been stirred by generations of distrust and fear.

One of the writers who was so contemptuous of the Highlanders had one thing to say in their favour: they were 'faithful and obedient to their king and country and easily made to submit to law, *if properly governed*'. When he was writing, during the ineffective rule of Robert II, the Highlands were not properly governed, and so they long continued. In the brief periods of active rule which were all that most Stewart kings enjoyed it was hard enough to find time to establish good rule in the Lowlands, and any progress made in the Highlands was speedily undone in the next minority. In 1428 James I summoned a number of chiefs to Inverness and there arrested them. He executed three of his captives and released the others after a brief imprisonment. Like other wise rulers, James saw that he could never control the west Highlands unless he cut their communications with Ireland, and an act of 1426 forbade ships to cross to Ireland without the king's special leave. In James II's reign the Lord of the Isles was in league with the 8th Earl of Douglas in the famous 'bond' which caused the king to murder Douglas. In 1461, after James II's strong hand was removed, the Lord of the Isles was 'usurping royal authority and the royal crown' by uplifting royal revenues and exercising the king's prerogative of granting pardons for offences. Next year, in collaboration with the exiled 9th Earl of Douglas, he made a treaty with England whereby he agreed, in return for payment of 100 merks yearly in time of peace and £200 yearly in time of war, to be an English agent and, in the event of an English conquest of Scotland, to share Scotland north of the Tay with his fellow-traitor.

After James III's minority was over, the government again turned its attention to the Highlands, and in 1476 the Lord of the Isles was deprived of the earldom of Ross and of Kintyre. It was left to James IV to carry the process further and in 1493 annex the lordship of the Isles to the crown, with which it still remains, to furnish one of the titles of the heir apparent, along with those he derives from the earlier patrimony of Bruces and Stewarts—Duke of Rothesay, Earl of Carrick and Baron Renfrew, as well as High Steward of Scotland. James IV led several expeditions to the west, and, with the support of his fleet, operated as far afield as Dunaverty in Kintyre, Mingary in Ardnamurchan, and the islands of Coll and Tiree. He also attempted to improve administration in the western isles, where, it was said in 1504, 'for lack of justices and sheriffs, the people are gone almost wild'. But his scheme was actually less ambitious than John Balliol's two centuries earlier, because the sheriff and justice for the north isles was to sit no nearer the islands than Inverness or Dingwall; in the south the seat was to be at Tarbert or at Campbeltown, which had ready access from the Firth of Clyde.

Permanent machinery for administration throughout the west was not yet going to be provided by additional royal officers. Besides, while the king could capture strongholds, he could not furnish royal troops to garrison them. For administration and the custody of castles alike, therefore, the answer was the employment of local magnates, and this reign saw the further advancement of two great families, the Campbells of Argyll and the Gordons of Huntly. Colin Campbell, the descendant of a landowner who had received lands on Lochawe as a reward for his support of Robert Bruce, now received some of the forfeited lands of the Lord of the Isles, along with the custody of Castle Sween, and also land on which to build a castle at Inverlochy near Fort William. He had already acquired the lordship of Lorne by marriage, and he now laid the foundations of an ascendancy which was in time to be more dangerous to the crown than the lordship of the Isles had ever been. The Campbells extended their influence, sometimes by the acquisition of land or office, sometimes by marriage, throughout much of Perthshire and even as far afield as Angus, Ayrshire and Nairnshire. Similarly, the Gordons, Earls of Huntly, who originated in the Lowlands, became governors of the castle of Inverness and hereditary sheriffs of Inverness, and a member of their kin acquired the earldom of Sutherland by marriage, so that

Page 159 The judges of the Court of Session in 1962

Page 160 Old houses at Pittenweem: (*above*) before restoration; (*below*) after restoration by the National Trust for Scotland

their sphere of influence extended from Aberdeen to the Pentland Firth. Such families, with private ends to serve, were not necessarily interested in the preservation of order, for it was disorder that gave them their opportunities: it was not by keeping the peace that they could earn their reward, but by putting down breakers of the peace, which is not quite the same thing. On the death of the 3rd Earl of Argyll in 1529, his son claimed a position like his father's, on the ground that 'I and my friends have as great experience in the daunting of the isles as any others of the realm, and especially for the destruction of those inobedient to the king's grace and the rewarding of them that make good service to his highness'. The king chose instead to make use of Argyll's enemy Alexander of Islay, who accused Argyll of deliberately fomenting mischief in order to give him an opportunity to destroy 'the inobedient'. In 1540 James V made an ambitious cruise to Orkney and the western isles. The chiefs never seemed to learn a lesson, and submitted as tamely to be kidnapped by James V—and again, later, by James VI—as they had been by James I.

By this time the Highland problem was taking on a new complexion. Descriptions of the Highlanders before 1400 said nothing of the existence of 'clans', a feature which no later writer would have omitted. The term *clann* properly means children, and in Gaelic notes written in the Book of Deer in the late eleventh or early twelfth century, *Clann Chanann* and *Clann Morgainn* were ruling family-groups descended from a common ancestor; located as these families were in Buchan, they have no connection with later Highland 'clans'. We hardly hear of 'clans' again until 1396, when a feud between two clans was decided by a conflict at Perth between thirty champions from each.

At some stage the term clan extended its meaning to embrace the followers of a chief to whom most of them were not related by blood. Among a people much attached to kinship as the basis of society, bards, who were the custodians of tribal myths, origin-legends and pedigrees, fabricated genealogies to give fictitious foundations to associations which in truth developed from community of interest or tenurial connections. Thus the clan system was no obstacle to the assimilation of incomers, and with the settlement of colonists or conquerors a supposed kin-basis was furnished for a society actually consisting of vassals and conquered people living under immigrant lords. There was no difficulty about accepting as a chief the descendant of some Englishman or Frenchman who had acquired a Highland estate. It is clear, for example, that the clansmen of Frasers, Grants or Gordons, must have included many people who had been there before those families arrived. But even the leading MacDonalds, descended from twelfth-century chiefs, cannot have been the progenitors of the bulk of their clansmen, whose forebears were there before the chiefs.

The main basis of the clan, not as a fictitious kin but as a social, economic and military unit, owed much to the geographical isolation of exclusive, self-sufficient communities. The lordship of the Isles had provided some kind of inter-clan organisation, and its disappearance, by removing a focus which may have been an element of stability and unity, increased the significance of the individual clans. A chief's dependants looked to him to organise their social, economic and military existence, perhaps even their survival against foes: and, while the leading men in the clan might be related to him by blood, the others would regard him as 'the father of his people', at first merely in a figurative sense.

In James VI's reign there were some novel features in government policy, appropriate enough under a king who was no man of violence but a devious tactician and strategist. Lowland contempt for the Highlanders was as strong as ever: in 1579, when a Midlothian farmer complained to the Privy Council about injuries to his animals and ploughmen, he remarked that it should not happen in a district which, being 'near the seat of justice should be peaceable' and set an example to the 'far Highlands' where nothing better could be expected. James shared this prejudice: the Highlanders on the mainland, he conceded, were 'barbarous for the most part, and yet mixed with some show of civility', and could be controlled through their chiefs; but the only course to follow with the Islanders, who were 'utterly barbarians', was to 'root out and transport' them and plant colonies of law-abiding Lowlanders. James envisaged the resumption, after 300 years, of the policy of colonisation and burgh-making which his ancestors had carried out elsewhere and which had come to an end with John Balliol's proposed new sheriffdoms in the west. Colonisation was attempted in Lewis, with almost complete failure, and the king's proposals for additional burghs in Kintyre, Lochaber and Lewis did not come to much either. But policy in the Highlands took on a new complexion after 1603. For centuries the English government had tried to subdue Ireland, while the Scottish government had tried to subdue the west Highlands; but the disaffected in one country were apt to find countenance in the other. As far back as the treaty of Northampton (1328), the English king promised not to intrigue with the Celtic subjects of the Scottish crown in the western isles, while the Scottish king undertook not to ally with the Celts of Ireland, and James I, as we saw, was also aware of the problem. If anything it intensified in the sixteenth century. A single family—MacDonald or MacDonnell of Dunivaig and the Glens—held land in Antrim as well as in Islay and Kintyre; it was a matter of debate whether the island of Rathlin, off the Antrim coast, was Scottish or Irish; and Highlanders were active in Ireland as mercenaries. In short, there was an Anglo-Scottish problem, and concerted action became possible after 1603. The strategic problem was solved (though other problems, still with us, were created) when the plantation of Ulster by Lowland Scots cut off the Irish Celts from those of Scotland. A small-scale parallel on the Scottish side was the one successful Jacobean 'plantation' in the west Highlands: the Earl of Argyll introduced Lowlanders into a new burgh at Campbeltown and settled some in his chief town, Inveraray.

The Argyll Campbells were further aggrandised on the fall of the MacDonalds of Dunivaig and the Glens after an unsuccessful rebellion in 1615. Almost simultaneously, the Mackenzies of Kintail were invested in the island of Lewis and, with lands stretching from that island across to Cromarty, became comparable in importance to the Campbells and the Gordons. But one of the novelties of Jacobean strategy was the rejection of the policy of elevating certain families or clans at the expense of others. The clan itself was now recognised as a unit, and chiefs were acknowledged as responsible to the crown for their clans. A leading agent of royal policy was the Bishop of the Isles, who was not an hereditary magnate with dynastic interests to serve, but essentially a crown servant. In 1609, at Iona, he met nine chiefs who came from places as far apart as Islay and Harris and he prevailed on them to adopt a code of 'statutes' against inter alia the carrying of firearms, the encouragement of bards who kept alive old feuds, and excessive consumption of spirits. This was all very well—if it could be put into practice—for clans settled on lands of which the chief was the landlord. But clans who insisted on acknowledging chiefs who were not their landlords were much harder to control. The most notorious of them was the 'wicked and unhappy race' of Clan Gregor, who were well placed, on the boundaries of Perthshire and Argyll, for raids into the Lowlands and retreat into wild fastnesses. For them the only fate was to be extermination.

Oddly enough, it was only after Jacobean policy offered the prospect of solving the Highland problem that Highlanders began to intervene in national affairs in a way which went far beyond sporadic raiding. In 1644, Charles I, confronted by a coalition of Scottish Covenanters and English Parliamentarians, commissioned James Graham, Marquis of Montrose, to command his forces in Scotland. Montrose failed to raise troops in the Lowlands, but he gathered a Highland army and found allies in a force led by a Scoto-Irish captain, Alasdair MacDonald, whose followers included expatriate Highlanders set on vengeance against the Campbells who had dispossessed them of their ancestors' lands in Kintyre and Islay. In a whirlwind campaign, Montrose won half a dozen victories over the covenanting armies and sacked Aberdeen and Dundee. Nothing quite the same had ever happened before, nothing even remotely resembling it had happened since Harlaw in 1411, and the bitterness against Montrose is explicable on the part of Lowlanders who had long been accustomed to peace and now saw their lands and towns devastated by wild 'Irish' from both sides of the North Channel. When Montrose was defeated at Philiphaugh (1645) a bloody revenge was taken, even on the women and children who followed his camp and on prisoners who had surrendered on promise of quarter.

Six years later, Scotland was overrun by Cromwellian armies. Two of their five great forts were at Inverness and Inverlochy, and the latter had particular responsibility for the west Highlands. It was remarked that 'there is not one robbery all this year, although formerly it was the trade they lived by to rob and steal', and another contemporary observed that 'at no time were the Highlands kept in better order than during the usurpation'.

A campaign similar to that of Montrose was threatened in 1689, when another Graham—John Graham of Claverhouse, Viscount Dundee—raised many clans for James VII after he had been superseded by William of Orange, but was killed in the moment of victory at Killiecrankie. The almost hysterical dread of Highlanders, and a determination like that of Cromwell to discipline them, lay behind the massacre of Glencoe in 1692, when one small clan was singled out as an example of the consequences of persistent disorder and dubious loyalty to the new king. More bloody massacres had taken place before in the course of Highland feuding and Glencoe might have been forgotten like them but for the existence of interests determined to embarrass King William's government, which had earned unpopularity on other grounds. Jacobites, Cameronians, Episcopalians, all had their reasons for antipathy, and there were also those moved primarily by rivalry with the Master of Stair, William's secretary of state. A commission of inquiry was at length set up in 1695 and it attached most blame to Stair, who was removed from the office of secretary but received a remission from his master for any fault he had committed.

Highland intervention came yet again, in the Jacobite risings of 1715 and 1745. It was partly for economic reasons that Montrose, Dundee and the Pretenders made an appeal to Highland clans, who saw their campaigns as opportunities for a revival, on a grand scale, of the traditional collection of booty in the Lowlands. There were, however, other reasons. It is sometimes said that the hereditary rights of kings made a special appeal to Highlanders, accustomed as they were to the rule of hereditary chiefs, but it is hard to square this with two facts: active loyalty to the house of

Stewart was in truth something of a novelty in the Highlands; and even now the cause appealed to only certain clans. An ecclesiastical element was important. The Presbyterian church established after the fall of James VII had little support in the central and west Highlands, or indeed at first in any area north of the Tay. While few Presbyterian Scots favoured a Stewart restoration, most Roman Catholics did, and so did many Episcopalians; and the clans who supported the Jacobite risings were Episcopalian or Roman Catholic.

The Fifteen had a good deal of support in the north-east, Fife, Lothian and the south-west, as well as in the west coast and isles and in the centre and north. The Forty-Five was much less broadly based. The north-east was still important, and in Perthshire many recruits were raised by a few enthusiastic chiefs and lairds. However, the north mainland and the outer isles were this time mainly on the government side, and the chief strength of Prince Charlie's army lay in Appin, Glencoe, Lochaber, Lochshiel and Moidart, the lands of clans of Stewarts, MacDonalds and Camerons, hereditary foes of the Hanoverian and Presbyterian Clan Campbell, who were hated for their successful aggrandisement. The picturesque impressions of Prince Charlie marching at the head of an army of kilted Highlanders, first to victory and then to defeat, and of Prince Charlie among the heather, guarded by incorruptible Highlanders and saved from capture by Flora MacDonald from Skye, have led to an erroneous identification of the Highlands with Jacobitism. Chatter about 'the clans' being defeated at Culloden ignores the fact that there were only some 5,000 men in the Jacobite army that day, when the population of the Highlands must have been about a quarter of a million. It was not a military defeat that transformed Highland society.

The fact is that the social structure of the Highlands was outdated. A chief granted large tracts of land in lease or 'tack' to men of substance, often his kinsmen. The leaseholder or 'tacksman' then let smaller holdings to the rank and file of the clan, and lived on the surplus by which the rents he received exceeded the tack duty he paid to the chief. The object was to maintain the maximum number of tenants on the clan territory, and the system had developed when a clan's very existence might depend on its ability to defend itself, and its wealth might depend on the number of thieving hands available to raid its neighbours. Any question of the standard of living obtainable from agrarian operations was secondary, and population outran subsistence when, with the growth of law and order, raids on the Lowlands could no longer provide subventions. Observers were unanimous that the Highlands had more people than they could support, especially as agricultural methods were inefficient and the habits of the people were not such as to make the best of a poor soil and an adverse climate or to facilitate the introduction of industries. From this period Highlanders began, almost for the first time, to enter the Lowlands in peaceful fashion and seek employment there, often in seasonal agricultural work but also in menial occupations in the cities. Down to this point, as lists of the inhabitants of any Scottish district readily show, there had been little intermingling of the two races.

A transformation of Highland life had begun before 1745, and would undoubtedly have been completed had Jacobitism never existed. The measures taken after the rebellions were not the main factor in bringing about change, though what they accomplished was not negligible. The principle of demilitarising the Highlands was adopted after the Fifteen and, under General Wade's command (1724–43), arms were seized (though many remained concealed) and members of clans loyal to the government were recruited into companies which in time became the Black Watch Regiment. By roads linking Crieff, Dunkeld, Inverness and Fort William, Wade provided ready access for troops to at least the eastern Highlands. After the Forty-Five there were renewed measures for demilitarisation, and this time the wearing of the kilt, which savoured of a military uniform, was forbidden. There were also acts aimed at reducing the powers of chiefs over their followers.

But social and economic changes had more far-reaching effects than legislation. Normal commercial landlordism was superseding the old relation of chief and clansmen: a landlord who no longer looked for armed retainers or received services from his clansmen expected a more substantial money income. The tacksmen were now seen as unnecessary middlemen who drew off a proportion of the rental, and the process of eliminating them began in the 1730s. If, alternatively, a chief retained the tack system but ignored the claims of kinship and tradition and put the leases up for auction, a new tacksman who came in as the highest bidder found that he could pay his tack duty more easily if he took up cattle-raising on his own account and turned the tenants out. Whichever course was followed, the landlords profited, but in either event there was dispossession, either of tacksmen or of subtenants. Another change which was beginning before the Forty-Five was the introduction of various industries—lead mining, iron smelting (using local timber and imported ore) and linen manufacture—in an attempt to provide peaceful occupations. Some agricultural changes began too, including the introduction of the potato.

After the Forty-Five, those changes were intensified. On estates which had belonged to chiefs who had followed Prince Charlie and which were now administered by crown commissioners, the clan structure vanished, and when the chiefs recovered their estates after forty years neither they nor their clansmen wanted to go back to the old ways. On these annexed estates, tenants received leases, but they were debarred from sub-letting, so that the tacksman could not re-emerge. The commissioners made regulations to ensure good husbandry, they spent money on roads and bridges and, in association with the Board of Manufactures, encouraged linen production. Wade's work was continued in a more extensive network of military roads, and after 1800 commissioners of Highland Roads and Bridges improved and extended communications still more, now for peaceful traffic.

Hitherto the Highlands had been mainly a cattle-raising area, but from the 1760s sheep farmers from the Lowlands introduced new breeds of sheep, and within half a century this movement spread all over the Highlands. At that time the industrial revolution was leading to a concentration of population in towns, and the rising demand for mutton and for wool to be manufactured into clothing meant that the change-over to sheep led to an enormous, though temporary, increase in the value of some

Highland estates. But the advance of sheep always involves the retreat of men, and tenants were dispossessed in favour of a handful of shepherds.

In the allocation of arable land, too, there were changes. Hitherto a farm had usually been let to several families, with holdings scattered in intermingled strips, but now separate holdings or crofts of arable land, each worked by one family, were created, combined with common rights on pastureland. As the population grew, the crofts tended to be subdivided into ever smaller units, and, while it was true that by growing potatoes a very small croft could sustain life in a good year, it could not maintain the cattle on which tenants had relied for a money income to cover their rents and other necessities.

In the same period employment was provided along a large part of the west coast and in the islands by the kelp industry, the manufacture of alkali from the burning of seaweed. It flourished especially in the years just before and after 1800, when there was a heavy duty on imported alkalis and the wars with France disrupted imports. After the war ended in 1815, and the import duty was reduced, the kelp industry rapidly became almost extinct.

Both the crofting system and the kelp industry led to an increase in population, especially in the outer islands. Sheepfarming had a contrary effect, but over-all the number of people in the Highland counties continued to increase: Perth and Argyll were to reach their maximum in 1831, Inverness in 1841, Sutherland and Ross in 1851.

As soon as the notion was rejected that the land should support more and more people, irrespective of their standards of living, there was bound to be a drastic redistribution of population. The problem was illustrated in Sutherland at the beginning of the nineteenth century. Most of the county was used for cattleraising and low-quality farming, which barely provided subsistence even in good seasons. The noble family who owned nearly the whole county decided that it would be sounder policy to turn the inland districts over to large sheep-farms, which would require only a few hands, and re-settle the people in crofts on the coasts, where they could supplement the produce of the land by fishing. Such planning, however, paid insufficient attention to human wishes. The tenants saw themselves driven from what they regarded as their ancestral homes; in the process of removing them there was some needless brutality, and men from inland glens did not take readily to the unfamiliar and perilous occupation of fishing. The county did become an exporter of wool and mutton, the fishing industry was expanded, roads opened up the county and the people were relieved from near-starvation conditions. But much bad feeling was engendered, and the 'clearances' have furnished propaganda ever since.

But what were the alternatives, if a still increasing population was not to starve? Crofts were being subdivided; there was too little employment to supplement what they yielded; epidemics of disease and bad seasons were fatal to both the food and the fuel of the crofters. In 1836-7, when the peats failed and there was no money to buy coal or wood, the only thing was to burn the turf and timber of houses: lots were drawn to determine which house should be demolished for fuel, and then lots drawn again to determine in which remaining house the dispossessed family should be accommodated. Almost £80,000 was raised by relief committees in the cities and used to provide potatoes, meal and blankets. Worse was to come in 1845, when the failure of the potato crop led to famine. Landlords spent great sums in relief, and some of them were ruined in consequence. The government was slow to act, but in 1847 a Board of Destitution was set up to organise the employment of Highlanders in railroad construction and in the making of the so-called 'Destitution Roads'.

The period was that of the great famine in Ireland, where the failure of harvests, especially in 1846 and 1848, led to a twenty per cent decline in the population. Much of it was accounted for by emigration, but the number of deaths (less from actual starvation than from attendant diseases) has been put as high as 800,000. The lesson was obvious, and the percentage of holdings of less than five acres dropped in a decade from 45 to 15½. Scotland was fortunate in that the growth of the population was checked by less painful means and that it was not a single major disaster which caused a reconsideration of crofting policy.

In the second half of the century the subventions for the Highlands came mainly from landlords. The old landlords, often descended from clan chiefs, found their estates quite uneconomic, and sold out to men whose wealth came from their English estates or from business. To them a Highland estate did not need to be profitable: it was a status symbol, it provided them and their guests with deer-stalking, game-shooting and salmon fishing and on it they were prepared to spend lavishly. But deer-forests required if anything fewer hands than sheep-farms, and they led to further depopulation. Sometimes the removal of tenants did no more than rectify the previously grossly inflated population, but sometimes it almost stripped an area of people altogether. Even so, several areas were still over-populated.

When the next crisis came it again arose as much from natural causes as from any act of man. In 1882 there was a general failure of the potato crop, gales ruined the grain crops, the price of cattle fell and the fishing was poor. The Highlanders themselves did not throw up a leader, and were probably not capable of doing so, for they had always depended on leadership of chief, tacksman, priest or minister. Consequently the agitation which arose was largely directed or inspired from the Lowlands and it lost all sense of proportion and reality. A kind of anti-landlord complex prevailed and pseudo-historical fantasy idealised a past age when land was vested in the clan and chiefs were the source of largesse. The idea was fostered that one day the land would be in the hands of 'the people'. Thus a demand arose for more land for cultivation, and both in Skye and Lewis there were land-raids, when crofters seized grazings and started to cultivate them. In 1883 a commission was appointed to inquire into the condition of crofters, and in 1886 came the Crofters' Holdings Act, which granted security of tenure, permitted the bequest and assignation of crofts, appointed fixed rents, arranged for out-going tenants to have compensation for improvements and provided for enlargement of holdings; and a Crofters' Commission was set up to superintend the operation of the new regulations. The crofter, in short, received the advantages of ownership without its liabilities, and landlords, it seems, were permitted to exist principally so that they could shoulder half the rates and pay compensation to out-going crofters. The Commission also acted as a Land Court, but in 1911 that court was reconstructed, with jurisdiction throughout Scotland and not only in the crofting counties: its chairman has the status of a judge of the Court of Session and it performs a very useful function in dealing with many problems which arise in communities of smallholders.

For a generation and more it was thought that the Crofters Act had settled the problems of the Highlands. But for some time now it has been apparent that it did no such thing. To give tenants security while freeing them from any control over the use to which they put the land resulted in crofts being neglected. There was not even any obligation on a tenant to live on his holding, and the trouble came to be not absentee landlords but absentee crofters, who abandoned cultivation and used the land only to graze sheep. Recent legislation has attempted to rectify such abuses, but with only partial success. There has also been talk of turning the crofters into proprietors, but crofters who have in effect heritable possession, often for a nominal rent unaltered despite inflation, are not enthusiastic, unless they intend to sell building plots at inflated prices. A persistent difficulty has been that at least the smaller crofts were never intended to provide a living, but, as part-time fishing declined and part-time employment in the merchant navy ceased to be practicable, there was a dearth of subsidiary occupations. One approach has been through the amalgamation of crofts and the allocation to individual crofters of a proportion of the common grazing, accompanied by re-seeding, so that crofting can provide a livelihood.

The last of the wealthy landlords who could afford to ladle out money on an uneconomic estate was an exceptional one—Lord Leverhulme, who after 1918 acquired the whole of Lewis and Harris and spent in all about £1½ millions on various schemes, only to find himself frustrated by suspicion and reluctance to co-operate. In general, subsidies from landlords vanished after 1918. The state came in, in various ways and to an increasing degree, with old age pensions (1908), a national health service, subsidised transport, free medical care and other services for schoolchildren and all the other benefits now known as social security; and it also provided subsidies, grants and loans to encourage hill cattle, sheep-raising, land improvement, house-modernisation and so forth. There is some reason to believe that Highlanders and Islanders showed conspicuous ingenuity in wringing the utmost out of unemployment and sickness benefits, as well as from grants. Yet the depopulation of the Highlands and Islands has been greater under the welfare state than it ever was under innovating landlords. The population of Sutherland, despite the 'clearances', reached its maximum in 1851 and did not experience a catastrophic fall until after 1911.

The Highlands and Islands Development Board, set up in 1965, was empowered to make grants and loans to stimulate the economy in every possible way. The three main fields in which it has operated have been fisheries, manufactures and tourism, but such generalised headings hardly do justice to the enormous scope of the activities it has assisted, ranging as they do from fish-farming, piers and processing plants, through crafts and industries (including leather, clothing, plastics, quarrying, printing and jewellery) to hotels, the social activities of residents and recreational facilities for visitors. The Board has, besides, under-taken a vast amount of publicity in London and overseas by participating in exhibitions and trade missions. In fourteen years it disbursed some £53 million to over 5000 ventures and it estimated that it had created or preserved over 15,000 jobs. It approached its work with understanding and a real feeling for the needs of the area. Its total budget may seem meagre, but many think it better to spend small sums in ways which do not disrupt the local way of life and which make use of local resources, rather than to introduce vast industrial complexes which might as well be in the industrial Lowlands.

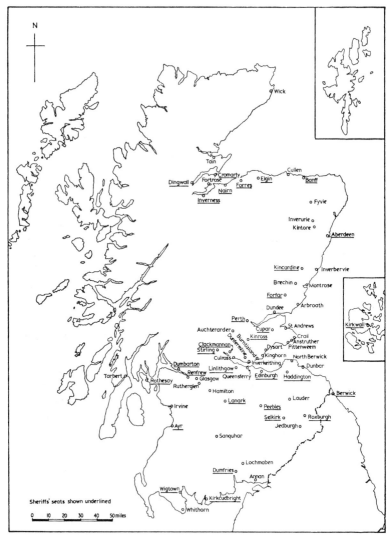

N

Wick

Tain
Cromarty
Fortrose
Dingwall   Forres   Cullen
Nairn   Elgin   Banff
Inverness
Fyvie

Inverurie
Kintore
Aberdeen

Kincardine   Inverbervie
Brechin   Montrose
Forfar
Dundee   Arbroath
Perth
Auchterarder   Cupar   St Andrews
Kinross   Crail
Clackmannan   Anstruther
Stirling   Pittenweem
Culross   Dysart
Kinghorn   North Berwick
Dumbarton   Inverkeithing
Renfrew   Linlithgow   Dunbar
Rothesay   Glasgow   Queensferry   Edinburgh   Haddington
Rutherglen
Tarbert   Hamilton   Lauder   Berwick
Irvine   Lanark   Peebles
Selkirk   Roxburgh
Ayr   Jedburgh

Sanquhar

Lochmaben
Dumfries   Annan
Wigtown
Kirkcudbright
Whithorn

Kirkwall

Sheriffs' seats shown underlined

0   10   20   30   40   50 miles

Medieval burghs

CHAPTER 8

The Church

Christianity reached south-western Scotland by the fifth century, and its beginnings are associated with the name of Ninian and a church he is said to have built at Whithorn in about 400. In 563 a monastery was established at Iona by Columba, one of several Irish monks who were at work at that time among their fellow-countrymen in Dalriada and among the Picts. Ninian, a Briton, was a direct product of the christian Roman Empire, but the Irish missionaries were also indirectly its products, for Ireland had been converted by Patrick, a native of Roman Britain. However, the church in Britain and Ireland was cut off from Rome by the invasion of the pagan Anglo-Saxons and it developed certain peculiarities.

In the year of Columba's death (597), Augustine, sent by the pope to introduce christianity to the Anglo-Saxons, arrived in Kent. The pope meant him to have authority over the bishops of the Britons, but he found that neither they nor the Irish would accept Roman usages or acknowledge him as their archbishop. Consequently, when monks from Iona established themselves in the Anglian kingdom of Northumbria and encountered a mission from Kent, there was a direct conflict. The points ostensibly at issue were the date of Easter and the manner of tonsuring the heads of the clergy, but what was really at stake was papal authority. At the synod of Whitby, probably in 663, the king of Northumbria gave his ruling in favour of Rome, and the Irish monks had to withdraw. Within half a century the king of the Picts submitted to Rome and Iona itself capitulated.

By the time the Irish and the Picts united to form the kingdom of Alba (844), Scandinavian attacks had destroyed Iona, and the church of the united kingdom had its headquarters for a time at

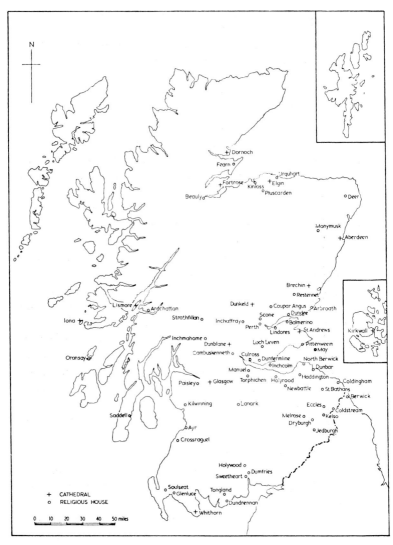

N

Dornoch
Fearn
Urquhart
Fortrose
Kinloss Elgin
Beauly Pluscarden
Deer
Monymusk
Aberdeen
Brechin
Restennet
Dunkeld
Coupar Angus Arbroath
Scone Dundee
Strathfillan Inchaffray Balmerino
Lismore Ardchattan Perth Lindores
Iona Inchmahome Dunblane Loch Leven St Andrews
Cambuskenneth Pittenweem
Oronsay Culross May
Dunfermline North Berwick
Manuel Inchcolm
Paisley Glasgow Torphichen Holyrood Dunbar
Haddington Coldingham
Newbattle St Bathans
Saddell Kilwinning Lanark Berwick
Eccles Coldstream
Ayr Melrose Kelso
Crossraguel Dryburgh
Jedburgh
Kirkwall

Holywood Dumfries
Sweetheart
Soulseat Tongland
Glenluce Dundrennan
Whithorn

+ CATHEDRAL
o RELIGIOUS HOUSE

0 10 20 30 40 50 miles

Medieval cathedrals and religious houses

Dunkeld and then at St Andrews, a name which shows that Scotland had turned its back on the Celtic west and, by adopting an apostle of the universal church as its patron, had entered the main stream of European life. The fact that in the eleventh century King Macbeth went on pilgrimage to Rome shows that the Scots did not regard themselves as schismatic. However, in their comparative isolation they had escaped the effects of reforms which were changing the church elsewhere.

It is not surprising that Malcolm III's wife Margaret, brought up partly on the continent and partly in England, thought there was a good deal amiss with the Scottish church. However, she does not seem to have tried to recover the revenues of monasteries which had become the hereditary property of laymen, and she continued the royal patronage of the Culdees, who were in effect corporations of priests living in communities but also serving local churches. It was easier to introduce changes in worship and discipline than to interfere with vested interests.

Institutional reform came in the following century, especially under David I. New monasteries were lavishly endowed by the kings and nobles for the reformed orders which had become fashionable on the continent and in England. David was later to be reproached as 'a sair sanct for the croun' whose munificence to the church impoverished the monarchy. But he was not devoid of worldly wisdom. Primarily centres for an ordered round of praise and prayer, the monasteries were oases of stability, but there were more material benefits, if only because it was in the interest of the monks to exploit the economic value of their property by developing sheep-farming, working coal-seams, creating harbours and founding burghs. It was even to the royal advantage, in that the court could reside in religious houses instead of being at the expense of building palaces.

Equally important were innovations in non-monastic organisation. Local churches had previously been maintained, at least in the south and in the Pictish areas, in association with some kind of territorial organisation, and had sometimes been handed over to Culdees, but now there was a vast programme of building parish churches, served by resident priests and maintained by the teinds

177

or tithes paid by the parishioners, and many churches up and down the country still show twelfth-century Norman work. Each bishop, assisted by archdeacons and rural deans, became responsible for the supervision of the parishes within a territorial diocese. Cathedrals were erected at the bishops' seats, each with a chapter of canons.

Although the Scottish church had had a 'head bishop' since the ninth century, the reorganisation of the twelfth did not provide it with an archbishop, and the Archbishop of York claimed Scotland as part of his province. The pope for a time supported York, but the Scottish kings resisted and seem to have been supported by the churchmen, although most of them had come from Norman England. In 1192 a papal bull formally conceded that the Scottish bishoprics (except Galloway, which remained in the province of York) were subject directly to the pope and not to any archbishop. A later bull vested central authority in a provincial council, composed of the bishops and selected clergy. It was not until 1472 that Scotland obtained an archbishop, at St Andrews; Glasgow followed twenty years later.

Possibly Scottish churchmen feared that English political encroachments might destroy their ecclesiastical independence. At any rate, in 1306 Robert Bruce, though fresh from murdering his rival in a church, was supported by bishops at his inauguration. While there may have been no more unanimity among the clergy than among the barons, and while many churchmen, especially abbots whose monasteries lay in the path of each English invasion, were ready enough to come to terms with England, Bruce continued to receive valuable aid from clerics. Their organisation to some extent operated whatever the political situation, and the king's competent propaganda department was evidently directed by the Abbot of Arbroath. Many years before that department drew up the Declaration of the Barons it had drawn up a declaration which, with unquestionable exaggeration, proclaimed that 'the bishops, abbots, priors and the rest of the clergy' would adhere to Bruce, with whom, it was said, 'a faithful people will live and die'.

During the Great Schism (1378–1418), when two popes, and

for a time three, competed for the allegiance of western Christendom, England supported the pope at Rome while France and Scotland, not unexpectedly, supported his rival at Avignon. Later, however, when France withdrew its support from Benedict XIII, the Scots persisted in adhering to him, and believed that ultimately no other nation did so: it may have flattered their national vanity to think that they had a pope of their own. During the schism local machinery had to be strengthened, and the Scottish estates ordained that appeals which normally went to the pope should meantime be heard within Scotland. On the other hand, pope and anti-pope were attempting to maintain the customary splendour from reduced constituencies, and therefore pressed all their powers to bring in money. Thus, when the schism ended, the pope was accustomed to exploiting his authority and the Scots resented his encroachments.

The right to elect bishops, which in early times had belonged to the clergy and people of the diocese, along with the king or a local magnate, had in the twelfth century been transferred to the cathedral chapters, while the right to elect an abbot belonged to the monks of his house. But in practice the voice of the king or some other layman had usually been effective in the choice of bishops and abbots alike. From the fourteenth century, however, the pope began to extend his power over appointments, and James I and later kings passed acts to check papal aggression. The king, who contended that, since prelates served him as officials and councillors, he ought to have a say in their appointment, was ultimately successful in obtaining recognition of his right, first to be consulted when promotions were made (1487) and in the end actually to make nominations.

Support for the national cause in war or opposition to papal control over appointments did not imply objection to the principle of papal authority. It might indeed be said that the Scots had no objection to papal power as long as it was not too effective. But there is other evidence of something like autonomy. In the reign of James IV there was a movement to create a native 'use', with 'additions and legends of Scottish saints', and the king—not any ecclesiastical authority—ordained that service books framed by the bishop of Aberdeen should supersede 'books of Salisbury use' (which predominated in England).

By about 1220 interest had turned from monks to friars, especially at first the Dominicans or Friars Preachers (Black Friars) and the Franciscans or Friars Minor (Grey Friars). They served the people as preachers and confessors, and their houses were nearly all in burghs and not in the thinly populated countryside. The foundation of friaries continued sporadically into the early sixteenth century, but by that time the fashion was to invest in collegiate churches, where a corporation of priests and choristers conducted services with ceremonial and music impossible in an ordinary parish church and catered for the increasing demand for the saying of masses, especially for the souls of the departed. Some of the collegiate churches were parish churches raised in status, others were entirely new foundations, others again—St Salvator's at St Andrews and King's College at Aberdeen—were associated with universities. Concurrently, the burgesses were enlarging and adorning their town churches. These fashions suggest a loss of confidence in religious orders with headquarters overseas, a strengthening of national and local patriotism and even an element of anti-clericalism. Collegiate churches could be dominated by the founder's family; bishops established university colleges over which they retained some control; and burgesses endowed proprietary chaplainries, where they could appoint, discipline and dismiss the chaplains.

The church was becoming increasingly top-heavy in the sense that its resources were concentrated in a limited number of institutions. The bulk of the revenues of many parishes was granted to abbeys, bishoprics or cathedrals, and ultimately nearly ninety per cent of the parishes were 'appropriated', to the detriment of the spiritual wellbeing of the people whom they were supposed to serve. That the church was a wealthy institution anyone could see who observed how an abbey, with its great complex of church, cloister, domestic buildings and gardens, dominated the country landscape and could vie with the castles of the nobility, or who noted how in a town a great church contrasted with the humble houses, mainly single-storey and with

thatched roofs, and caught the eye far more than the only other
public building, the tolbooth or town house. The total annual
revenues of this wealthy corporation must have been worth some
£400,000. But this vast sum represented the income of only some
3,000 clergy, in a population of perhaps 700,000. And even
among the clergy there were enormous inequalities: bishops and
abbots had their thousands, cathedral dignitaries their hundreds,
but hardly any parish priest had an income running into three
figures and the income of some barely reached two.

The church had pretensions in keeping with its material
splendour. How did 'Excommunication' sound in the mouth of
a Scottish priest?

I dissevir and partis thame fra the kirk of God and deliveris
thame quyk to the devill of hell, thare perpetually to remane
condampnit in body and saule. . . . And thare bodeys that
happinnis to dee under this cursing to be cassyn furth to
doggis and beistis and nothir to be erdit in kirk nor kirk-
yaird. . . . I forbid al Christin man and woman til have ony
cumpany with thame. . . . I tak fra thaim and cryis doune al
the gude deidis that ever tha did. . . . And as the sounde of
this bell gais fra your eris and the lycht of this candle fra
your sycht sa mot thare saulis gang fra the visaige of God
Almychty and ther gude fame fra the warld.

An institution with such powers might seem cheap even at
£400,000 a year. But what would happen when men began to
doubt the sanctions which lay behind such a 'cursing'?

All could see that much was amiss. If a parish priest was going
to make ends meet, he had either to accumulate several livings or
engage in some secular occupation, and in either event the
parishioners would be neglected. Equally, starvation wages did
not attract men able to instruct the people by either precept or
example. Prelates had the education to fit them for a lucrative and
highly competitive profession, but they were no better than the
parish priests in morals or spiritual zeal. Equally, while vicarages
did sometimes remain in a family and even pass from father to

son, this abuse too was more conspicuous among dignitaries.

Such irregularities should have been checked, but dispensations for almost any breach of canon law could be obtained—at a price —from the papal court. Moreover, one result of the pope's surrender to the king over appointments to prelacies was a series of scandalous appointments, one of them of James IV's eleven-year-old illegitimate son to the archbishopric of St Andrews. Worse was to come. James V, at the age of twenty, obtained a papal dispensation for the promotion of his three sons, one of them begotten in adultery, to any ecclesiastical benefices. The papacy was so manifestly an obstacle to good government that even men otherwise conservative in their views thought there was little to be said for it.

In monasteries, the idea of community of property had been lost sight of: each monk now had his individual 'portion' or share of the revenues, his own 'chamber' or apartment, and his own 'yard' or garden. This comfortable livelihood could even be granted to a man who was not a member of the community, for a monk's portion in Melrose was given to a surgeon to encourage him to sew up casualties in Border warfare. Men were too selfish to spend money on structural maintenance, and there is ample evidence of the damaged or even ruinous state of churches. When monks complained that 'if the kirk be not repaired this instant summer, God's service will cease in winter', they were the victims of a prevalent malaise. The whole situation was in some ways reminiscent of the eleventh century, before the reforms of the Margaretsons.

Possibly these reforms had never wholly penetrated to the Celtic west. It is one of the ironies of history that, by what seems like perversity, it was the Irish and some of the west Highlanders who were subsequently most devoted to Rome. In the Middle Ages some of the parish churches in the Highlands had to serve enormous stretches of wild country, and there was not a single friary, not a collegiate church except at Kilmun on the Firth of Clyde, and no monasteries outside Argyll. As the sees of Argyll and the Isles were without consecrated bishops for long periods, discipline must have collapsed and there cannot have been adequate administration of the sacraments, let alone preaching and instruction. The most significant late medieval monuments are not church buildings but a large number of tombstones, decorated with arresting sculptures. In their commemoration of the departed and in their association with important local families they fit into much the same context as the collegiate churches of the Lowlands, but they are more informative about the ties of kinship than about the level of piety, and flaws in the Latinity of the inscriptions suggest that educational standards were not being maintained.

A challenge to the church on theological grounds went back at least to the period of perplexity during the Schism, when Scotland received a taste of heresy from the England of Wyclif and the Bohemia of Hus, and from that period there may always have been 'lollards' who denied the validity of the mass and the priesthood. Then, in the 1520s, the teachings of Luther arrived through the trading links of the east coast burghs. The church and its censures were no longer respected, and the bearer of letters of 'cursing' might now be dragged by the hair of his head from the very altar. Belief in justification by faith left no room for trust in the efficacy of the mass or the other 'works' which the medieval system had encouraged.

Few thought that the church needed all its revenues, but there was no agreement on a scheme for redistribution. What was required was the restoration to the parishes of the teinds which were their proper patrimony. But what was going on was rather a division of the spoils. The crown was drawing money from the church by direct taxation, scions of royal and noble families were being appointed to wealthy prelacies, and clerics of all ranks were feuing their lands to laymen and granting their teinds in lease. This secularisation did nothing to make the task of reformers easier.

By the death of James V there were sufficient sympathisers with the Reformation to form a government which permitted the reading of the Bible in the vernacular. One question was, could there be reform without revolution? The existing system was not wholly lacking in vitality, for some of its institutions were still attracting fresh endowments for the saying of masses. Besides, efforts at reform from within were made. Under the primacy of John Hamilton, who was not opposed to doctrinal modification in a Lutheran direction, three councils of the Scottish church (1549, 1552, 1559) passed statutes for the strict examination of clergy, regular visitation by bishops, more preaching and instruction, and repair of churches. Perhaps it was difficult to take this seriously when the bishops themselves were showing little sign of reforming their own lives, and it was noticeable that, apart from a modest increase in the minimum stipend, nothing was done to redistribute revenues in favour of the parishes or interfere with vested interests. The long conflict with Rome petered out in a situation in which the Archbishop of St Andrews performed many functions hitherto reserved to the pope, the crown made appointments with hardly even formal acknowledgement of the pope's rights, and, while there was much talk about the powers of a general council, papal authority was ignored.

In August 1560 Parliament repudiated Rome, forbade the celebration of mass and adopted a reformed 'Confession of Faith'. The English *Book of Common Prayer* was introduced and the more radical *Book of Common Order,* which had been used by English exiles in Geneva, soon appeared. But once more, as Queen Margaret had found, it was easier to change doctrines and worship than to tamper with institutions, so that for a time the Reformed Church was left with only a congregational organisation.

The Reformers knew what they wanted. In the first *Book of Discipline* they claimed all parochial revenues for the ministers, schools and the poor, and the lands of the bishops for the universities and for the superintendents who were to exercise oversight. The lands of the monasteries were tacitly relinquished to the existing holders (mostly now laymen), but all other competing claims were disregarded. In their proposals for organisation the Scots picked and chose among the models offered by other reformed churches. In advocating the election of ministers by congregations and the appointment of superintendents who would have neither the canonical consecration, the wealth nor the places in Parliament of pre-reformation bishops, they were following the example of Denmark. The local kirk session of elders to exercise discipline and deacons to control finance followed a pattern agreeable not only to Calvin and the French Protestants but to many Lutherans and some Anglicans. The one feature in which the Scots showed originality was dictated by the political situation. As long as the Lords of the Congregation governed, the control of the christian community in the church could be exercised through the estates of the realm or even the privy council, but when Mary returned from France in August 1561 and continued to go to mass it was evident that neither her Parliament nor her Council could be regarded as the 'godly' governors the reformers sought, and a new device had to be found. Recourse was had to a General Assembly in which the christian community was represented by three estates, in the manner of a parliament: there were nobles and lairds, burgesses chosen by town councils, the superintendents and such ministers as they might select.

Many of the achievements of the Reformation are obvious: the Bible in the language of the people; the participation in worship of a congregation with a service-book and a psalter in their hands; the restoration of the cup to the laity; clerical marriage; the revival of church life in the parishes; the efficient oversight of clergy and churches; and—not least—the elimination of abuses. The whole concept in worship was of a kind of corporate priesthood, vested in the people. The Communion ceased to be something done by the priest alone, at the altar, and became a corporate act, in which minister and people assembled round a table. In Baptism, likewise, the emphasis was not on a priestly rite but on the reception of the child into the christian fellowship. Marriage, too, was a matter for the community, and for that reason was to be celebrated on Sunday in face of the congregation. In discipline, the penance imposed by the individual priest gave way to the penance imposed by the kirk session. The minister was seen as the delegate of the people, deriving his authority, under God, from them and not from the bishop or superintendent who gave him formal admission. This eminently sensible idea at one stroke eliminated all the hocus-pocus which has bedevilled so much discussion of the ministry in later generations. The greatest compliment which has been paid to the Reformers, and the measure of their success, has been the

185

way in which almost all churches, including now the Roman Catholic, have come to adopt practices which they advocated.

The dispossession of holders of church property which the Reformers' schemes envisaged did not commend itself to the nobles and lairds who supported them. By a compromise reached early in 1562 a third of most ecclesiastical revenues (except those in Argyll and the Isles, which must have been regarded as beyond government control) was taken over by royal officers, partly to augment the revenues of the crown—which thus acquired a vested interest in the Reformation—and partly to pay the ministers of the Reformed Church; the other two-thirds generally remained with the existing possessors, whether they were clergy or lay commendators. The result was a situation not paralleled in any other country. The doctrine and worship of the reformed congregations were alone officially recognised, and financial provision had been made for them. On the other hand, the entire structure of the old regime remained intact, stripped of spiritual functions but still possessed of the bulk of its wealth and with some administrative functions. Bishops still sat in Parliament and Council, exercised jurisdiction in matrimonial cases, received presentations from patrons and appointed men to livings. They were forbidden to say mass—some of them, it has been remarked, 'had no desire to be troubled with that or any other duty'—and had in law no religious functions unless they served in the reformed church. Three of them did so serve, and contemporaries had no difficulty in identifying bishops and superintendents: 'I understand,' one wrote, 'a bishop and superintendent to be but one office; and where the one is the other is. . . . To take away the office of a bishop, that no bishop be in the kirk, would be to alter and abolish the order which God hath appointed in His kirk.'

It has been said that 'the principal reason why the ancient church structure changed so little was that the aristocracy'—and it might be added, the crown—'had found ways to make that structure pay, and they would tolerate no change'. There is a good deal of truth in this, but it leaves out of account the moderate outlook of the Scottish reformers. It is certainly misleading to think of a precipitate revolution. The monasteries were not, as often said, 'suppressed'; recruitment ceased, and the abbey churches, except in so far as they were parish churches, fell out of use, but the monks retained their quarters and their 'portions' as long as they lived. Friaries were closed, but the friars were pensioned off. A considerable proportion of the priests served in the reformed ministry, not infrequently in the parishes where they had served before. Nor were the reformers guilty of wholesale destruction of church buildings. The ruined churches of Scotland are mainly the consequence of English invasions, the selfishness of pre-Reformation clergy, violence in times of civil strife, the ravages of time and weather and the activities of nineteenth-century restorers. The concern of the Reformers was to preserve and repair the churches they needed, not to destroy them.

The funds available to the reformed church from the thirds were inadequate, and on the accession of James VI (1567) it became the law that only men qualified to serve in the reformed church should be admitted to parsonages and vicarages, so that the two structures which had existed since 1560 would merge. On the same principle, it was decided in 1572, with general approval, that ministers should be appointed to vacant bishoprics and exercise the same powers as superintendents, subject to the General Assembly.

Presently, however, the presuppositions on which the organisation of the reformed church had rested were challenged, and controversy broke out between Presbyterians, insisting on the equality of ministers, and Episcopalians, who upheld the office of bishop. In England the cause of the bishops and the *Prayer Book* ultimately triumphed and the Puritan opposition was driven out; in Scotland it was the Presbyterians who in the end prevailed and it was the Episcopalians who became nonconformists. But that was not to happen until 1690. The superficial appearance is of two alternating systems: episcopacy in 1584, presbytery in 1592, episcopacy in 1610, presbytery in 1638, episcopacy in 1661 and presbytery in 1690. But there were many phases of compromise, and the two parties were comprehended within one church.

The foundation of Scottish Presbyterianism is usually attributed to Andrew Melville. The Reformers, it might be said, did not disapprove of bishops, but only of bad bishops; to Melville the only good bishop was a dead bishop. His campaign, marked by the second *Book of Discipline* (1578), proceeded to the logical conclusion that the admission and supervision of ministers were to be in the hands not, as hitherto, of bishops or superintendents, but of courts or committees, especially the presbytery, a new body which was to operate within an area smaller than the diocese: episcopacy, in short, was to be put into commission. But this was not Melville's only novelty. The Reformers had been intensely anti-clerical: the three estates, in the General Assembly, were to rule the church, while at parish level laymen, elected as elders for only a year at a time, were not only to discipline their fellow members but even—in theory at least—depose their minister. Melville reverted to clericalism. There were, he said, Two King-doms, and the lay community should have no say in ecclesiastical affairs. Elders were to be appointed for life and to become 'ecclesiastical persons' like ministers, while the general assembly was to be reconstituted so that it would consist only of ministers and the new life-elders.

King James VI believed that the church formed part of a Single Kingdom over which he, his Parliament and Council, ruled, and bishops, whom he nominated, would be his most apt agents in church government. His power was limited, and by a statute of 1592 he had to authorise the Presbyterian system. It was only after much tactical manoeuvring that he succeeded in taming the assembly and exiling Melville, who had told him to his face that he was only 'God's silly vassal'. The powers of bishops were stage by stage restored, ultimately (in 1610) with an assembly's ap-proval; but kirk sessions operated as before and presbyteries continued to perform important functions. It was essentially a compromise, which met with a fair degree of acquiescence.

Not content with this, James decided to modify Scottish wor-ship along English lines. Between 1615 and 1619 three draft liturgies were prepared, the third of them approximating to the *Prayer Book*. Concurrently, the king brought forward the Five Articles of Perth (1618): observance of the chief holy days; private administration of Communion and Baptism; a rite akin to episcopal confirmation of children; and kneeling at Communion. The last aroused violent opposition among a people to whom it savoured of the 'papistry' they had denounced so fiercely: 'We abhor and detest all kind of papistry. . . . We detest and refuse the usurped authority of that Roman Anti-christ, his five bastard sacraments, his devilish mass, his blasphemous priesthood, his desperate and uncertain repentance, his general and doubtsome faith, his worldly monarchy and wicked hierarchy.' James did gain a reluctant consent to his Articles, but he realised that he had gone too far and withdrew the proposed new liturgy.

James understood his people. His son, Charles I, had left Scotland when he was three and had no first-hand knowledge of the country. Besides, with the pliant James ecclesiastical questions were matters of expediency; with his obstinate son they were matters of conscience. Some of Charles's aims, ironically enough, were in line with those of the reformers—an educated ministry, a school in every parish, the restoration of church buildings and the payment of generous stipends—and, like the proposals of the reformers, they led to a clash with the nobility. James had been far too wary to make strenuous efforts to recover church property from lay hands, but Charles issued a revocation whereby all church revenues must be put at his disposal. He did provide machinery to increase stipends—machinery which survived until the twentieth century—but he did it at great cost. Although the scope of his revocation was whittled down, he had induced a sense of insecurity in nearly every landholder in Scotland. Besides, in order to embellish his Scottish capital, he created a bishopric of Edinburgh, insisted that the church of St Giles should be transformed into a cathedral, and gave instructions for the erection of a new parliament house nearby. These manifold requirements drove Edinburgh to bankruptcy at a time when the whole country was undergoing the unpleasant and novel experience of regular and heavy taxation.

Financial grievances were linked with a growing uneasiness at the manipulation of Parliament and with the jealousy which was aroused by the prominence of bishops in the Council and the appointment of the Archbishop of St Andrews as chancellor—the first clerical chancellor since the Reformation. Extravagant rumours circulated: the clergy were to possess a third of the wealth of the kingdom, and the king would appoint forty-eight abbots to sit in Parliament and swamp the house. The nobles, threatened with the loss of property and influence, had for the most part little contact with their distant king, and those who were around him were out of touch with Scottish opinion. The question was, how could their grievances be put convincingly before their sovereign? Parliament, subject to royal manipulation, was useless, and when a supplication was prepared which complained about constitutional, financial and ecclesiastical policy and was eloquent of the distrust felt for the 'mystical ends' of the high church clergy, the only result was the trial for treason of a noble who had handled it. The nobles began to think of making common cause with the ministers who opposed the king's ecclesiastical innovations.

In 1633, when Charles was in Edinburgh for his Scottish coronation, an act was passed enabling him to order the clergy to wear surplices, an altar with candles on it was erected in the abbey church of Holyrood and the *English Prayer Book* was read in the church of St Giles. The project of a prayer book for Scotland was revived. Before the book had even taken final shape, the Scots were arbitrarily commanded to use it, in terms of a Code of Canons, issued in 1636 by royal proclamation, which also forbade extempore prayer, ordered the rearrangement of churches to provide for an altar and made no mention of kirk sessions, elders or presbyteries. The *Prayer Book* was not devoid of concessions to the Scots, for example the substitution of 'presbyter' for 'priest', but it permitted the presbyter, when consecrating the elements at Communion, to stand before the altar like a priest saying mass.

When the book was read for the first time in the cathedral of St Giles on 23 July 1637 there was a riot. Seven months later came the National Covenant. In its forefront was an old anti-popish covenant of 1581, designed to appeal to the populace, and this was followed by a long recital of statutes which the king was held to have infringed. At the core of the document was an appeal from Charles's innovations to the rights of 'free assemblies and parliaments'. Much of it was redolent of the antiquarian studies of a lawyer, but it appealed to the notion, implied long before in the Declaration of Arbroath, that the Scots were a Chosen People. Now Scotland was seen as the New Israel, 'the little young sister' who should take her place—apparently through a bigamous union—along with 'the church of the Jews', as 'the bride of Christ, the betrothed Virgin, joined to God by a marriage covenant never to be forgotten'. It has been said that the Covenant was a device to remind God which side he was on, and the conviction that their cause was God's cause immensely strengthened the resolution of the Covenanters.

The Covenant did not condemn episcopacy, but an assembly at Glasgow later in 1638 decided that episcopacy was to be 'abjured'. The assembly was an instrument of the nobility and gentry, for the 'elders' present consisted of 17 peers, 9 knights and 25 lairds and there were 47 burgh representatives. The royal administration collapsed in the face of the estates of the realm arrayed behind the Covenant. With money furnished by the burghs, the Covenanters raised an army in which peers and their sons were colonels, lairds were captains, lawyers were the general's bodyguard and the privates were 'stout young ploughmen', accustomed to following their lairds. It looks amateurish, but there were many professional officers who had served on the continent and found that, with the Thirty Years' War petering out, they could be better employed at home, and the army was more than a match for the levies which the king raised from his restive English subjects. Not only had Charles to give way in Scotland, but attempts to find money to fight the Covenanters caused him to summon the English Parliament, after a lapse of eleven years, and in 1642 the English Civil War began. While some Scots thought that they should now support the king, who had conceded their demands, most of them believed that their own revolution could best be assured by a Solemn League and Covenant (1643), whereby they agreed to support Parliament on the understanding that the churches of England, Scotland and Ireland should be brought to uniformity 'according to the Word of God and the example of the best reformed churches'. The Scots, who had proclaimed in the second

Book of Discipline that they would become 'an example and pattern to other nations', had no doubt where 'the best reformed church' was to be found, but the English were not so sure. Thus, when a Westminster Assembly of Divines drew up a *Confession of Faith, Directory of Public Worship, Catechisms* and *Form of Church Government*, they were accepted by the Church of Scotland but proved unacceptable in England, where Congregationalism prevailed. The Scots had miscalculated. Therefore, when the English went on to execute Charles I, the Scots agreed to support Charles II on condition that he took the Covenants. But their adventure into England on his behalf ended in defeat at Worcester (1651), and Scotland was conquered by Cromwell, whose administration sent the General Assembly packing.

After the king came back in 1660, synods, presbyteries and kirk sessions continued, but the General Assembly was not revived. Instead, legislative power and appellate jurisdiction lay with the bishop in synod, executive authority very largely with the presbyteries, but all under the direction of Parliament and Council. There was no general reordination of men in Presbyterian orders, the forms used for ordination and consecration were not Anglican and confirmation by bishops was not practised. Besides, worship continued much as it has been under the Covenanters. This was again a compromise.

But it was at variance with the Solemn League, to which some Scots were fatuous enough to adhere despite the obvious preference of England for its own ecclesiastical system. This caused conscientious difficulties for those who saw the Covenants as contracts made with God and permanently binding. Besides, ministers who would not accept the place now accorded to bishops, or attend synods they convened, were deprived, numbering more than a quarter of the total. The congregations of those deprived ministers, who were heavily concentrated in the southwest, absented themselves from the parish churches and instead worshipped in conventicles, often in the open air. The government tried alternating doses of repression and concession, in the end with fair success. But a remnant, known as Cameronians, remained irreconcilable, and when the Roman Catholic James VII succeeded they refused to acknowledge him. The government on its side took proceedings against more moderate Presbyterians, whom it quite unjustifiably blamed for the Cameronian excesses.

James VII, in his anxiety to favour his co-religionists, the Roman Catholics, granted a general toleration, comprehending the Presbyterians, and this was fatal to the existing establishment. Many who were Presbyterian in sympathy but had previously acquiesced in episcopacy now opened their own meeting-houses and even set up presbyteries and synods, so that a kind of 'shadow' system was already in existence by the time James was deposed and succeeded by William of Orange. The situation was, however, confused. For one thing, the logical Solemn-Leaguers or Cameronians would not acknowledge an uncovenanted William any more than an uncovenanted James. On the other hand, William saw as clearly as James VI had done that episcopacy might be politically preferable to presbytery. However, the Scottish bishops felt they could not violate their oath to James by acknowledging William, and the Presbyterian majority among William's supporters prevailed on him to restore Presbyterianism (1690).

This was not, however, a victory either for the Covenanters or for Andrew Melville's principles. The Covenants were shelved and the reason given for the establishment of Presbyterianism was not that it was founded on the Word of God but that it was 'agreeable to the generality of the people'. Parliament, far from abdicating its functions in the church, merely acted at this juncture in favour of presbytery just as thirty years before it had acted in favour of episcopacy. Contemporaries were in no doubt that what one parliament had conceded another might withdraw. Nor did the settlement introduce freedom of worship or toleration, and the Presbyterians, who were only a small minority among the ministers, resisted the king's wish for genuinely representative assemblies. The exclusive claims of the Church of Scotland were as firmly upheld now that it was Presbyterian as they had been when it was Episcopalian. Its liberal complexion in later times has earned for seventeenth-century Presbyterians a reputation for holding principles which in truth they detested.

But the church was not in practice inclusive, for some Episcopalians refused to be absorbed and the Cameronians repudiated a settlement by which 'prelacy' was established in England. Moreover, within the Church of Scotland as now established there were divergent opinions. There were those who, while not rigid Covenanters, felt that the covenants had been too lightly laid aside; and there were those who, while they accepted the parliamentary decision for presbytery in 1690, were not prepared to accept the continued interference of Parliament, and especially (after 1707) a parliament at Westminster, in church affairs. There were theological differences too: while 'Evangelicals' adhered to the strict doctrines of Calvin, especially on the subject of predestination, the 'Moderates' were more liberal, and others moved towards a religion from which the supernatural had been largely eliminated to make it little more than a code of ethics. In this situation it was not improbable that patrons (whose rights, abolished in 1690, were restored in 1712) would appoint ministers whose sermons would not be agreeable to conservative congregations.

The First or Original Secession Church, which broke away in 1733, was based on conservative theology and a revival of the Covenants. It split in 1745–7 because some of its members scrupled to take an oath in which burgesses had to acknowledge 'the true religion presently professed within this realm' and which, the precise contended, implied an acceptance of the establishment. Each section—Burgher and Anti-Burgher—split again at the end of the century into 'Old Light' and 'New Light' sections, this time over the question of the power of the magistrate in matters of religion and the duty of the state to enforce ecclesiastical discipline —a somewhat academic question in a non-established church.

About the middle of the century disputes over patronage became more serious, and ministers who sympathised with the claims of congregations began to refuse to take part in the admission of ministers presented by patrons. This led directly to the formation in 1761 of the Second Secession or Relief Church. It represented the 'voluntary' principle, that the church should not seek state support but that each congregation should take responsibility for the maintenance of its church and minister.

The establishment, thus rid of disturbing elements, accommodated itself to parliamentary authority, patronage and the changing thought of the times. The period saw a growing attachment to 'reason', which sometimes involved rationalism in the sense of a denial of the supernatural but always meant at least a distrust of emotion and 'enthusiasm'. The 'Moderates' who ruled the assembly emphasised cultural, intellectual and social attainments and shocked the precise by playing cards and attending theatres. However, towards the end of the century a wave of religious awakening touched all ranks of society. It represented a new kind of evangelicalism, quite at variance with both the Moderate distrust of 'enthusiasm' and the antiquated politics and theology of the Seceders. By this time there was a political awakening as well, and the aspirations associated with the early stages of the French Revolution encouraged a new humanitarianism more in tune with the warmth of the Evangelicals than with the coolness of the Moderates.

Conflict emerged on such issues as foreign missions and the needs of the churchless masses in the growing towns. The Evangelicals were enthusiastic for mission in every sphere, and raised money for the provision of additional chapels to supplement the parish system, while the Moderates looked askance at moves which threatened to withdraw congregations from their legal parish ministers. Patronage again became a much-canvassed grievance, partly because it seemed contrary to the liberal thought which advocated popular rights in the franchise and partly because it was believed to perpetuate the domination of the Moderates; but it was the law of the land. As the Evangelicals rose to ascendancy, the Assembly proceeded to challenge statute law, and cases arose in which the civil courts pronounced its decisions illegal. The more determined Evangelicals therefore decided to renounce the state connection, and in the Disruption of 1843 about thirty-nine per cent of the ministers gave up their emoluments to 'cast themselves on such provision as God in His providence may afford'. About a third of the people followed them, and the Free Church of Scotland was formed. With wealthy and influential support it was able to erect churches and schools

195

throughout the land in something like duplication of the entire ecclesiastical and educational system. The Free Church had a large Highland following, and provided the Highlands with perhaps more adequate ministrations—when necessary in the Gaelic tongue—than they had ever known before.

The Disruption was the greatest of the secessions, but it was also the last. Already there had been indications of a different trend, for two sections of seceders had combined in 1820 in the United Secession Church, another section was readmitted to the Church of Scotland in 1839 and in 1842 two other groups formed the United Original Secession Church. Four years after the Disruption the Relief Church combined with the United Secession to form the United Presbyterian Church. The Free Church then attracted into its fold in 1863 the majority of the United Original Secession and in 1876 the majority of the Reformed Presbyterians or Cameronians. Thus, by the end of the century, there were three large Presbyterian bodies—the Church of Scotland, the Free Church and the United Presbyterian Church; and three small ones—the minorities of United Original Seceders and Reformed Presbyterians who had declined to enter into unions, and the Free Presbyterians, who had broken away from the Free Church in 1893 on theological grounds.

The next stage came in 1900, when the United Presbyterian and Free Churches joined in the United Free Church. The United Presbyterians had stood for the 'voluntary' principle, but the Free Church, although it was in practice maintained by its own people, had adhered to the principle of establishment. Therefore a minority in the Free Church—the 'Wee Frees'—refused to go into the union and, claiming to be true to principles which the majority had repudiated, successfully asserted its right, in a lawsuit which went to the House of Lords, to the entire property of the Free Church. The intervention of a royal commission was then necessary to arrive at an equitable division of the endowments.

The United Free Church was a serious rival to the establishment, for it could muster 1,700 ministers against 1,400 in the Church of Scotland. Therefore, when negotiations for union began between the two, what was required was little less than the surrender by the Church of Scotland of its whole historic position, and almost complete victory for all that the Free Church had contended for in 1843. One old-standing grievance had been eliminated as long ago as 1874, when patronage was abolished. In 1921 Parliament in effect abdicated its ecclesiastical authority by conceding that the Church of Scotland had the 'right and power, subject to no civil authority, to legislate and to adjudicate finally, in all matters of doctrine, worship, government and discipline'. (However, no steps were taken to abolish the oath by which the sovereign undertakes to maintain the Church of Scotland as it was in 1690, and it has been argued that even now the Church is not free to abolish synods or revive episcopacy, for example.) In 1925 the system whereby parish ministers were maintained from the teinds or from dues paid in place of them was swept away, and with it went the duty of the heritors to maintain the church and manse. Although large funds, derived from a charge on land, continue to be drawn by the Church of Scotland, it had made a great financial sacrifice, for the income from this source was in effect 'frozen' at its 1925 level, whereas the teinds had fluctuated with the price of victual in a way that compensated for inflation. It was not wholly logical that a charge should be imposed on every landowner for the support of a church no longer subject to Parliament, a church in whose affairs the landowner has no voice unless he happens to be a minister or elder. However, taken along with other minor changes, these measures of 1921 and 1925 satisfied the scruples of the majority in the United Free Church, and only a small minority declined to enter into the union.

Although the reformers had been anti-clerical, post-reformation church life had been dominated by the minister. From a lofty pulpit he preached a long sermon and delivered long prayers which were themselves partly didactic. The only part the congregation took was to join in the singing of the metrical psalms, which alone were permitted, to the exclusion of hymns composed by mortals. Instrumental music was abhorred and the singing led by a precentor. For generations he would read a psalm line by line and the people sing a line at a time after him—a practice needless in Scotland where most people could read, but originally imitated from the Puritans of England, where people were generally illiterate. Throughout the eighteenth century and into the nineteenth public worship did not include even the reading of the Bible and still less the recitation of 'set forms' like the Creeds or the Lord's Prayer. Celebrations of Holy Communion were infrequent, and the most conspicuous feature of sacramental worship was the gathering of large numbers of people for a joint service—the 'holy fairs' or 'jostling, promiscuous assemblies' where reverence and devotion were at a minimum. Strict oversight of private morals was exercised by the ministers and the kirk sessions of elders, and public worship was enlivened by the denunciation from the pulpit of the 'penitents' whose offences had been discovered.

In the last hundred years and more, however, the ordered reading of scripture has been restored to public worship, sermons have become shorter and in some churches the service has taken a more liturgical character, with congregational recitation of the Lord's Prayer and the Creeds. Service-books were reintroduced by individuals and societies in the nineteenth century, a *Book of Common Order* was officially approved in 1940 and a revised version in 1979. The psalms were supplemented first by metrical paraphrases of scripture and then by successive hymn-books which comprehend a wide range of christian praise and devotion. The restoration of better musical standards and the introduction of choirs and organs had for a time the effect of making churches look rather like concert-halls, but in the twentieth century churches have been planned in such a way that the focus is unmistakably on the Holy Table. Doctrinally, the *Westminster Confession* retains an official position, but subscription to its terms in detail is no longer required. The harsh kirk session discipline was for the most part quietly laid aside in the course of the nineteenth century, but the stern austerity of earlier days lingered on in the Highland districts where the Wee Frees and the Free Presbyterians have most of their members, and those churches are noted for their forthright pronouncements, made wholly without fear or favour, on moral issues.

In the eighteenth and nineteenth centuries there had sprung up a number of denominations, all broadly evangelical in outlook—Methodists, Congregationalists and Baptists—but none of them gained a large following and none can be said to stem from a central Scottish tradition. The Episcopal Church, however, has a history linking it directly with the Church of Scotland which existed before the parliamentary establishment of Presbyterianism in 1690. The Episcopalians who agreed to acknowledge Queen Anne and the Hanoverian kings enjoyed toleration from 1712, but a great many of them clung to Jacobitism right down to the death of Bonnie Prince Charlie in 1788. For those 'non-jurors' there were phases of prosecution, especially in the aftermath of each Jacobite rising, and they did not qualify for toleration until 1792. The two sections of the Episcopal Church— those tolerated under the Act of 1712 and the former non-jurors—drew together thereafter and ultimately organised their church under seven bishops, who retain among them the titles of the fourteen historic sees. The nineteenth century saw a general tendency towards conformity with the Church of England, and statutes of 1840 and 1864 qualified Scottish clergy for office in the English church. But, while this Scottish church came to look like a branch of the Church of England, it has always been completely autonomous. Its system of government is democratic: congregational business is managed by an elected vestry; in the Representative Church Council and the Diocesan Councils lay men and women are present, approximately equal in number with the clergy, to direct administration; clergy and laity elect the bishops; and lay members sit on synods, where decisions are taken on canons and liturgy.

After the Reformation, the Roman Catholic Church, as a regularly organised institution within Scotland, hardly existed until the 1690s. Nothing had been done to rally the opposition to Protestantism which was strong in some parts of the country, and in the early seventeenth century Roman Catholic effort was virtually extinct. Missions conducted by Irish Franciscans between 1619 and 1637 claimed spectacular numbers of converts, but most of them subsequently lapsed and other efforts were so intermitten that by about 1680 the total Roman Catholic population wa estimated, by a friendly observer, as no more than 12,000. As a result of a more sustained effort which began in the 1690s considerable gains were again claimed, but the total number does not seem to have exceeded 30,000 until after 1800. The situation was then transformed by the great immigration from Ireland, and in a hundred years the number of Roman Catholics increased twentyfold. Over the whole country the nominal strength rose to over 15 per cent of the population, and in certain districts in Strathclyde it exceeded a third.

A survey made in the late 1950s shows that some 60 per cent of the adult population of Scotland were members of one church or another. There were well over twenty denominations, but of the total church membership 63.5 per cent belonged to the Church of Scotland and 25 per cent to the Roman Catholic Church, while no other body could claim more than about 3 per cent. Nominal membership, however, is a different thing from active support: on the average Sunday only one in four of the adult population attended a church service, but a third of those who attended were Roman Catholics and only one in eight attended a service of the Church of Scotland. A census a hundred years earlier showed that nearly one in three of the entire population went to church and the Presbyterian attenders outnumbered the others by five to one.

The question of a wider union was under consideration almost immediately after the achievement of the union of 1929, but the only success so far has been the absorption of the remnant of the Original Secession by the Church of Scotland in 1956. There have been to date five rounds of talks with Anglicans, with no results in the way of union, though collaboration and mutual recognition have gone a long way, especially at local level, and 'areas of ecumenical experiment' have been recognised. Conversations between the Church of Scotland on one side and the Congregationalists and Methodists on the other also proved abortive. Multi-lateral conversations involving the Church of Scotland, Episcopalians, Congregationalists, Methodists, United Free Church and Churches of Christ have done a lot of exploratory work but have not yet produced any unions. One difficulty is that the

Church of Scotland had not so far had no make any changes in its doctrines, worship and discipline for the sake of union: it had in effect simply absorbed or swallowed the Secession, the Relief and the Free Churches and inevitably hoped to use the same technique again. The rejection of proposals for union with Congregationalists and Episcopalians gave little ground for believing that the Church of Scotland would readily make concessions to the very minor bodies which alone, apart from the Roman Catholics, now remain outside its allegiance.

CHAPTER 9

The Economy

Long before the resources of Scotland were fully and efficiently exploited they were already providing food, clothing and fuel for a modest population. On the pastures there grazed cattle and sheep to yield skins, wool, tallow, immense stores of cheese and butter, and the bone and horn from which useful articles were made. On mountain, forest and moor there was abundance of game which furnished hides and flesh, there was wood and peat for fuel, turf and stones for building. The enormous exports of skins, hides and fleeces suggest that there can have been no shortage of meat. The cultivated land produced the grain which gave the people their bread, their meal and their ale, and in good seasons produced a surplus for export. The seas, lochs and rivers so abounded in fish that men spoke of 'fishy Scotland'.

In both Highlands and Lowlands, cattle—many of them to serve as or to breed draught-oxen—were far more important than sheep; the latter were often kept only in very small numbers, for the sake of the ewes' milk rather than for mutton or wool, and even sheep-rearing areas like the Border hills did not carry what would now be reckoned a proportionately heavy sheep stock. The universal cereal was oats; bere (a kind of barley) was widespread, and there was wheat in all the east coast areas south of the Moray Firth, as well as in the central belt and Ayrshire.

Internal trade was hardly necessary, for town-dwellers had their own cattle and strips of arable ground, so that basic foodstuffs and raw materials did not need to be brought in from the countryside. In larger burghs, however, local supplies either of foodstuffs or of skins and hides for the glovers and shoemakers would not suffice, and, besides, fish and salt must always have been brought from the coast to inland burghs.

Overseas commerce was more important, though few necessities had to be imported, except corn in time of dearth. As there was a scarcity of fodder in winter, the custom was to slaughter at Martinmas all cattle not required for breeding or haulage and to live during the winter on the 'marts' or salted carcases; the temptation, in the spring, to kill off some of the miserable survivors was checked by a close season for flesh eating in Lent, which was maintained even after the Reformation. Among the significant imports, therefore, were spices and other garnishings to render salt meat palatable. So far as drink was concerned, Scotland produced its own ale and beer, but the import for which we have most evidence in early times is probably wine, if only because there was a celebrated case about a large bill left unpaid by Alexander III to his wine-merchant. Likewise, the clothing produced in Scotland was of mediocre quality, and finer materials, including silks, had to be imported. Not least among imports was iron, for little native ore was used.

In return for goods not produced at home, the Scots sent overseas the surplus of what was primarily a subsistence economy —wool, fleeces, hides, skins and fish. The outstanding export in early times was wool, which went especially from the Tweed valley through Scotland's greatest town, Berwick, where the spacious mouth of the Tweed gave immediate access to the open sea, an important consideration in the days of sail. Alexander III was able to pledge the customs of Berwick (it is not said for how many years) for no less than £2,197. But other east coast ports, from Leith to Dingwall, were flourishing in a more modest way. There was a significant incident in 1247, when a ship, designed to transport crusaders from France to the Holy Land, was built at Inverness for Count Hugh of St Pol, whose wife was related to the Scottish king. The vessel caught the admiring attention of an English chronicler, and we may be sure that the count did not entrust its construction to a bunch of novices. There must have been practised shipwrights at Inverness, no doubt using timber floated down Loch Ness and the River Ness.

There was a good deal of trade with England, largely by sea with east coast ports. The proximity of English markets became so attractive as to nullify the effects both of political hostility and of legislation designed to keep Scottish raw materials at home and encourage native manufactures; Scottish wool was always welcome in England, and English cloth welcome in Scotland. This was plain in the sixteenth century. In 1546, although the two countries were at war, 'all the merchandise and victuals' from south of Forth were said to have been sold in England. Fish, too, found a market in England: in 1555 a northern laird complained that he would have got half as much again for his fish if he had been able to sell them there. Native consumers alleged that English demand drove up prices and that the best Scottish produce was diverted to England.

To France went wool, cloth and salt fish, in return for wines from Gascony and various delicacies and luxury articles. The Low Countries were early established as the chief outlet for Scottish exports. By 1296 the Flemings had a depot in their Red Hall in Berwick, and from the next century a port in the Netherlands—Middelburg, Bruges or Veere—was the Scottish 'staple', through which the principal exports passed and where a 'conservator of Scottish privileges in Flanders', appointed by the Scottish crown, guarded the goods and interests of Scottish merchants. To the Low Countries the Scots sent wool, skins and hides, and later coal, salt, cloth, stockings and herring, in return for spices and clothing. German merchants had their Scottish headquarters in the White Hall at Berwick in the thirteenth century, and when Wallace liberated Scotland in 1297 he wrote to Lübeck and Hamburg telling them that they could resume their trade. That there was already commerce with Norway is indicated by a clause in the treaty of 1266; in later times corn (in time of plenty), cloth, skins, coal, salt and fish went to Scandinavia and the Baltic in return for corn (in time of dearth), iron and prodigious quantities of timber. By the end of the Middle Ages wine was coming from Spain as well as from France. Another trade which probably developed relatively late was that between the Firth of Clyde and Ireland, which received linen, cloth, stockings, herring and coal.

For the thirteenth century there are figures for royal and ecclesiastical wealth which make possible some comparison with

England and suggest that Scotland was as prosperous then as it ever was. The surviving remains of castles, abbeys and cathedrals carry the same message. Scotland had shared fully in romanesque architecture as it had been developed by the Normans, and Kirk-wall Cathedral, Dunfermline Abbey, the parish churches of Dalmeny and Leuchars, and many more up and down the country, could have been built anywhere in western Europe; nothing shows more clearly how fully Scotland shared in a great cosmopolitan civilisation. In the thirteenth century the pervading impression is of the integration of Scotland into European culture. Ecclesiastical architecture moved into the First Pointed phase, and the quality at its best is very good, though it seldom equals the finest work in other lands. This was also the first period of conspicuous secular building in stone. Castles like Bothwell, Caerlaverock and Kildrummy indicate something like opulence: Scottish magnates had a taste and refinement matching that of magnates elsewhere. In the account of Edward I's progress through the country in 1296 there are illuminating phrases: 'Perth, a fine town', 'Forfar, a castle and a fine town', 'Montrose, a castle and a fine town', 'Aberdeen, a fair castle and a good town'; and only once, in a tour lasting from 18 March to 22 August and taking him as far north as Elgin, was the English king unable to find suitable quarters under a roof.

Medieval farmers can probably be credited with having enough sense to know what level of production they should try to achieve. No foresight could anticipate a wet and stormy season, which could mean starvation, for even local shortages were serious when the means of moving food about the country were limited. The effect of the weather must always be kept in view, though we do not have adequate information until the early seventeenth century. At that time we know that the weather was on the whole better than it had been for some time, and one can only speculate about the extent to which the success of James VI's government was due to better weather and consequent material prosperity. It is certainly true that the less favourable conditions in the second half of the century, winding up with several bad seasons in the 1690s, had political repercussions.

But in medieval times it was war with England which hit the economy hard. The fertile south-east felt the brunt of almost every English attack, and from time to time English armies burned and plundered further up the east coast. Cornland lay unsown, flocks and herds dwindled. As wool and hides were scarce for export, foreign trade fell away and imports could not be obtained. People were not likely to build better homes or improve their land when all might be destroyed, and more likely to hope that a turn in the fortunes of war would give them an opportunity to recoup their losses by raiding England. Agrarian pursuits became as discouraging in the Border country because of war as they were in the Highlands because of weather. As late as the sixteenth century English attacks caused the place of Haddington among the Scottish burghs to drop from fifth (in 1535) to fifteenth (in 1557), and it was not thought worth while to put a good roof on the church of Ayton, which lay in the path of invading armies, 'for fear of the Englishmen'.

However, the very simplicity of the economy made it resilient, and, given even a short period of peace, there was rapid recovery. In David II's reign, when there was peace after war had been almost incessant from 1296 to 1356, the king was able to raise very large sums from the customs and had a revenue probably exceeding that of any later medieval king. There was an even more marked recovery in the latter part of the fifteenth century, when the country enjoyed more settled conditions and England was preoccupied with the Wars of the Roses. Berwick was finally lost in 1482, but its place as the main port for the south-east had already been taken by Leith, and it was for this reason, as well as the ability now of Lothian farmers to harvest their crops without interference, that Edinburgh at this stage became the capital of the country. Many new burghs were established—68 burghs of barony between 1450 and 1513. There was a fresh interest in fishing, with acts in 1471 and 1493 to encourage the construction of fishing boats. The burghs were now paying a fifth of a taxation —half as much as the amount paid by that wealthy corporation the church and half as much as that paid by the crown tenants.

After a long recession, ecclesiastical building flourished once more. The fashionable collegiate churches, of which Rosslyn Chapel is an outstanding example, were a kind of status symbol on which Scottish barons were willing to expend considerable sums. Equally, fine burgh churches reflect growing prosperity. Among secular buildings, the towers of nobles and lairds, while lacking external refinement, have some sophisticated internal work. The finest royal buildings were not to come until the reign of James V, but the royal quarters at Stirling Castle were extended and James IV, not content, as his predecessors had been, to 'live in digs' with the monks of Holyrood, built the first royal palace there, as well as erecting part of Linlithgow Palace. James III patronised both musicians and artists—the earliest painting which has survived in Scotland dates from his reign and consists of altar panels prepared for Trinity College Church, in Edinburgh. Such an expanding economy bred culture, and among James IV's subjects were three of Scotland's greatest poets—Robert Henryson, William Dunbar and Gavin Douglas. Literature enjoyed official encouragement and patronage, and the printing press was introduced in 1508. When this Golden Age came to an end at Flodden, the English noted with admiration both the equipment of the Scots and their lavish provisions in food and drink—which were much enjoyed by the victors, who for three days had had no beverage but water.

The poverty of medieval Scotland has been exaggerated, mainly because travellers' tales are easier to quote than the more reliable evidence of records. Possibly medieval Scots took pleasure in pulling the legs of inquisitive visitors, much as islanders probably pull the legs of the sociologists and folklorists who descend on them today. One fifteenth-century visitor had heard of a tree producing fruit which, on falling into water, turned into geese, and when he asked its whereabouts was told that it existed only in Orkney—which, as the Scots knew, but he did not, was almost treeless. Others were told that the solan goose or gannet incubated its egg by covering it with its foot, and one of them improved on this by deriving 'solan' from 'sole on'. It is perhaps understandable that visitors who were introduced to Scotland through the bald hills of the Southern Uplands reported incorrectly that the land was 'destitute of timber', but, although Scotland hardly had walled cities on the continental scale, no one who used his eyes at all should have said that the 'towns have no walls'. Native Scots who had been anglicised, like John Major, were as mischievous detractors of their own country as were visitors.

Anyone who takes the trouble to go beyond travellers' tales soon discovers that they wrote a lot of nonsense. There was, for example, extensive native woodland, and some pains were taken to conserve it. In 1488 a baron court decreed that a tenant in East Lothian should forfeit his lease because he had destroyed trees, and in 1568 a licence was granted for the planting of trees as part of a project for making a forest in Glenfalloch for the keeping of deer and horses. The planting of trees was often a condition in a lease or a feu charter. The trouble, it seems, was not lack of trees but difficulty of transport, for, with the exception of Inverness and Perth, to which timber could be floated down by loch and river, Scots burghs found it easier to obtain supplies from Norway.

John Major's greatest blunder was his allegation, repeated by almost every later writer, that Scottish tenants had no security of tenture. The truth is that the heredity which prevailed so strongly everywhere else in Scottish life was equally conspicuous in tenancies and that continuity was the norm. Leases for life were quite common, but even when the formal lease was short—from one to five years—it was constantly renewed to the same tenant or his heirs on the same terms. Rentals of monastic houses show many examples of holdings being passed on in the same family for generations. It was not exceptional that in 1540 a tenant of Glenluce held land which had previously been held by his brother, his grandfather, his great-grandfather and his great-great-grandfather. Tenancies which endured for generations were the 'kindly tenancies', a phrase in which 'kindly' is related to 'kin' and means hereditary. On such a tenant's death his heir obtained his inheritance by being 'rentallit' or entered on the rent-roll of the estate.

In the late sixteenth and early seventeenth centuries the Scottish farmer, free alike from 'malice domestic' and 'foreign levy', could at last sow his seed with some confidence that no human agency would prevent him from reaping his crop. On the church lands, hereditary proprietors took the place of prelates who had been under the temptation to put immediate profit before the ultimate good of the estate. For lesser men, feu charters, conferring proprietorship, to some extent superseded leases, and were expected to encourage the erection of better buildings, the extension of cultivation, the construction of dovecots, orchards, pleasances and warrens. Contrary to what is often stated, it was commonly sitting tenants who obtained feus. There are indications, too, that arable land was being extended at the expense of pasture: settlers were expressly authorised to 'ryve out and win' new corn land, and they were converting 'the bestialls' girse' or the beasts' pasture into arable. A more commercial nexus began to supersede the keeping of tenants who paid small rents but rendered services, and if tenants were to pay higher rents they had to improve their land and grow heavier crops, so the quality of the land began to be improved by the use of lime.

The sixteenth and seventeenth centuries saw other changes. With Anglo-Scottish peace and the personal union, the Borders, from being a hotbed of reivers, became a route for peaceful traffic, while east coast shipping was safe from English attack; though Scotland's involvement in England's continental wars made it vulnerable to foreign warships. Development was interrupted during the covenanting period, when armies marched and counter-marched; civil war gave opportunities for raiding commerce at sea; and Scotland raised three great armies in little more than three years, to see them destroyed at Preston, Dunbar and Worcester. Scottish trade with the Baltic reached its lowest recorded level in 1651. The Cromwellian union established free trade between the two countries, but Scotland, wasted by war and by intolerable taxation, was unable fully to profit, and economic legislation was framed to suit England. But before and after that troubled period the economy flourished. Determined efforts were made, with some success, to develop manufactures, especially linen and woollen cloth but also glass, leather, soap, sugar, paper, hardware, pottery, ropes and gunpowder. By the end of the century linen was said to be 'the most noted and beneficial' of all

Scottish industries, and it certainly provided one of the most conspicuous exports, especially to England. Pastoral farming was now making a novel contribution to exports, in the shape of the vast number of cattle on the hoof with which drovers took the road to England. When England thus figured increasingly as an outlet for Scottish exports, it is not surprising that many imported luxuries now came from there rather than from the continent.

Once again a changing economy was reflected in a changed architecture. The predominant secular building of the early seventeenth century was a modification of the tower-house, which became increasingly refined and sophisticated and lost much of its defensive character. But already residences with little or no pretension to fortification were appearing, for example the Earl's Palace at Kirkwall, c1600. After 1660 the purely residential dwelling finally prevailed, and Kinross House (1684–95) antici-pated the classical styles of the eighteenth century.

Although the economy remained predominantly rural, there were developments in the burghs. Nearly as many burghs of barony received charters between 1661 and 1707 as had obtained them in the whole preceding century, and, although some were only 'parchment' burghs—a kind of status symbol for their owners—they demonstrate afresh the interest of the nobility in economic progress and represent a movement against the mono-polies of the royal burghs, inroads on whose privileges were made in this period. In the sixteenth century, Edinburgh's assessment for taxation had sometimes equalled the combined figures for the next three burghs—Dundee, Perth and Aberdeen—and its propor-tion of a total burgh taxation usually amounted to a fifth or quarter, while its proportion of the total customs might amount to over a half. After 1603 it remained the regular meeting place of Parliament, central law courts and Privy Council, and the king's commissioner to the Scottish Parliament resided there in the Restoration period. The city was therefore still a great centre of consumption and it maintained or even increased its lead over other burghs. But the most significant change was that Glasgow's share in a taxation rose from four per cent to twenty per cent and its place among the burghs, which had been fifth in 1594, was second (though still a very poor second) before the Revolution. Its expansion was partly a consequence of the pacification of the Highlands and of the settlement of Ulster, but American trade was beginning to have a noticeable effect.

Trade with America was, however, contrary to English law. English attempts to curb Scottish trade caused many complaints, and these were not alleviated either by Scottish success in smuggling—whether across the Border or across the Atlantic—or by the fact that Scotland was pursuing a similar protectionist policy. Scottish obsession with the need to expand trade, and a sense of frustration caused by English restrictions, led directly to the foundation in 1695—the same year which saw the foundation of the Bank of Scotland—of the Company of Scotland trading to Africa and the Indies, which was responsible for the unfortunate Darien venture.

The economic progress of Scotland in the seventeenth century has received insufficient attention, partly because the Whig interpretation of history has left its legacy in the view that all good things started with the Glorious Revolution and its sequel the Union. But there is another, less subtle, explanation. Henry Gray Graham wrote an eminently readable, but singularly mischievous, book, *The Social Life of Scotland in the eighteenth century*, which painted a black picture of pre-Union Scotland. One of Graham's notorious howlers was his statement about the Education Act of 1696, 'Never was there a wiser law, and never was a law more studiously disregarded.' Somewhat similarly, he would have us believe that Scotland was almost entirely without roads and wheeled transport until the eighteenth century. The truth is that from Columba's days numerous references to carts and carriages can be found, some of them in documents relating to the building of the many medieval bridges, which postulate the existence of roads or at any rate of serviceable tracks. By the late seventeenth century coaches were already commonplace for men of wealth and position. Again, people prefer to repeat an old saying purporting to show that once a farmer had paid his rent and set aside his seed he had only a third of his crop left—'ane to gnaw and ane to saw, and ane to pay the laird witha' '—rather than look at records

211

which show what the yield actually was and how much of it was swallowed up in rent. Another feature which again requires correction is the extent of woodland: apart from old native timber, landowners began in the seventeenth century to experiment with imported trees.

The economic advantages of union, when it came, were not at once apparent. The abolition of customs between England and Scotland meant that English manufactured goods, often of better quality and in any event produced on a larger scale and in consequence cheaper, were able to drive Scottish manufacturers out of business. Over much of the country there was half a century of something like stagnation in every sphere save agriculture, and only after that was the economy adjusted to new conditions. But trade with America, previously possible only surreptitiously, now lay open. The Clyde became the main channel for the import of tobacco into Britain. Most of it was for re-export to the continent, since the colonies themselves were forbidden to export tobacco except to Britain and other British possessions. In exchange for their exports, which included sugar and rum as well as tobacco, the colonists wanted to import manufactured goods, for they themselves had few manufactures and were indeed forbidden to manufacture some of their own raw materials. In the Clyde area there therefore developed manufacture of wrought-iron work, leather goods, pottery, crystal, ropes, shoes, hats and furniture.

Linen, however, was especially important. In 1727 acts were passed providing for the supervision of the industry and placing funds (available in terms of the Treaty of Union) at the disposal of the Board of Trustees for Manufactures, which offered prizes and subsidies and arranged for instruction by skilled craftsmen. The many processes connected with the industry—the preparation of the raw flax, spinning, weaving, bleaching and dyeing—were, one or more of them, carried on in nearly every parish in the kingdom. Spinning long remained a part-time domestic occupation for women, but weaving, while still done in the home, came to be full-time and to be concentrated in areas like Glasgow, Paisley, Dundee, Dunfermline and Perth, while the finishing processes were even more localised. The production of linen cloth rose about twelve-fold between 1728 and 1800. It would hardly be an exaggeration to call the eighteenth century the linen era in Scottish economic history. A second bank, the Royal, had been founded in 1727, and a third started, significantly as the British Linen Company, in 1746.

The phase in which the main pillars of the Scottish economy had been tobacco and linen came to an end when the American War of Independence (1776–83) brought about the collapse of the tobacco trade. After the war the Americans were free to ship their tobacco anywhere and Scotland lost its massive import and re-export trade. The industry which largely took its place was cotton manufacture. Glasgow capital and English inventive genius—Hargreaves, Arkwright and Crompton with their spinning jenny, water-frame and mule—happily combined with Scottish natural resources in the shape of water power, Scottish skill acquired in linen manufacture, and Clyde shipping to bring in the raw cotton. Within a few years there were many cotton mills by Scottish riversides, especially in Renfrewshire and Lanarkshire.

The eighteenth century no more than foreshadowed the future growth of the heavy industries. Coal mining had been hampered by the difficulty of keeping the mines free of water and by inadequate transport except between places on the coast. The steam engine provided pumping machinery, and railroads, on which wagons were drawn by horses, linked pits to the coast. At the end of the century, canals made an important contribution, and soon steam power was applied to the railroads. More of a novelty than coal was the foundation in 1760 of the Carron Iron Works. They represented a combination of English capital and technical skill with Scottish business acumen and were designed to exploit Scottish natural resources, in this instance native iron ore, coal and wood, as well as water power, which was used to blow the blast for the furnaces and drive the machinery. It was not, however, until the invention of the hot blast in 1828 that Scottish ores became competitive, and until that happened iron was a very poor third, after cotton and linen, among Scottish products.

Eighteenth-century 'improvement' was conspicuous in agriculture. Root crops like turnips began to be cultivated on a large scale and new grasses were introduced to yield abundant crops of hay. As cattle and sheep could now be adequately fed in winter, stock could be improved by breeding heavier animals. Farms became larger, consolidated holdings taking the place of the old intermingled rigs; fields were enclosed by dykes; the old communal system of farming was superseded; and the new crops made rotation possible. Leases became more general; labour services fell out of use, and the ground was systematically drained and cleared of stones. Afforestation made enormous strides; not only were rows of beeches and chestnuts planted round the mansions, but vast areas of mountainside were covered with larch. Better implements, like threshing machines and a more efficient plough, made their appearance. Thus equipped, Scottish farmers made a great deal of money at the end of the eighteenth century and the beginning of the nineteenth, when the French wars meant that imports had to be restricted, armies had to be clothed and fed and the navy supplied with salt meat. All the time, too, the growing population of the towns had to be fed.

The most conspicuous urban development was the growth of Glasgow, from about 12,000 at the time of the union to 100,000 a hundred years later. It was only in this period that Glasgow first became a port, with the deepening of the Clyde to make it really an artificial waterway, and at the end of the century the opening of the Forth and Clyde canal connected Glasgow by another artificial waterway to the North Sea. Eastern Scotland had derived much less direct benefit from the colonial trade than the west, and some of its manufactures had been depressed by English competition, but once economic revival reached the east, by the middle of the century, Edinburgh began to extend beyond its medieval bounds, over bridges spanning the valleys to south and north, into George Square (1766) and the 'New Town' from 1767.

There had been legislation on roads in the seventeenth century, providing for free labour on their making and maintenance, but better arrangements were made in the eighteenth, when a long series of acts set up turnpike trusts and empowered them to levy tolls on vehicles and apply the proceeds to the care of roads.

However, it was not until the end of the century that the principles of good road-making were understood. Then came rapid improvements, accompanied by the building of the handsome bridges of Rennie and Telford, some of which now carry traffic with a weight and bulk of which the designers never dreamed.

The domination of cotton continued until roughly the middle of the nineteenth century. About seventy-five per cent of the output came from mills in Lanarkshire and Renfrewshire, and there was an especially heavy concentration in Glasgow and its immediate neighbourhood. After 1800 power was increasingly applied to weaving as well as spinning, but some handloom weavers long continued to make a good living from specialised products like the famous Paisley shawls. This great industry was suddenly shattered, like the tobacco trade before it, by an American war, this time the Civil War (1861–5), which cut off the supplies of raw cotton. After the war, recovery was only partial, for Lancashire became the British centre of cotton manufacture, and only certain specialised branches of it continued to flourish in Scotland.

Linen production became increasingly a full-time occupation carried on in factories, mainly in Fife and Angus. A new textile, jute, became the main industry of Dundee, while Kirkcaldy concentrated on linoleum. The manufacture of 'tweed', which had begun to develop in the Borders at the end of the eighteenth century, also expanded.

In this period, however, the emphasis came to be on the heavy industries. The output of coal, required for steam engines in factories, locomotives and ships, iron smelting, heating, the making of gas and later electricity, rose from $7\frac{1}{2}$ million tons in 1854 to 39 million in 1908. After the invention of the hot blast in 1828, the number of furnaces smelting iron more than doubled in ten years and production rose more than 500 per cent. By 1860 a million tons of pig iron were being produced annually, mainly in Lanarkshire and Ayrshire. Interest later began to focus on steel, the efficient manufacture of which began about 1860. In a single decade (1879–89) steel almost completely superseded iron in shipbuilding.

Clydeside took a foremost place in the production of steamships

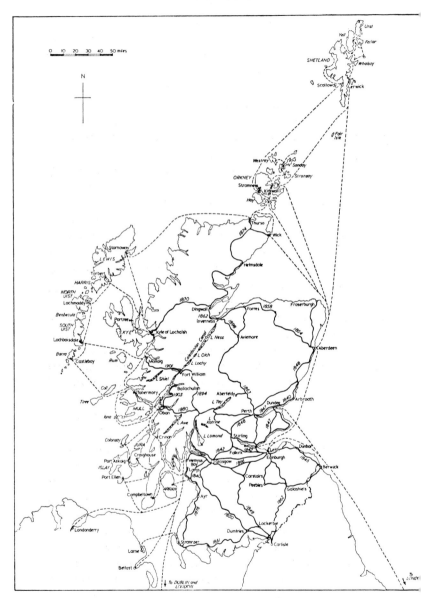

The main rail and steamer routes c 1900

and locomotives, many of them for export to all parts of the world. For some time engines were fitted in wooden hulls, but when metal prevailed the Clyde had the raw materials and the skilled labour of iron workers. Between 1859 and 1889 the tonnage of shipping built on the Clyde showed a tenfold increase and came to represent a third or more of British tonnage. Not only steamships, but some of the finest and fastest sailing ships—the clippers, apparently first designed in Aberdeen to meet the challenge of steam—came from Scottish yards.

There were other uses for Scottish natural resources. Quarrying, especially of granite in Aberdeenshire, was one, and another was the production of oil from shale, which had a brief but brilliant career, mainly in West Lothian, at the end of the nineteenth century and the beginning of the twentieth and which left the enormous red 'shale bings' which were such striking features of the landscape. Among lighter industries, the manufacture of paper grew rapidly and Scotland was famous also for printing and book-production. Brewing and distilling were put on a commercial footing at the turn of the eighteenth and nineteenth centuries and provided substantial exports.

In the farmyard the ubiquitous steam engine operated threshing-mills, and engineering skill provided reaping machines and other mechanised implements. The growing urban population increased the demand for farm produce and improved transport facilitated its supply. But agriculture did not flourish after 1846, when the Corn Laws were repealed and the British farmer was no longer protected against the competition of wheat which could come more cheaply from the plains of North America. Later, Scottish stock-raising met similar competition as frozen and canned beef and mutton came from South America and New Zealand. As a result of mechanisation and competition the fraction of the population employed on the land fell from a third in 1800 to a twentieth in 1911, and many people moved either into the cities or overseas. The decline in agriculture was matched by an unprecedented development of fisheries. Herring were latterly being caught in prodigious quantities and salted for export (in 1907 to a total of 2½ million barrels), while steam trawlers were able to reap a harvest of white fish from distant grounds previously inaccessible.

The improved roads and the canals had just reached their maximum efficiency when they were almost put out of business by the railways and the steamship. Most of the main railway lines in the populous parts of Scotland and connecting Scotland with England came into operation between about 1830 and 1850. Expansion to the north and west came later—Inverness 1863, Kyle of Lochalsh 1870, Thurso 1874, Oban 1880, Fort William 1894. Nowadays, when so many lines have been closed and railway traffic is worse than secondary, we are apt to forget the enterprise, capital, engineering skill and above all manual labour which went to railway construction, involving high and exposed routes and the bridging of lochs, rivers and estuaries.

The islands, and the west and north mainland, benefited from steam navigation which, using inland lochs as well as the sea, opened up the Highlands and Islands as nothing else could have done. Water was not only a highway between one part of Scotland and another; shipping carried Scottish manufactures to the ends of the earth. As vessels rapidly increased in size and power they concentrated in a few large ports. Glasgow became the third port in Britain (after London and Liverpool), docks and wharves were developed at Leith, Dundee and Aberdeen, and at Grangemouth a new port was created which ultimately displaced Leith as Scotland's second port. Meanwhile all round the shores the little harbours declined into fishing ports or passed out of use altogether. After World War I, when coal became more costly, coastal traffic declined, and since World War II the competition of road transport has gone a long way to drive it out of business.

The period between about 1830 and 1860, when both cotton and heavy industry counted, was possibly the best period ever in the Scottish economy. The later concentration, which by 1911 meant that there were nearly 1½ million employed in heavy industry and only 165,000 in textiles, though it brought temporary prosperity, was a disadvantage in the long run: had a more mixed economy persisted subsequent troubles might have been avoided. The general pattern in the nineteenth century was one of spectacular expansion, of great opportunities for Scots and of fortunes accumulated by shrewd and thrifty men who had begun with no capital but their brains. Yet there were booms and slumps. There was a financial crisis in 1824-5 and hard times in the 'hungry forties', when there were poor harvests and weavers were finding conditions more difficult than ever, partly because hand looms could not compete with power looms, and partly because wages were forced down by the employment of women and of Irish immigrants. On the other hand, in the 1850s wars in the Crimea and in India absorbed men and stimulated certain branches of industry, and a general increase in prosperity in Britain coincided with a commercial crisis in the United States. At the end of the 1860s there was distress as the cotton industry declined, and there was depression once more about 1875-9.

The population of Scotland as a whole, little more than a million in 1707, increased during the nineteenth century from just over a million and a half to nearly four and a half. But many counties were showing a decrease long before 1900, whereas the big cities and even medium-sized towns were showing spectacular increases. Lanarkshire increased tenfold and by 1911 had nearly as many people as the whole of Scotland had had in 1801. Most of the additional people had moved in from the rural Lowlands and the Highlands, but part of the increase was due to immigration. With the potato famine in the 1840s, Irishmen by the thousand crowded into central Scotland and since they were fleeing from starvation they were content to accept any wage and to put up with any conditions. In the same period many Scots, often of the most intelligent and enterprising type, were emigrating.

World War I was a watershed in Scotland's economic history. After 1918 the tale was of serious unemployment in the heavy industries, contraction in exports and chronic depression. Yet at least two factors would in time have altered the Scottish economy even had there been no war. In the nineteenth century, Britain's rapid industrialisation had given her an advantage over lands only partially or not at all industrialised, with the result that practically the whole world was a market for the products of her heavy industry. But as industrialisation spread through most of Europe, to America and ultimately to Asia, Britain's former customers became self-supporting and even competitors. Scotland, with her greater concentration on heavy industry, felt the loss more than England did. Another factor was the dwindling of some raw materials. Native supplies of iron ore were well on the way to exhaustion by 1914, and many of the collieries, especially in Lanarkshire, had reached a point where they could no longer be worked economically. Already by 1914 the expansion of Scottish industry was losing momentum and production levelling off.

During the siege conditions of the war, agriculture had of necessity been expanded, but when peace came and the government reverted to something like a laissez-faire policy, farmers had again little protection against imported foodstuffs, and there was renewed contraction. Changes similar to those which militated against heavy industry affected the fisheries, for markets shrank and Scotland's resources were depleted. The great continental markets for cured herring were never fully recovered after 1918, and it became increasingly apparent that, wherever the elusive herring were, they were not on the old grounds whence they had been taken in such prodigious quantities before 1914. Attempts to expand the home market had only limited success. Increased demand for white fish for the fried fish trade benefited chiefly the larger English trawlers, which brought cheaper and coarser fish from more distant grounds where few Scottish trawlers operated.

While some of the causes of economic decline might have been foreseen before 1914, there were sectors in which the decline was caused by sheer bad luck. The linen industry, for example, had built up an outstanding reputation for quality, but after 1918 it languished and textile towns like Dunfermline were as depressed as some of those which concentrated on heavy industry. The principal cause was that the linen tablecloth, the pride of Victorian and Edwardian households, went out of fashion. Supplies of cheaper material could be obtained more readily from Belfast. It was another piece of bad luck that certain important new industries, especially the manufacture of motor cars and aircraft, found their centres in the south and that Scottish firms which had been active enough in the infancy of those manufactures were driven out of business. Somewhat similarly the coal industry declined as oil became the fuel for ships, locomotives and power stations.

However, when all qualifications are made, it remains true that the war had direct effects in producing recession. Concentration on armaments, and the turning over of factories to war production, had led to dislocation. Moreover, during the war Scotland's old overseas customers had to turn to other suppliers, and new commercial links were apt to survive after Scotland was again in a position to compete. Labour, too, was disrupted by mobilisation for the forces, and of the men who returned from active service not all were eager to resume their former employment. The process of recovery and readjustment was made more painful by psychological factors. Support for the war had been stimulated by high-sounding slogans about 'a war to end war' and 'a war for democracy'; the League of Nations was established in an atmosphere of optimism which now seems fatuous beyond belief, and promises had been held out that after the war Britain would be 'a land fit for heroes to live in'. The returning ex-servicemen found that conditions fell far short of their expectations. In their disillusionment they were not likely to wait patiently for economic adjustment. These material and psychological circumstances combined to produce emigration on an unprecedented scale. Between 1921 and 1931 nearly 400,000 people left Scotland, not far short of double the exodus in any previous decade. And at the 1931 census Scotland's population showed a drop for the first time since records began.

Simple arithmetic suggested that emigration would relieve unemployment. But it was all too often men of skill and initiative who emigrated, and their removal disturbed the balance of the labour force. Scotland had already suffered heavily by war casualties, certainly in numbers but also, less calculably, in leadership. Such losses, by death and emigration, must have been one reason for the lack of enterprise of which Scots were often accused. Whereas they had been in the forefront of every technical advance during the era when the steam engine was developed, it was not so in the era of the motor car and the aeroplane. The intellectual resources of the nation were, it would seem, dwindling at the same time as its mineral resources. However, it was becoming irrelevant to blame Scottish management for failure, as the direction of industrial effort was slipping away from Scotland altogether into large combines with headquarters south of the Border. In the railways the pattern was evident to all. Scotland's railway system was run by five Scottish companies, each attracting its own loyalties from passengers and staff, until 1920, when the Scottish network was merged into two British companies, with headquarters in the south. But it was equally true elsewhere. Of a total investment of £84 million in new firms between 1945 and 1970, £66 million came from overseas, mainly the United States, and £17 million from England. Before 1914 very few major Scottish enterprises were owned and directed in England or America, but now the ownership of 40 per cent of them lies in England and of 15 per cent in North America. Most of the remainder, the ownership of which remains in Scotland, consists of smaller concerns.

The question whether lack of initiative and energy had deeper roots is not easily answered. Each generation is apt to see a decline in moral stability and self-reliance. But it remains true that in recent times too few Scots have risen to a concern for the well-being of the nation as a whole. One can only speculate how far the fostering of class-consciousness has been detrimental, but it is certainly true that sectional interests now prevail. The results of nationalisation have been disappointing to those who recall the idealism with which it used to be advocated. We were led to believe that if men worked for the state instead of for profit-making firms, they would be inspired by the concept of service to the community, but industrial unrest has been as serious in nationalised industries as elsewhere. The concept of service has been equally lacking on the management side, for many railway lines which were useful but unprofitable were maintained by private enterprise but have been closed by British Railways. It has been argued that the effect of increased governmental activity in the economic field as well as in everything that goes by the name of social welfare has sapped self-reliance. One can say this without suggesting that the more energetic labours of earlier generations were altruistic. The truth is far otherwise. Scotland was for long a relatively poor country, where a competence could hardly be won without hard work, and, before the advent of sickness and unemployment benefit, a man either worked or wanted. The trouble is that this economic incentive no longer operates and a sense of responsibility to the community has not taken its place.

Underlying some of the recent difficulties is an imbalance of population. Although birth-rates fell, the prolongation of education, whether compulsory or voluntary, increased the number of young people not at work, the expectation of life rose and emigration took away the young and left the old. Thus, all in all, a smaller working population has to support a larger non-working population. Not only the enormous cost of education and social services, but all the problems of an economy in transition, fell on a diminishing number of workers.

The imbalance of population has been paralleled by an imbalance of employment. Figures for employment are certainly a rough and ready indication of the health of the economy. Thus, nothing can explain away the high average of unemployment between the wars, of never less than 10 per cent, still less the peak of nearly 30 per cent reached in 1931: equally, a figure like 4·3 per cent in 1973 (as against 6·5 per cent in 1972) suggested a sounder economy. But the improvement was largely in non-productive occupations like transport services, entertainment, education, administration and so forth. Full employment, which many now regard as an end in itself, can be attained by taking in each other's washing, but no one would call that a healthy economy.

However regarded, the scene between the wars was a dismal one, and some can discern little improvement since. But it has to be remembered that the heavy industry of the central belt was a development only of the last three-quarters of the nineteenth century, and may have been only a phase like the linen, tobacco and cotton phases before it. Equally, the centre of gravity, which moved from the east to the west in the eighteenth century, may return to the east. There has been, for example, the expansion of the Grangemouth area, based largely on oil, some of it brought across the country by pipe from a deep-water port at Finnart on Loch Long. It is noticeable, too, that Glasgow, which held its maximum population of about a million almost unchanged from 1921 to 1961, dropped to less than 800,000, though this was mainly because of the planned reconstruction of formerly congested areas and the pursuance of an 'overspill' policy which retained the population in the same region. The eastward move seemed likely to accelerate with Britain's entry into the European Economic Community and the developments arising from North Sea oil, which were expected to be at least as far-reaching in their effects as any previous industrial change had been. Oil did produce thousands of jobs in rig yards, steel mills and construction works, and employment for planners, bankers and even lawyers. In 1973 the percentage of unemployment in Aberdeen (and also in the Borders) was only 1-2, whereas in Lanarkshire it was 12-13. Not only did oil redress the balance in favour of the east, but it brought developments to areas in the north where industry on a major scale had not hitherto been known. It benefited the west as well, for rigs were built at Clydebank and platforms in Cowal and Wester Ross.

Some signs of fresh emphases could be detected even before World War II, and it has become clearer since then that over-concentration on heavy industry was to some extent being overcome. A wide range of lighter manufactures has been introduced or expanded—clothing, furniture, electrical equipment, cycles, office and refrigeration machinery, clocks and watches, and fountain pens. A factory to manufacture aeroplane engines started at Hillington during the war, and it and other similar factories in Scotland employed nearly 10,000. The British Motor Corporation (now British Leyland) opened a factory at Bathgate in 1961 and the Rootes firm (now Chrysler) established one at Linwood, Renfrewshire, in 1963. They had thousands of employees, but suffered from almost incessant labour troubles, and their future could not be said to be assured. Older industries which had survived alongside heavy industries, such as linoleum, and brewing and distilling, flourished. Whisky exports first topped the £100 million mark in 1965, a 50 per cent increase in five years, and in

1973 they exceeded £250 million. The old industry of paper-making was not so fortunate, partly because for Britain as a whole the position was deteriorating, with the British producers' share in supplying British demand dropping from 75 per cent in the 1960s to 60 per cent in 1973 and likely to drop further.

The heavy industries themselves were far from moribund, for production of pig-iron (now from imported ore) recovered in the 1950s to something like its pre-1914 level, and steel production rose higher than ever before. A deep-water port at Hunterston, on the Ayrshire coast, was intended to take vessels up to 350,000 tons to bring in ore for the steel works at Ravenscraig. Steel production stood at 3.1 million tons in 1973 and was expected to rise to 4.5 million as a result of developments then planned. Scottish production of coal, though it had dropped to little more than a quarter of the 1913 figure and the colliers which used to be constantly busy shipping it away were a thing of the past, was still substantial at 11 million tons, half of it going to the production of electricity; and the mines employed some 30,000. Ship-building exceeded 400,000 tons in 1957, but fluctuated wildly and was plagued by labour troubles as well as by the somewhat reckless, if well-intentioned, attempts of management to keep going by building at a loss. It is only right to say that the brighter aspects of the picture are somewhat offset when we remember that some of the activity was the result of the treatment which Scotland (except until 1974 Edinburgh) received as a 'development' or 'assisted' area: Scotland had been receiving almost two-fifths of the total Regional Development grants paid out to all such areas in the United Kingdom. However, for two or three decades the most impressive thing about Scottish industry has become its variety. A new source of power came with hydro-electricity, and yet another with nuclear energy, which was represented by stations at Hunterston, Dounreay on the Pentland Firth and Chapelcross, Annan.

There remained the older heritage of agriculture and fisheries. With a world food shortage Scottish agriculture expected an assured future, but it received no priority when land was required for housing or industry. While the exceptional efforts made to extend tillage during World War II were transient, agriculture did not slump after it as it slumped after 1918, for the total output was well above that of the 1930s. Livestock accounted for 42 per cent of the output (slightly more than half of the value being in cattle); livestock products 35 per cent (nearly two-thirds of this being milk); and crops 23 per cent (nearly half being potatoes). The total value was £280 million in 1971–2 and £325 million in 1972–3. Scotland is still probably self-sufficient in meat, potatoes and milk and could at a pinch feed itself, though in such a contingency the larder would have a changed look. The proportion of the population engaged in agriculture had halved since 1911, but this was largely because of mechanisation. With subsidies, guaranteed prices, improvement grants and loans, the government cannot be accused of indifference, but the future within the Common Market remained uncertain. Afforestation, too, has gone ahead, and the Forestry Commission has so extended its operations that the landscape of large areas has been transformed out of recognition, but a single pulp mill, near Fort William, sufficed to deal with the products. Fishing, while far more concentrated than of old and employing only a third of the number employed in 1911, was still important in certain centres: the total value of fish caught was £43·7 million in 1972, an increase of nearly £9 million on 1971, and Aberdeen remained Britain's third fishing port. But more and more foreign fishing vessels—Polish, Russian, Norwegian, German, Belgian, Danish and Spanish—continually worked in Scottish waters and new methods and apparatus led to disastrous depletion of stocks. One of the most disappointing features of Common Market policy was that it offered only temporary and limited protection to Scottish rights in Scottish fishing grounds.

CHAPTER 10

Society

Speculation about society in Scotland before 1100 has been based on the assumption that the various immigrants—Irish, English and Scandinavian—introduced the social habits of their homelands. This is not unreasonable, but the question remains how far such imports prevailed over the society and institutions of the Picts. We do know that when Norman influence was added after 1100 we find an amalgam of native and imported features. There persisted ancient dues known as *cain*, which seems to have been in the nature of a tribute rather than a tax or rent, and *conveth*, which was originally the maintenance provided for a king or lord on his progresses: both of those were of Celtic origin. But the king also levied customs on ships engaged in trade and he received *ferms*, which suggest Anglo-Saxon institutions. The leading magnates were still *mormaers*, whose style means 'great steward'; they make an occasional appearance in our scanty sources before 1100, and may well have been of Pictish origin. Their title was translated by the Latin *comes*, and this also represented the Anglo-Saxon 'earl', with whom the *mormaer* was equated. At a lower level there was the *toiseach*, who seems to have been either the head of a kindred or an officer in charge of an estate, or perhaps both. The title had probably come from Ireland, where it was and is well known. But there were also *thegns* or thanes, unmistakeably Anglo-Saxon, and there were *drengs*, who were Anglo-Scandinavian. The term *thegn* could denote either status or office: in this it was like *toiseach*, and the two seem to have been equated. But while the terms *toiseach* and *thegn* were imports, the system they represent may have been Pictish. The *drengs* vanish as mysteriously as they appear. The officers known as sheriffs appear on record from the 1120s, but the term is Anglo-

Saxon (*shire-reeve*) and they may have been introduced in the previous century.

Within this amalgam a pervasive change was taking place. Celtic society was based on the concept of kinship, either real or fictitious, and office and status had probably been determined by place in a family or tribe. However, Anglo-Norman influence introduced the concept that holders of lands and offices stood in a clearly-defined relationship to the crown. The change is clearest in land tenure. Before 1100 land, though privately owned, had been subject to certain burdens in favour of a king, a chief or perhaps an official, but there is no indication of the concept of superiority. By contrast, the essence of the feudal system was the granting of lands as a fief, to be held in return for service. The king, as the ultimate owner of all land, granted land to his vassals, who in their turn, as subject superiors, granted land to their sub-vassals, and so on down the scale, for in Scotland there was no check on subinfeudation. The superior, at whatever level, could retain certain rights, especially to administer the land while an heir was under age, to arrange the marriage of an heir and to receive a sum called 'relief' when an heir entered on his inheritance. Besides, the vassal, again at whatever level, held his fief in return for some consideration: military service, of knights or of archers; non-military service, such as acting as a janitor in a castle; a fanciful return, such as a rose or a pair of gloves; a nominal return, usually a penny a year 'if it be askit'; 'free alms', that is, the 'devout orisons and prayers' of religious establishments; or, finally, a simple money payment.

It was the money payment which persisted as land was increasingly granted 'in feu ferm' for the consideration of a 'feu duty', an annual sum fixed in perpetuity. In James II's reign Parliament urged that crown lands should not be leased, but feued, and that other superiors should be encouraged by this example. Then, before and after the Reformation, most church lands were feued. In time, this offshoot of the feudal system became the tenure by which most land—or house or flat for that matter—was held. Non-Scots, unfamiliar with it, seldom succeed in grasping the simple fact that the 'vassal' is the proprietor, who has ownership of the property, which can be inherited by his heir, bequeathed by will or sold. The 'superior' has no rights of property, but he was entitled to lay down conditions about the use to be made of the property. Under this admirable system, some superiors preserved amenity much more successfully than official 'planning' authorities have done. A device whereby heritable property is conveyed in return not for a large lump sum but for a modest annual payment has been very beneficial to purchasers, especially in times of inflation, and it should have been thought a useful help towards home ownership in the twentieth century. However, like so many old Scottish institutions, it has been condemned to death by those who fail to understand it and is in process of extinction.

The Scots had a liking for security, and the terminable lease never appealed much to them, especially for house-sites. They also coveted a security for their titles against the chances of war, tumult and accident. This they obtained in the Register of Sasines. The practice had long been to complete a title, after the grant of a charter, by an instrument of sasine drawn up by a notary public and relating that the granter or his representative had given sasine (*seisin*, possession) by handing over earth and stone or some other token to the grantee or his representative. When efforts to have such instruments recorded in a public register were finally successful in 1617 they gave Scottish proprietors a security enjoyed in few other countries, they proved a useful protection against fraudulent transactions and they simplified the task of historians in tracing the history of property and families. But Scotland, which had this admirable system of registration of conveyances for about three hundred years before anything of the kind was thought of in England, is now reproached for being backward in its possession of 'that cumbrous system', and the Register of Sasines, like the feuing system, is doomed. A great historian of English law once remarked, in a moment of unusual candour, 'If our lawyers had known more of Roman law, our law—in particular our land law—would never have become the unprincipled labyrinth that it became.' Scots land law never became an unprincipled labyrinth, thanks largely to the feuing system and the Register of Sasines. But Scotland is now being seduced into accompanying the English into their unprincipled labyrinth.

The feudal system, despite its importance and persistence, never determined the entire shape of society. At the top, the peerage developed from pre-feudal magnates. Such magnates existed chiefly, if not entirely, in ancient Pictland, for the 'Scotia' recorded in this connection did not always include Argyll, though that had been the original kingdom of the Scots when they came from Ireland. 'Scotia' contained a number of districts the origin of which puzzled even the men of the twelfth century, who tried to combine them to form a mystical total of seven and alleged that they took their name from seven brothers. One arrangement offers Caithness, Moray and Ross, Mar and Buchan, Angus and Mearns, Atholl and Gowrie, Strathearn and Menteith, and Fife and Fothrif. Some at least of those areas gave their names to the *mormaers* or *comites* or 'earls' already mentioned. The earliest earldoms south of Forth were Carrick, in Ayrshire, which seems to have been created in a predominantly Celtic part of the land in about 1200, and Dunbar or March, which was a kind of offshoot of the English earldom of Northumbria. The earl was not, even in that early period, owner of all the territory from which he took his style, for other estates were intermingled with his. The probability that his relationship was with the people of the district rather than with the land is strengthened by the fact that incoming Normans could acquire earldoms only by marriage with an heiress. On the other hand, by 1200 most of the earls were feudal vassals of the crown for their earldoms. When earldoms were next created, in the fourteenth century, they were distinctly territorial, conferred on the man who held the bulk of the land in some area and regarded as inseparable from the land. More honorific earldoms appeared from the later fifteenth century, and the title finally became merely a matter of status.

While incoming Normans were not made earls, they could be 'lords'. Admittedly, any 'baron', whether his estate was large or small, was also a *dominus* or lord. But there were certain vast lordships—Annandale, Galloway and Badenoch in particular—which are hard to distinguish from earldoms except that they lacked the mystique of antiquity. Bruce of Annandale, who held his lordship for service of ten knights, was not likely to be confused with a mere knight or even with a 'baron' who held his land for the render of a fraction of a knight.

The feudal system did not shape the lowest grades of society either. In at least the more fertile areas, social organisation centred largely round that essential implement of agriculture, the plough. The basic unit of land was the 'ploughgate'. It is sometimes equated with 104 or 120 acres, but it was really based not on precise measurement but on a notion of the area which a plough-team could cultivate. The primitive plough is said to have covered only half an acre a day, and it was only over a cycle of years that it could work anything like 104 acres. The ploughgate was divided into the infield, which received the manure from the farmyard and was perpetually tilled, and the much more extensive outfield, of which only one portion or another was cultivated intermittently. In some areas the unit was not the ploughgate but the 'davoch' (possibly of Pictish origin), which may have been the area which could receive a certain quantity of seed or produce a certain quantity of grain.

The plough normally required eight oxen to draw it, so the ploughgate was divided into eight 'oxgangs'; but the 'husband-land', consisting of two oxgangs, seems to have been thought of as the normal holding for one man—logically enough, for if the plough needed eight oxen it probably needed four men, one to guide it, one to goad the oxen, one to pull them on and one to remove obstacles from their way. The individual tenant, in short, was the husbandman, who supplied two oxen to the ploughteam, and the whole arrangement postulates the occupation of the ploughgate by four husbandmen, whose homes and steadings formed a 'toun'. Each had his own holding, but it was not consolidated: he had his scattered rigs or strips, so that the good and the poor land was equitably shared.

The husbandman was a rent-paying tenant, though part of his rent might be paid by so many days' work at seedtime or harvest, the carting of peats and occasional 'long carriages' with exceptional loads. He was a free man, who could leave the estate if he wanted to. But there were other men who were not free. The existence of genuine serfs, who could be bought and sold or handed over by gift, is attested by several documents, some recording proceedings for the recovery of fugitive serfs. The last vestiges of serfdom disappeared in the second half of the fourteenth century—two hundred years earlier than it did in England—and from that point there were only free tenants. However, besides the serfs there were men whose status is indeterminate: for example, it is not clear whether the bondmen or *bondi* were men in bondage or free farmers like Scandinavian *bönder*; and, while *nativi* can mean serfs, it may also mean men who were not personally in servitude but who were tied to the estate and could not leave it. Distinctions may not have been rigid. The serf shades off into the tenant who was tied to the estate, and he in turn into the tenant who was not so tied but who was at the landlord's beck and call for labour services. There was also a class of cottars, who each had only a cottage, a yard and perhaps pasture for a single cow and who were available as hired labour. There is no known connection between the serfdom of early times and the personal servitude of colliers, salters and, it would seem, some fishermen, which comes to view in the seventeenth century and was not abolished until Acts of 1775 and 1799.

In a rural society each family had to be largely self-sufficient. Besides growing his own food and producing his own fuel, each man was his own builder, his own carpenter, his own shoe-maker, literally his own butcher, baker and candlestick-maker. Something of this versatility may still be seen in crofting communities today, though to an ever diminishing extent, for ease of transport has facilitated purchase from shops or from vans or indeed by mail order. It may be doubted, however, if a completely undifferentiated society ever existed, for even in prehistoric times there was some specialisation, among metal-workers for instance. In the Middle Ages there was a rough-and-ready division into those who prayed—the clergy, and those who fought—the soldiers, who were all dependent for their creature comforts on those who worked. It is not mere speculation that communities of workers would therefore grow up around religious centres or castles, for many ecclesiastical establishments as well as royal castles were the foci of towns. While what have been called 'organic towns' thus grew by a natural economic process, others were artificially created by kings or magnates who saw advantages in having towns on their land: they drew higher rents, acre for acre, from land let in small plots to burgesses; the residents provided a reservoir of labour; the merchants and craftsmen who were encouraged to settle furnished the landowner's material needs.

One element in the population of a town would be craftsmen, who rendered skilled services and supplied manufactured goods—weavers, tailors, armourers, smiths, saddlers, carpenters, potters and so on. The other element would be merchants, ready to supply goods produced elsewhere. Such foodstuffs as had to be brought into the town from the countryside were disposed of at a market, usually a weekly market, for it would not have been worth anyone's while to keep a shop permanently open for the infrequent sales. Foreign trade was far more important, as was explained in the previous chapter.

Not only were craftsmen and merchants alike free men, but if a serf escaped and lived unchallenged in a burgh for a year he became free. 'Town air gives freedom', they said. But not all inhabitants of the burgh had equal status. Merchants were probably on the whole wealthier than craftsmen, their activities were more central to the burgh's *raison d'être*, and trade required more organisation than other burghal activities; the gild of merchants, the strongest corporate body in the burgh, therefore gained control of burgh government. A craftsman could become a member of the merchant gild only if he renounced his craft and 'all trade and occupation in his own person that is not comely and decent for the rank and honesty of a gild brother'. The merchants would accept him into their fraternity only if he would accept the standards of what was thought a superior social class: his wife and servants would 'use and exercise no point of common cookery outwith his own house' and would not 'be seen in the streets with their aprons and serviettes'. However, the craftsmen in time created their own gilds, which obtained 'seals of cause' or charters of incorporation, legalising the organisation of the craft, its charitable activities and its endowments of altars. Sometimes these gilds ultimately gained a share in burgh government, but it was secondary to that of the merchants.

While the burghs, with their specialised interests, corporate constitutions, separate representation in Parliament and collective organisation in the convention of royal burghs, to some extent stood apart from the rest of Scottish society, the differentiation must not be exaggerated. For one thing, most burgesses had their own interest in crops and herds and must have shared some of the countryman's concern over harvest prospects. But, in addition, many burghs were integrated with local landed society. Non-royal burghs, indeed, were proprietary in the family of the landowner who had founded them. But royal burghs, too, frequently had local lairds or nobles as provosts, in defiance of legislation designed to confine the office to active burgesses. It was also true that merchants who prospered were apt to acquire estates and so pass into the landed gentry or even the peerage. Scottish society was very fluid, and by the seventeenth century, when titles were somewhat lavishly conferred, there were many peers who were only a couple of generations removed from a plebeian ancestor.

Yet throughout the whole of Scottish society 'the kin'—blood relationship—was important. It is usually easy enough to see how a nobleman was associated with his own immediate kinsmen and with collateral branches of the house stemming from a common ancestor. It is, however, impossible to distinguish such demonstrable relationships from the potential relationship implied by a shared surname, and 'the name' became as important as 'the kin'. This, it must be said, could not apply so much in the Highlands, where until the seventeenth century it was only the leading families who had surnames; the rank and file were known by compounds of patronymics and epithets which, though they incorporated the Christian name of the father (with the prefix 'Mac-', or the suffix '-son') and perhaps also that of the grandfather or great-grandfather (with the prefix 'Vic-'), gave no clue to the bearer's more remote ancestry or distant kinship. It is not easy to recognise clan or family affiliations in 'Duncan McNicholl VcNeill or McLawrin', 'John McLawrin, son of Finlay Neilson',

'Neil Maklawrin Patriksoun and John McNeill Patriksoun, his brother', 'Alastair McAllane VcAne VcCoull' or 'Ewin Bane McEwin VcMartene'. Contemporary Lowlanders would at any rate be in no doubt that men so named belonged to a different society. The point is that the clan consisted of people bearing a great variety of names, and 'Clan X' was composed not of men bearing the surname X but of men, whatever their names, who followed the chief called X. In the Lowlands, however, surnames were all but universal by 1500 and formed an easily recognisable label, among descendants of English or Norman immigrants as well as among native stock. A good example of cohesion among bearers of the same name is found in 1565, when Queen Mary married Darnley, who belonged to the house of Lennox, always a rival of the house of Hamilton, and there was a rebellion in which 37 Hamilton lairds and 120 Hamiltons of lower rank are named as taking part. An indication of the attachment to the name appears in entails restricting succession to heirs bearing the name of the original grantee and in the practice whereby, when a female succeeded to an estate, her husband frequently took her name and transmitted it, and not his own, to their descendants. Entails laying down that lands should pass to heirs 'bearing the name and arms' of a certain family indicate the centuries-old link between the surname and heraldry, a matter on which the Lord Lyon King of Arms is still the authority. How far contemporaries were from thinking that the surname demonstrated kinship was illustrated in 1537, when the Angus Douglases were out of favour and it was suggested that their minor dependants should lay aside the name of Douglas and be called Stewart.

However, a magnate's following extended far beyond 'the kin' and 'the name'. A 'band' or bond might join one magnate to another, almost in the manner of a political alliance, or it might join a group of like-minded people for political, ecclesiastical or criminal purposes. There was also the bond of manrent, whereby a man of lower degree, in return for protection, undertook to support a great man in his quarrels. Besides, from the beginning of feudalism a vassal held land specifically on condition of service to his superior, and in the later Middle Ages pensions were sometimes granted with a view to creating a company of retainers. Below the level of feudal vassals, tenant farmers were brought into the connection. And finally there were those who, without necessarily having a tenurial link, had a tradition of service. It was by a combination of all these links, added to 'the kin' and 'the name', that a nobleman built up his following.

While the very great, acting in concert, often determined the politics of Scotland, lesser groups were famous—or infamous—for feuding and resistance to the law. Feuds were thus alluded to by James VI, who did so much to suppress them: they 'take up a plain feud, . . . to bang it out bravely, he and all his kin against him and all his'; but, as we have seen, it was not entirely a matter of 'the kin'. Borderers were often emphatic that 'the name' was the primary consideration, and one finds for example a feud in the 1570s between the 'surnames' of Brownfield (or Burnfield) and Haitlie. Elsewhere we cannot be so sure of what is involved, unless we have an actual list of names, as, for instance, when a round dozen of Cheynes were respited for a murder in 1578. When, in 1490, six score 'Murrays' were burned to death in the church of Monzievaird by their 'Drummond' foes, it would be rash to assume that all concerned bore those two surnames. The same would be true of the rivalry of 'Crichtons' and 'Maxwells' which in 1508 issued in a spectacular riot in Dumfries, in much the same way as 'Douglases' and 'Hamiltons' clashed in the 'Cleanse the Causeway' affray in Edinburgh in 1520. The existence of groups with their inherited feuds permeated every walk of life: in 1575 a minister of the reformed church sought an excuse for non-residence in his parish on the ground that it lay 'in the high parts of Sutherland', in the country of the Murrays, with whom his family was at feud, and that he could not reside there for fear of his life.

To the modern mind, the whole thing is apt to seem as disreputable as the gangs in which criminals organise themselves today. Yet the Scots took a sober pride in it. John Knox tells us that he had a 'good mind' to the Hepburns of Hailes, Earls of Bothwell, and would overlook their misdeeds because his father, his grandfather and his great-grandfather had all served under them. This connection, he added, was 'part of our Scottish kindness', part, that is, of the strength of kinship and heredity in Scottish society.

The relationship was neither dishonourable nor one-sided. The greater men did their part in seeing to the welfare of their dependants, not least by passing legislation in their interest. Reading the *Acts of the Parliaments of Scotland* one would never guess that a clique of magnates, or an ambitious king, was in control of affairs. Between 1449 and 1500, as the late Lord Cooper remarked, 'no fewer than ten separate acts were passed at brief intervals for the benefit of a class of the community described as "the puir tennentes" or "the puir people that labouris the grund, . . . whose heavy complaintes has ofttymes bene maid" '. Reign by reign there was a good deal of legislation aimed specifically at benefiting the lower classes, for example by liberating tenants from dependance on their landlords. One of James I's statutes forbade landlords to remove tenants unless they were going to take the land into their own hands. An act of James II ordained that when the ownership of land changed, tenants should continue to hold their farms at the old rents until their leases expired. Under James III it was ordained that tenants were not to be responsible for the debts of their landlords, and under James IV that when an estate changed hands the tenants were to sit at least until the following Whitsunday.

A policy pursued so long cannot be dismissed as if there were only isolated acts representing a bid by one king or another to buy support. The provision by James I, and again by James V, of an advocate for the poor is only one illustration of a concern for social justice. If tenants served their lords it was reasonable that they should get something in return. This social cohesion created by all the links between classes, combined with measures to provide social justice, must explain the absence from Scotland of the kind of social unrest which issued in the peasants' revolts and similar outbreaks familiar in England and other countries.

Hereditary succession permeated institutions. The heritable jurisdictions of lords of regality and lords of barony are well known, and so are heritable sheriffships. But inheritance was common elsewhere, though by custom rather than by law. It happened in the burghs. Sir George Ogilvy of Dunlugus was provost of Banff for at least thirty years and his son also became provost; the Learmonths of Dairsie, generation by generation, were almost invariably provosts of St Andrews. Complaint was made in Aberdeen about the 'unlawful usurpation' of the magistracy by 'the race of Menzeisses', so that the burgh was 'thralit to serve ane raice of pepill'. There was an amusing incident in 1664: John Ewart, former provost of Kirkcudbright, had been imprisoned in the town for refusing to pay the minister's stipend, but his son, who had now become provost, allowed his father 'to pass and repass as if he were not a prisoner', and the privy council had to intervene with an order for the removal of the elder Ewart to Dumfries, where he was not so fortunate as to have a son as provost. Heredity was one of the abuses in the church which was denounced by the reformers. Yet the Reformation did not at once eliminate it—though it did make it more respectable, since the solicitude of a married clergy for their kin was not scandalous. In the legal profession, whether on the bench or at the bar, it is hard to believe that skill and talent were so outstanding in certain families, generation by generation, that no abler men could have been found to fill vacancies. Even at the humble level of the sheriff-officer of Edinburgh, Roger Templeton was succeeded in the late sixteenth century by William Allan, who married his widow, and then by James Templeton, his son.

The traditional structure of Scottish society, in which various links joined together men of various classes under the leadership of the nobility, continued to shape the course of events until the seventeenth century. Indeed, it never did this more clearly than in the covenanting movement against Charles I, when the mass of the people followed the traditional leadership of the nobility. It was only after the restoration that the lower classes first acted without aristocratic leadership, in the Pentland and Bothwell Brig risings of 1666 and 1679. The result was military failure, but it was now plain that the old social ties were at last breaking down.

It will be readily observed that neither historic Highland clans, concentric in structure and as a rule based on the exclusive occupation of a limited territory, nor the more amorphous Lowland social groups, consisting though they did of members widely scattered and intermingled with men of different allegiances, have much connection with the so-called 'clan' of today, based on nothing more than identity of surname. The notion that such identity denotes a common ancestry cannot be entertained. As long as men were designated by genuine patronymics, whether of the 'Mac-' variety or the '-son' variety, the designation changed in each generation, and it was just a matter of chance in what generation the patronymic was 'frozen' to become a surname. Thomas Johnson, for example, may have decided to retain the patronymic of his father, Andrew Johnson, as his surname, but Andrew's father had been John Robertson and if a fixed surname had been adopted a generation earlier the descendants would have been known as Robertson and not as Johnson. Thus the belief that all Johnsons, or Robertsons, or Fergussons, are descended from the same John or Robert or Fergus is preposterous. Besides, as late as the eighteenth century a Campbell, for instance, might change his name to MacDonald on moving to a different area. But some modern 'clans', ignoring history, are based on nothing more subtle than the extraction of names from Directories—a device which appeals to those seeking money 'to buy back the clan lands'. Such bogus 'clans' are in keeping with the bogus 'clan tartans', which are nothing more than a commercial racket. Nearly all the patterns now in use are modern inventions and it is quite clear that when clans were genuine they were not associated with particular tartans.

The one achievement of the cultivation by Lowlanders of clans and tartans has been to efface old distinctions between Highlands and Lowlands, which broke down anyway with migration and intermarriage. There are nowadays far more people of Highland descent in the Lowlands than there are in the Highlands, and there are seldom perceptible differences between them and their Lowland neighbours. The broad distinctions which survive are between Highlanders in the Highlands and the people—whatever their origin—who live in the Lowlands. There are linguistic differences. The Gaelic language is now spoken by only some

65,000 people, chiefly on the extreme western fringe, but those Highlanders who do not speak Gaelic speak English. The Highlander who speaks Lowland Scots exists only on the stage. Many Lowlanders, especially of the lower social classes, speak dialects of Lowland Scots, differing substantially from standard English. The educated Scot in the Lowlands seldom succeeds in divesting himself of Scotticisms in accent and idiom, and very often sees no reason to try. He flatters himself that he pronounces the English language better than most Englishmen and certainly than broadcasters who offend his ear by their slovenliness, often leading to ambiguity: 'the Uganda Rasians', 'the wailing fleets of Rusher and Japan', 'we sor a pander at Longleat', 'Highlanders are always wining', and so on. It is easy to see why an American—and this is a fact—wrote of 'the Prince of Whales'. Foreigners, not surprisingly, sometimes say that it is easier to follow English when it is spoken by a Scot.

Recent settlers have been integrated to various degrees. The Irish immigrants of the nineteenth century arrived with different traditions and outlook and were in the main of a different church and they created problems, especially in the industrial areas where they predominated. Their descendants have largely been assimilated, but the adherence of most of them to the Roman Catholic Church gives them a considerable measure of cohesion which is encouraged by the religious segregation maintained in schools. Recently English immigrants have far outnumbered the Irish—about a quarter of a million of the inhabitants are of English birth—but they hardly form a community even in academic circles where they are so conspicuous. Italians who arrived in the nineteenth century to make a very significant contribution to social change by providing cafés as some substitute for the public-house, retain a good deal of individuality because of their religion, their association in the catering trade and their strong sense of family. Polish and Lithuanian miners who arrived in the nineteenth century, and additional Poles who came during World War II, have on the whole shown more signs than the Italians of integrating with the natives, and religious differences have not prevented a lot of intermarriage. The most recent arrivals, from Asia and the

West Indies, present problems which Scotland has never had to face before.

It seems unlikely that the distribution of Scotland's inhabitants changed much over the many centuries when the pattern of settlement depended mainly on the fertility of the soil, and as late as 1755 half of the people lived north of Tay, largely in the rich farm-lands of the eastern coastal plain. The industrial changes of the eighteenth and nineteenth centuries created an industrial belt, stretching north-eastwards from Ayrshire to Angus. Heavy industries were focused in the Forth–Clyde valley, though coalfields extended into Fife on one side and Ayrshire on the other; Fife and Angus flourished mainly on textiles. This industrial belt now contains three-quarters of the population.

With industrialisation came urbanisation. Until after 1707 no more than a fifth of Scotland's people can have lived in burghs at all, most burghs were mere villages, and the genuine townsman, wholly differentiated from the countryman, hardly existed outside a few large burghs. Now the typical Scot is a city-dweller. Not only is half of the population concentrated in less than a dozen large towns, but even outside the industrial belt there is a tendency to concentrate, for in almost any county in the Highlands and Islands the only areas with an increasing population are those containing towns.

The reasons are not wholly, perhaps not even mainly, material; they are largely psychological. Ours is an urban civilisation, our standard way of life is an urban way of life. The idea prevails that only in a town can anyone share to the full the benefits of the modern world. Not only do people therefore flock to the towns, but those who remain in the country tend to neglect local resources and look to the towns for all supplies. Instead of fishing in the surrounding waters, they wait for a fish-van from a town. Not so long ago every little community had its own bakery, but nowadays bread, buns and cakes—all hygienically wrapped— come from Glasgow, if not from London, with the depressing result that wherever one goes in the Highlands and Islands the same articles are on the tea-table. Some think it little short of a scandal that islands with good grazing rely on imported milk, either fresh or tinned. The revulsion against rural life has been encouraged by legislation designed for city-dwellers. One of the most disastrous regulations was that requiring all children to complete their schooling with a type of education which could be provided only in towns. Thus country-raised children, on reaching the age of twelve, were taken away from their parents and educated for an urban way of life; they seldom returned to the country. Not infrequently the parents, rather than see the family broken up, migrate to the town when the eldest child is ready for secondary school. Thus rural depopulation goes on, and problems of housing and employment in the towns are aggravated.

Scottish education long had its roots in the communities, whether urban or rural, and in past centuries it met varying needs with some flexibility. Monks, even in Celtic times, could read and write, and seem to have spent a lot of their time on the admittedly mechanical task of copying service-books, gospels and psalters. Later the educational attainments of the dignitaries of the medieval church could hardly have been possible without a substantial basic structure of local schools. Yet we are in the dark both about the precise means by which clerics received their rudiments and about the numbers who profited from the schools which existed. The evidence that there had been schools in Celtic times comes mainly from the survival into the twelfth century of men with such styles as *ferleginn* (a man of learning and an instructor) or 'ruler of the schools', who were presumably by that time titulars enjoying revenues which had once been set aside for education. In the same century, however, we also find references to genuine schools, as opposed to laicised Celtic survivals. The role of the abbeys in education has been misunderstood: while they had to educate their own novices—and down to the Reformation all, or nearly all, monks could at least sign their names—it was not their business to conduct schools for outsiders. Consequently, when we find an abbey with the patronage of a school and the right to nominate the master, the school may originally have had a separate existence and then been granted to the abbey as a source of revenue in much the same way as a parish church was 'appropriated'. The cathedrals were more important agencies than the monasteries, for most cathedrals which were in centres of population had grammar schools and song schools. But, whatever the part played by the church, there was a tendency, even before the Reformation, for schools to pass under the control of town councils. All in all, we have definite evidence of about sixty schools in medieval Scotland, but our records are far from complete and it is likely that every Scottish burgh had a school. The first Scottish Education Act, passed in 1496, presupposed the availability of schooling. Lairds of substance were to send their eldest sons to a grammar school, on pain of a fine of £20, which might be equivalent to £2,000 today, until they acquired 'perfect Latin'.

The Reformers, in their first *Book of Discipline,* had an ambitious scheme: every parish was to have a school; every town a grammar school; in the ten towns where superintendents had their headquarters there was to be a 'college' teaching logic, rhetoric and languages; and at the top of a four-tier structure the universities were to be reorganised. Schooling was to be available for all, and indeed was apparently to be compulsory—but only until it was seen whether children were 'apt for letters and learning'; the Reformers did not propose to waste time on the uneducable. Schooling was not to be free: the commonwealth should not be burdened with the cost of educating those who could afford to pay for it, and bursaries were to be given according to a kind of means test.

More came of these proposals than is often believed. The new presbyter was a graduate and, unlike the old priest, could be an effective educational agent. From the earliest days of the reformed church some ministers drilled children in the Catechism, taught them to read the Bible and the prayers in the *Book of Common Order* and even instilled some Latin and French. The ideal of a school in every parish was never lost sight of. No legislation to put it into effect was passed until 1616, when there was an act of the privy council on the subject, followed by an act of parliament in 1633. Other acts followed in 1646 and 1696. The king might quarrel with the General Assembly, ministers might wrangle about the rights and wrongs of bishops and presbyteries, but king,

General Assembly, bishops and presbyteries were at one on the need for education. The hope that a substantial share of the ancient ecclesiastical endowments would become available for education was indeed thwarted, though for a time schoolboys and students were endowed with revenues which had formerly been used to pay priests to say masses, and some of the ecclesiastical revenues turned over to burghs were used for educational purposes.

But even before the first of the seventeenth-century acts was passed there were many parochial schools, and as early as 1611 the synod of Fife ordained an assessment for their maintenance. In burghs, the existing grammar and song schools continued and there were English schools and French schools. Education was not confined to boys, but girls do not seem usually to have been admitted to the grammar schools and were instead in the charge of 'vulgar schoolmasters', as distinct from the Latin grammarians. A study of records of the 1570s gives the impression that it was usual for a town to have a grammar school: such schools are mentioned at Dunkeld, Canongate, Edinburgh, Stirling, Dingwall, Deer, Dunfermline, Perth, Aberdeen, Linlithgow, Leith, Elgin, St Andrews, Chanonry of Ross, Kirkwall, Falkland and Haddington. In the seventeenth century it is equally plain that it was usual for a country parish in the Lowlands to have its school. For example, out of 88 rural parishes in Fife and Perthshire, no less than 68 had schools. The standards were high, too: in 1690 there were in the county of Angus no less than 35 schoolmasters teaching Latin.

Until the foundation of Scotland's own universities, the Scot who wanted advanced education had had no choice but to leave home, either for England or the continent. The war of independence interrupted movement to England, but in the late fourteenth century Scottish students were obtaining licences to proceed to English universities, though not all of them went: perhaps the receipt of a licence was itself regarded as a qualification. However, from 1378 to 1418 England and Scotland were supporting rival popes, and Scottish students, regarded as schismatic in England, went largely to French universities, especially Paris. Then from

1409, France, too, was in a different camp from Scotland, and Scotland's first university, at St Andrews, received its bull of foundation from 'Scotland's Pope', Benedict XIII, in 1413. Two more universities were founded later in the century—Glasgow in 1451 and King's College, Aberdeen, in 1495, while St Andrews was strengthened by the foundation of St Salvator's College in 1450. Expansion continued in the early sixteenth century, with St Leonard's and St Mary's Colleges at St Andrews. At the Reformation, the universities of Glasgow and Aberdeen languished, but new vigour was imparted to Scottish academic life by Andrew Melville, principal of Glasgow and then of St Andrews. A fourth university was started at Edinburgh in 1583 and a fifth in Marischal College, Aberdeen, in 1593.

The general thesis behind the fashionable concept of 'The Scottish Enlightenment' is that before 1707 Scotland was an uncultured backwater, with stunted political institutions and dominated by religious bigotry, but that after the union light and civilisation flowed in from the south to absorb the vitality of a people who had ceased to be preoccupied with ecclesiastical controversy and had not yet found an outlet in politics. This is a hangover from the Whig view of history, which thought that all good things started after the Revolution. The truth is that few have taken any trouble to find out about Scottish culture before the eighteenth century: if they did, they would find that the achievements of the 'Unenlightened' were not inconsiderable. The parish schools, or the best of them, gave boys enough Latin to fit them for the universities, and the universities tempered the wind for those who were not adequately prepared. University education was cheap, bursaries were available and academic terms suited to boys who had to spend part of the year earning. The availability of sound education at every level, combined with social mobility and a lack of class consciousness, meant that Scotland could draw on the natural ability of men of all classes. The 'ignorant yokel', so familiar a figure in English literature if not in English life, has no existence in Scotland in either literature or reality.

Before the act of 1872, which for the first time made schooling compulsory, there were 942 parish schools, and that is as near as may be to a school for each parish. But the parish schools were far outnumbered by a variety of others. There were the grammar schools in the burghs, numbering 54, and alongside them had developed 23 academies, with a more liberal curriculum. In many burghs there were also charity schools of one kind or another, mostly transformed in the nineteenth century from boarding establishments into day schools. Mainly in the Highlands and Islands were 283 schools founded by the Scottish Society for the Propagation of Christian Knowledge, established in 1709. Far and away the largest category of schools were 'adventure schools', to the number of some 1,500, in which the teachers were supported purely by the fees of their pupils. They varied enormously, from institutions in towns which provided education at least as good as that in any grammar school, to a room in a village where an old man or woman was ready to impart, in return for a few coppers, the little that he or she knew. Then there were nearly 200 Gaelic Schools, founded by societies set up in Edinburgh, Glasgow and Inverness in the early nineteenth century with the object of preserving Gaelic in the Highlands. If some believed that it was important to encourage a particular language, others believed that it was important to instil particular religious doctrines, so there were about 1,000 church schools. It is not surprising that Roman Catholics and Episcopalians established their own schools, but the Free Church was equally opposed to the established church's privileges, so it also set up schools. The Church of Scotland took up the challenge and, not content with its position in the parish schools, organised its own schools. Besides these voluntary efforts there was also, in the nineteenth century, a certain amount of official effort to authorise additional schools in large or populous parishes, and these extra schools numbered 336. There were also industrial schools; there were the 'ragged schools' which provided free meals for the very needy and were sometimes called 'soup kitchen schools'; and there were factory and colliery schools, run by employers for their young employees.

It could hardly be called a system. But Scotland had at least 4,400 schools, and some put the figure as high as 5,000. In the large towns, where the sharp population rise in any event exceeded the capacity of the schools, too many small children were at work and there had been an immigration of illiterate Irish, and in parts of the Highlands and Islands schools were scarce. But over the greater part of the country nearly all the males, at least, could read and write. The Argyll Commission, whose findings led to the Act of 1872 for compulsory schooling, reported that four-fifths of the children were at school. In 1855, when the new marriage registers came into use, nine-tenths of the men and three-quarters of the women were able to sign their names—proportions which tally with an over-all figure of four-fifths of the people receiving some schooling.

The Act of 1872 did not make education free, for fees were still exacted (those of paupers being paid by the parochial boards). Nor did it lead to an increase in the number of schools; on the contrary, many of the voluntary agencies and adventure schools felt that they were being bowed out and closed their doors, so that the number of schools actually dropped by several hundreds. What was worse, it was another thing to make compulsion work: in 1897 only seventy-six per cent of the children were at school, and as late as 1908 the percentage was only eighty-two—approximately the same proportion as before 1872.

The payment of fees in the board schools was in general abolished in 1894. In 1872 there had been no firm age limit up to which education had to continue, for children who had attained a certain proficiency could leave, even if they were only ten. The age became fourteen, without exception, in 1901, and was raised to fifteen in 1945 and sixteen in 1972. Since 1908, when boards were permitted to provide meals, transport, maintenance and books, and compelled to provide medical inspection, the scope of education has extended to become in effect children's welfare.

The Act of 1872 was concerned chiefly with what is now called primary education, and when the school boards were set up the only institutions resembling secondary schools which they administered were a few burgh schools which had been transferred to them. In the course of time, especially as the leaving-age was raised, the school boards had to extend their operations, at first by adding secondary departments to existing schools. The parish was as a rule too small a unit for secondary education, and the boards were reluctant to incur additional expense, but they were driven to expansion by the need for providing teachers, who were trained through the pupil-teacher system.

What is now called further education, mainly of a vocational nature, has a long history, both in specialised institutions and in evening classes. The Anderson Institute, founded under the will of a Glasgow professor who died in 1796, was intended to be less academic than the traditional universities. The Edinburgh 'School of Arts for the better education of the Mechanics of Edinburgh' was founded in 1821 and two years later the Glasgow Mechanics' Institute grew out of a Saturday evening class. Statutory provision was made for evening continuation classes by the Act of 1872, and power for compulsory attendance at day continuation classes dates from 1918. But the great expansion in this field came only after 1945, when for the first time there appeared a number of colleges which really represent a 'tertiary' level between secondary school and university.

Denominational schools in general remained independent of the school boards, and the churches continued to take the main responsibility for the training of teachers, but in 1905 the Education Department took over the training colleges of the Church of Scotland and the United Free Church, leaving the Episcopalians and Roman Catholics with their own colleges. In 1918 denominational schools were transferred to the new Education Authorities, which gave grants, regulated the curriculum and appointed the teachers (who had, however, to be approved by the appropriate church authority and give religious instruction as before).

The liberal attitude of the 1918 settlement to the denominational schools was characteristic of a general recognition that not all children required the same education and that parents should have freedom of choice. There were the schools fully integrated into the board system; the church schools with their privileges; schools administered by the boards but charging fees; former charity schools which retained a good deal of independence but received grants from public funds; completely independent day schools; and a few boarding schools on the lines of English 'public schools'. This remarkable variety, which avoided sharp distinctions, is now being eroded. Local authorities no longer charge fees in any schools or allow selection of pupils by merit: the aim was to gather all the children from a district into a single 'comprehensive school'. Nearly all the Episcopalian schools have been closed on one pretext or another. The Roman Catholic schools are under threat. The grant-aided schools were confronted with the choice between absorption in the local authority system or shouldering the heavy financial burden of becoming self-supporting. Thus Scotland may have, in place of the old gradations, a sharper division between two kinds of schools—the state-supported 'comprehensives', and independent schools for the children of parents who are willing, in the old tradition, to make sacrifices for their children's education. It is too early to assess the merits of the 'comprehensive' system in itself, and opinion remains divided. But some feel that the abler pupils are neglected for the sake of the weaker and 'under-privileged', and already there is talk of a kind of selectivity in reverse by removing disruptive elements from the 'comprehensive' schools to special institutions. Meantime many schools were grossly under-staffed, thousands of children were having only part-time education and no remedy was in sight for truancy, delinquency and vandalism.

The universities have undergone many changes since the seventeenth century. In the eighteenth, Latin was abandoned as the language of lectures and a system of professors, each responsible for a subject or subjects, was substituted for the old system whereby a 'regent' conducted the same class through all subjects for the whole of its academic life. This made it easier to widen the curriculum, but it was not until the nineteenth century that a great variety of additional subjects was introduced and specialisation by both teachers and students became usual: there were many new chairs and new degrees in law and science as well as honours degrees; research was encouraged and research degrees were instituted. Numbers increased markedly at Edinburgh in the eighteenth century—300 students and 8 professors in 1700, 1,200 students and 21 professors in 1800—and the ramshackle old buildings were superseded by the present Old College from 1786 onwards. Expansion went on in the nineteenth century, and in 1870 it was Glasgow's turn to move from its old quarters to Gilmorehill. Women were admitted in the last years of the nineteenth century. At that period the ratio of university students to the whole population was six times as high in Scotland as in England and twice as high as in Prussia. There was no doubt about the desire for a university education, and the many bursaries (mostly awarded by competitive examination) were supplemented from 1901 by the munificence of Andrew Carnegie, who hoped to ensure that no Scot was debarred by poverty from a university. Until 1860 the two colleges of Aberdeen had continued to be separate universities, and indeed, although St Andrews had colleges, the general pattern of Scottish universities has been unitary and not collegiate.

The universities have lost much of their independence because, especially since the Second World War, the sums derived from endowments and fees have had increasingly to be supplemented by government grants, which now make up nearly nine-tenths of the income. Between the wars the total number of university students was about 10,000, and by 1990 was over 50,000. The increase has arisen partly from the incorporation in the universities of previously independent institutions like veterinary and dental colleges, but it owed a good deal to the availability of grants, which went far beyond the dreams of Andrew Carnegie. There are now eight universities—though two of them are upgraded technical colleges and one, at Dundee, represents a hiving-off from St Andrews, so that Stirling is the only completely new foundation. English students often prefer a Scottish university to English 'Redbrick', the US sends large numbers of both undergraduates and postgraduates, and others come from the European continent, Asia and Africa.

Like education, the care of the poor had traditionally been a function of the church as the agency of Christian charity. Although from the late sixteenth century authority had been given by statute for the levying of an assessment for poor relief, few parishes operated one until after 1800 and the main burden remained with the kirk session. The law was clear on two points:

responsibility for a pauper lay with his parish of origin or at any rate his parish of 'settlement'—that is, where he had lived for a specified period; and, while relief was to be given to the aged, the sick, the maimed and the deformed, there was none for the able-bodied poor or unemployed. The poor fund at the disposal of a kirk session derived partly from 'mortifications' or bequests, fines exacted by the session from delinquents, fees paid at baptisms, marriages and burials and the charge made for the hire of a 'mortcloth' or pall; but the main source was the collections taken in church (which, in the days when stipend, church and manse were provided by the heritors, were not required for congregational expenses). From the meagre collections, however, consisting too often of the smallest coins or even of base money, only tiny sums could be paid. The system was not inadequate in a mainly rural society where cash was unimportant and neighbourly concern could be relied on to provide food to keep body and soul together. But its breakdown was almost inevitable as people concentrated in the growing towns. Urban parishes could now hardly avoid adopting assessment for a poor rate, and this in turn attracted paupers to the towns and increased the burden. The Disruption of 1843 was the final blow to the old system: now that the majority of the inhabitants of Scotland were no longer members of the established church, it seemed hardly fair that its kirk sessions, drawing reduced collections, should retain the exclusive duty of giving poor relief.

A new Poor Law of 1845 at last superseded one of 1672 and made such provisions that it became almost essential for a parish to impose an assessment. Paupers were to be rigorously removed to their parish of birth or settlement, and this relieved the towns somewhat. Poor relief continued to be administered on a parochial basis until well into the twentieth century, but in time a distinction was made between different kinds of poverty and responsibility gradually taken over by the central government. For example, the pauperism which arose simply from old age was alleviated with the introduction of the Old Age Pension in 1908. Then unemployment—the problem of the able-bodied poor—was dealt with through Unemployment Insurance. As 'Public Assistance', the successor of Poor Relief, became 'National Assistance' and finally all-round social security, the relief of poverty became a function of the central government.

Urbanisation also meant problems of public health, for refuse heaps still accumulated in the streets in the medieval manner. Crowded tenements, some of them looking on to sunless and malodorous 'closes' and all of them without water-supply or drains, were breeding-grounds of disease. Unhealthy conditions arose also from fishmarkets and slaughterhouses, as well as from vermin of all kinds. Visitations of the plague, which in earlier times had caused many deaths, had ceased, and the last known cases of people actually dying of starvation in bad seasons occurred in the 1690s. Another ancient scourge, smallpox, had been very largely eliminated by the introduction of vaccination at the end of the eighteenth century. But other diseases succeeded the older ones. The nineteenth century was the era of the 'fevers', especially typhus and cholera, epidemics of which caused thousands of deaths in 1832, 1848–9 and 1853–4, and in the late nineteenth century and the early twentieth tuberculosis took its toll. Fresh air was the best specific against some of those diseases, but to prevent others a piped water supply and drainage were essential. In Edinburgh, water had been brought into the town from springs at Comiston in the late seventeenth century, to supplement local wells, but the introduction of water to houses came later, and only in the late nineteenth century did it become the invariable practice to lead water into every house or flat as it was built. Glasgow, long dependent largely on polluted streams, was furnished with an ample supply of pure water from Loch Katrine in 1859, and this had an immediate effect in reducing the death-rate. Under various Acts of Parliament local authorities were empowered to insist on the notification of infectious diseases, to appoint medical officers of health and to remove nuisances which might be a danger to health.

As to housing conditions, difficulties arose from the very merits of Scottish buildings, which were solidly constructed of stone and too often lasted until they deteriorated into slums. It is true that a tall tenement occasionally fell down, the best known instance

being in Edinburgh, where the cry of a boy buried in the debris—
'Heave awa', lads, I'm no deid yet'—has been immortalised. But
usually they had to be pulled down, and it was here that local
authorities first intervened, for from the 1860s onwards the worst
slums were demolished and broader streets laid out. The building
of new houses, however, long remained a matter for private
enterprise, which did provide houses in such numbers that by
1914 there was a large surplus. Between 1861 and 1911 the
number of one-roomed houses was halved, and it ceased to be the
practice to build blocks in which the plumbing was shared among
households.

It was indeed usually possible for a working man who had
steady employment to better his position, to rent a more com-
modious house or even (with assistance from a building society)
to buy one. But the Scots as a nation were reluctant to spend an
adequate proportion of their earnings on housing, and the refusal
of some of them to pay reasonable rents has continued, right down
to the present, to complicate the situation. Since World War I the
provision by private enterprise of houses to let has not been
economic, and the burden has fallen on local authorities. They
have not yet succeeded in producing a surplus such as private
enterprise had by 1914, but it was not clear if the shortage now was
one of houses in general or merely of good-quality subsidised
council houses. Certainly many council houses in less desirable
areas long remained unoccupied. More than half (57.6 per cent) of
Scottish families lived in council houses, and those who had old-
fashioned ideas about morality in public life were critical of councillors who were themselves council-house tenants and voted to
keep their own rents down. In 1973 the percentage of owner-
occupied houses in Scotland was only 27·3, as against 51·6 in
England and Wales. As a consequence of the attitude of successive
governments to private ownership, every Scottish town has acres
—Glasgow seems to have miles—of substantial stone-built blocks
which have become derelict but which could still be in good
condition if legislation had not made it economically impossible
for the owners to maintain them. The Scottish tradition of town-
dwellings was the tenement or block of flats. Between the wars the

English model was preferred and in council estates gardens were thrust on tenants who neglected them. Since 1945 the tradition of flat-dwelling has revived, in the shape of blocks twenty and thirty storeys high. Almost 39 per cent of Scottish households lived in flats, as against a British average of only 12.6 per cent.

CHAPTER 11

The Last Twenty Years

It seemed at the beginning of 1974 that the year would be likely to prove little short of revolutionary in the political field. At the general election of February the Scottish National Party, which had thrice struggled to obtain a single seat and had for the first time achieved a second in 1973, suddenly gained a total of seven. In what had in the past been regarded as normal circumstances, with one of the major parties commanding a substantial majority, seven seats – a tenth of the Scottish representation – might have been dismissed as nothing more than a proof that legislative devolution required consideration; but in a parliament where there was something like a stalemate, seven seats seemed a lot and it was, besides, evident that there would have to be another election before long. When the Labour party went to the country in October, it was officially committed to setting up a directly elected Scottish assembly. This put it in a somewhat stronger bargaining position than the Conservatives, who were as yet undecided, but it was well known that a large section of the Labour party had not undergone any real conversion, and it was not only cynics who thought that Labour's only aim was to fend off the SNP. It was hardly surprising, therefore, that in the general election the Nationalists gained a further four seats, to bring their total to eleven, and ran second to Labour in some traditional Labour strongholds.

This unprecedented SNP success, the precise reasons for which may be detected by future historians, along with the fact that at Westminster the Labour government had an overall majority of only three, appeared to transform prospects for devolution. It seemed as if the Home Rule movement, after a century and a quarter, had emerged from the pattern of waves and troughs in which it had wallowed in the past. The government, dependent in the house on the support of Nationalists and Liberals, and threatened in the country by the SNP advance, could do no other than try to halt the drift of its supporters and the loss of its dominating position in Scotland, though many Labour members were still not enthusiastic about devolution. The Conservatives, equally, were shaken out of their entrenched position, and were prepared to consider a directly elected assembly in place of some more innocuous measure of appeasement, though among them the divisions went deep and the number of convinced devolutionists was small.

The government did not take long to produce a White Paper and subsequently a bill. These dealt with both Scotland and Wales, although Wales was offered far less than Scotland – and, it was to be abundantly proved, wanted even less than it was offered. The combination of Scotland and Wales was a curious device, the reason for which seems obscure, and it did nothing to endear the proposed measure to Scots, who never did take kindly to having their country bracketed with Wales, because Wales, unlike Scotland, was never an independent kingdom, was embodied into England by conquest and was for long a fully integrated part of England. Besides, it was so evident that the Labour party as a whole was still lukewarm that in December 1975 a 'Scottish Labour Party' was formed, with two MPs, to press for devolution in the context of a radical socialist policy. The Scotland and Wales Bill was finally lost in February 1977. But the Labour administration had now entered into a formal pact with the Liberals and could not retreat on the devolution front. A separate Scotland Bill was there- fore framed, providing for the setting up of an assembly in Edinburgh, comprising 142 members, with legislative and adminis- trative powers in certain fields of health, social welfare, education, housing, local government, transport, physical planning, agriculture and fisheries and the law and legal system. This was impressive, but under every heading there were important exceptions, e.g. control of drugs and medicines, social security benefits, the univer- sities, the voting system for local government councils, railways and air services, motoring offences, forestry and sea-water fisheries. Not only did the reservation of those functions to Westminster reduce the scope of the proposed assembly, but the assembly was to have no revenue-raising powers and its acts were to be liable to amendment or repeal by the UK parliament, in which the 71 Scottish members were to remain. With what seemed either reckless optimism or, according to one's point of view, cynical disregard for the sovereignty of parliament, the former Royal High School building on the Calton Hill in Edinburgh was designated as the meeting-place of the proposed assembly and expensive alterations to it were put in train.

The Scotland Bill was ultimately passed, but before that happened that opinion was changing once more. Some thought it was evident that the performance of the SNP members at Westminster was neither impressive nor encouraging; some began to suspect that the impetus towards Home Rule was once more going into a trough and, given time, would go away; some began to be bored with the whole prolonged business; and others considered that at a time of continuing economic crisis the London parliament should find something better to do. Dismay at the prospect of legislation from Edinburgh was expressed most strongly in Shetland, which was prepared to consider a whole range of alternatives, from the retention of its existing relations with Westminster to becoming completely independent. There was also the question of a possible reaction from the side of the English, who might rebel when they found that the 71 Scots at Westminster could vote on all English issues whereas the English MPs could no longer vote on all Scottish issues.

At the very least, it was hard to dispute that such a far-reaching constitutional change as the Scotland Bill should not be made simply by a bare majority in parliament, and the measure therefore contained provision for a referendum; it was then argued, further, that a bare majority of the electorate who happened to turn out on polling day should not be final, and an amendment provided that the referendum should not be decisive unless at least 40 per cent of the persons on the electoral roll voted in favour of the assembly. In view of the way opinion had been changing, few were surprised that the referendum, on 1 March 1979, did not produce the necessary 40 per cent, though not many would have predicted that only slightly less than 33 per cent would vote 'Yes'. Of the voters who went to the polls, those who supported the assembly outnumbered the rest by 77,435 (1,230,937 for, 1,153,502 against) but only 64 per cent of the electorate voted and the percentages for and against were thus 32.85 and 30.78. The geographical division was interesting. The regions known since 1974 as Strathclyde, Central, Fife, Highland, Western Isles and Lothian voted 'Yes', the last by only 800 votes; Dumfries and Galloway, Borders, Grampian, Tayside, Orkney and Shetland voted 'No'.

Possibly the most remarkable feature in the whole proceeding was this: after a century and a quarter of intermittent agitation against the union barely a third of the Scottish electorate were prepared to countenance even a modest measure of devolution. That the referendum figures in no way distorted Scottish opinion was shown at the parliamentary elections in May 1979, when the SNP lost all but two of their seats and their percentage of votes slumped from 30 to 17. Clearly the country had been through one of the repeated patterns of waves and troughs, and public opinion was still volatile: had the referendum been held perhaps two years earlier, the percentage would almost certainly have been very different. The reasons for the change seem clear: some voters had no doubt awakened to ramifications of devolution which had not occurred to them earlier and feared that, even if it were desirable in itself, it might indeed lead to the break-up of the United Kingdom, which they thought undesirable; many objected that Scotland, already saddled with community, district and regional councils and a Westminster Parliament, and faced with the prospect of a European Parliament in addition, was going to be the most over-governed, and perhaps the most expensively governed, of nations; others asked what kind of people were likely to seek election to the manifestly second-class office of membership of the Edinburgh assembly, and did not like the answer; others again were frightened off by the possibility of the domination of Clydeside radicals on one hand or sentimental Celtomaniacs on the other.

But while Scottish voters had been volatile on the issue of devolution, the general election of May 1979 showed that they were more constant on other issues than were the voters elsewhere in Britain. Labour support in Scotland increased (from 36 per cent to

42 per cent) when there was a substantial swing to the Conservatives in England. In Britain as a whole, the Conservatives had a majority over Labour of 71 and an overall majority of 43. But in Scotland, Labour had 44 seats, Conservatives 22, Liberals 3 and SNP 2. The Scottish Labour party, so recently formed, was eliminated. The Conservatives had increased their percentage of the vote from 25 per cent to 31 per cent and gained 7 seats (but lost 1 to Labour), Labour had gained 5 seats. Conservative and Labour gains alike were mainly at the expense of the SNP. There was if anything a sharper contrast than ever between Labour preponderance in the industrial belt of the lands draining into the Clyde and the Forth, where the Conservatives had only 7 seats out of 48, and the constituencies lying north and south of it; in the vast areas to the north Labour had only three seats, and the three most southerly constituencies also rejected Labour. There was no mistaking the persistence of the conservative north and of the independent attitude of the central and western Borders.

A few weeks after the general election, the voting for the European parliament showed a stronger trend to the Conservatives (or Unionists), who won seats in traditionally Labour areas, and – to general surprise – the SNP was successful by a narrow majority in the Highlands and Islands constituency. However, as only 33% of the electorate chose to vote, those results could hardly be thought significant.

The demonstration by the general election in May of Scottish fidelity to Labour did nothing to make the Labour party in England more enamoured of any change which would remove Scottish members from Westminster. They preferred to count that in the future as in the past the Scottish Labour vote might impose a Labour government on the United Kingdom despite a Conservative majority in England. However, such a calculation was hardly relevant in the short term, for the immediate result of the election of May 1979 was the formation of a Conservative administration under Margaret Thatcher. The Scotland Act, which the referendum had discredited, was duly repealed, and all that emerged from the commotion about devolution was a Conservative promise to try to initiate all-party talks on the constitutional position. Politically, therefore, the quinquennium which had encouraged expectations of something like revolution had produced no substantial change. Another use was found for the former Royal High School building on the Calton Hill.

But if constitutionally the policy was 'No change', the economic changes of the 1980s were disastrous. It had been possible to suggest that, in historical perspective, the economic history of the inter-war period and some of the years after World War II might emerge as nothing worse than one or two earlier periods of adjustment – like the transition from linen to cotton and the transition from cotton to heavy industry – which had been painful at the time but which had in the end produced a healthy economy on a new basis. However, by the 1980s it was much more difficult to have such confidence, because, wherever one turned, the picture seemed to be of an economy in decay, and what was especially depressing was that new enterprises, which had for a time seemed full of promise, came to grief.

The doubts expressed on page 224 about the prospects of the automobile factories at Bathgate and Linwood proved to be justified. The same was true at Fort William: there had been jubilation when the Wiggins Teape pulp mill came to Lochiel, attracting as it did a ceaseless traffic of juggernauts on the roads and promising an assured future for the West Highland railway, but in six years it had gone. The Cromarty Firth was a graveyard of blasted hopes and failures – an oil refinery with ancillary activities, an industrial complex with a designed population of a quarter of a million, an aluminium smelter, a yard for the fabrication of oil-rigs and platforms, even the century-old naval base at Invergordon: 'with one exception, all major projects mooted since 1981 have not materialised' (Marinell Ash, *This Noble Harbour* [1991], p. 271).

Further north, in Caithness, there was the Dounreay nuclear reactor, where, it had been said, 'Britain's nuclear future was being forged'. For a time it employed about a fifth of the working population of the county and it made Thurso a boom town. By 1992 it was on the point of being designated 'a listed building', to be preserved as an historic monument. Even hopes that there would be a spin-off by the reprocessing of other countries' fuel seemed unlikely to be realised in the face of the agitation aroused by the widespread terror of anything 'nuclear'. The lasting survival may be of only some smaller enterprises which are in Caithness mainly because Dounreay proved that the place is not off the map. An example of similar unfulfilled expectations, even farther north, was the shipping of frozen fish direct from Scalloway to America, which began in 1967 and lasted for over twenty years, with a peak of 4500 tons in 1971, but ceased in 1990 owing to diminishing stocks of fish.

At the other end of the country great hopes were held out of the transatlantic airport at Prestwick, for its remarkable freedom from fog made it competitive with airports nearer Edinburgh and Glasgow, but it was not provided with adequate links by road and rail and by 1992 it had almost ceased to function except for freight. The steel works at Ravenscraig near Motherwell had been planned under government auspices when steel was a nationalised industry, but their opening was long delayed by industrial disputes and it was admitted at the outset that the plant would be less economic than its Japanese competitors. Then in June 1979 it was announced that the work force in the modern steel foundry at Craigneuk, very near Ravenscraig, opened in October 1978 at a cost of £7.2m, would have to be reduced by a quarter as it was working to less than half its capacity and was uneconomic. Ravenscraig itself staggered on, under repeated threats from now denationalised British Steel, against whom the government could not intervene, until it was closed in 1992. It made matters worse when it was rumoured that the port of Hunterston in Ayrshire, which had been designed for the export of Scottish steel and of automobiles made in Scotland, was instead going to be used for the import of foreign coal. Coal-mining had long been in terminal decline and in the decade 1967-77 the number employed in mining and quarrying fell from 53,000 to 33,000. The psychological shock of learning in 1990 that only one deep coalmine remained operative was profound, and the continuation of some opencast extraction of coal was hardly a consolation.

The government could not be absolved from all blame for what was happening in the management of coal, and still less could it be absolved for what was happening in the management of the railways and the distribution of resources between rail and road. It seemed nothing short of lunacy that the new bridge over the Dornoch Firth should not carry a railway line and should thus make the railway hopelessly uncompetitive. In 1956 the village of Helmsdale had more than 100 railway employees; by 1992 there were 100 miles of track, from Dingwall to Thurso, with no staff on platforms. The arguments for and against the upgrading of the A1 all the way to Edinburgh and for and against the extension of rail electrification beyond Edinburgh might be more debatable, but opinion was so irritated that both sides of the case were unlikely to be appreciated. It was much the same with defence: the retention or extinction of Scottish regiments was a matter only of sentiment, but it was possible to raise more enthusiasm on that issue than on the future of Rosyth Dockyard, which had serious economic implications.

The overall picture of an economy heading for disaster had been sufficiently illustrated in the Report of the Clyde Port Authority for 1978. The total tonnage of imports and exports fell from 19 million in 1974 to 9 million in 1977 and 1978; each year the proportion of imports to exports was in a ratio of about 6 to 1; and it hardly brightened the picture to note that the port charges, levied on a dwindling number of vessels and cargoes, almost doubled in the period. It looked like catastrophe.

It was not indeed all gloom. The oil industry, in its various facets, brought an enormous amount of highly profitable activity to some east coast ports. In Grampian region, where most of mainland oil activity took place, by 1992 the average weekly wage for manual workers was £319, compared with £265 for Scotland as a whole and £285 for Britain. There was a boom in office property in Aberdeen (where in 1992 the Harbour Board, with a pre-tax profit of £7.2m, planned a £14m development on the site of the defunct shipbuilding yard). Montrose, Dundee, Methil and Leith were other ports which profited, but the greatest gains were in Shetland (where a terminal costing £1.3bn was created) and, to some extent, Orkney. Initially there was some disappointment that, although Britain now had its own oil, the commodity, far from becoming cheaper and more plentiful, became scarcer and dearer. There was uneasiness that the income it generated was being squandered instead of being salted away with a view to investment against the 'rainy day' when oil would finally run out, and fears were often expressed about the prospective length of life of the industry. That continued expansion was still envisaged was shown when in 1991-2 BP invested £650m in a second loading-berth at Hound Point, Dalmeny, whence ever-larger tankers carry away oil piped from North Sea oilfields. Prospects, with new fields likely to come on stream, extended well into the next century.

At the same time, it sometimes looked as if oil was going to prove in some ways the disappointment of the century. The oil had come, the oil would reach its peak, the oil would go, and it was hard to be certain that Scotland was going at the end to be much better off. The construction phase, which for a time provided a lot of new employment and continued activity in certain places, did not realise all the hopes which had been held out. The oil-fabrication yards at Kishorn in Western Ross and at Stornoway were closed, and as early as 1979 it was announced that nearly 1200 of the 1600 employed at the Nigg yard on the Cromarty Firth would have to go. In 1992 massive redundancies were announced at Ardersier, near Inverness, and it was evident that both Nigg and Methil also faced serious problems. The prosperity was thus possibly short-lived, but perhaps the psychological effects were most damaging. We were so often told, 'Just wait until the oil begins to flow... Just hold on for a year or two until oil makes its impact'. But what those encouraging noises amounted was to lead people to think that once oil arrived there would be no need for further endeavour; they could just rest on their oars and allow the oil to do the rest. Consequently there was no incentive to effort. Of course, apart from the expected (but never realised) effect on the balance of payments, it was thought that oil revenues could contribute to plans for reinvestment in industry; but there was no point in assisting production in Scotland when people now preferred to buy cars from Japan, ships from Korea, radios from Taiwan and books (even books on Scottish History) from Hong Kong.

Developments elsewhere, if less spectacular – and less controversial – than oil, were more positive. The production of whisky had risen by 25 per cent between 1967 and 1977, when the exports were valued at £660m (about a sixth of total Scottish exports), and in 1991-2 there was an increase of approximately 10 per cent in exports overseas, though there was some decline of sales in Britain. Alongside the continuing popularity of that ancient liquid there was a novel and almost incredible expansion of the bottling of another liquid – Scottish water. In ten years British consumption of bottled water rose from about nil to about 500m litres; imports from overseas fell off by about a third, while Scottish production made up a large proportion of the shortfall. Another novel way of exploiting a natural resource of which Scotland has a superfluity has led to a perfect 'rash' of projected super-quarries all over the north and west, to extract the aggregate for which there seems to be an insatiable demand: Glensanda, designed in 1981 and in ten years producing 10m tonnes, shipped away from a jetty capable of taking a ship of 120,000 tons, is on a site previously consisting of a mass of pink granite, a ruined castle and some other derelict buildings, tucked away in the wilderness area of Morvern on the west side of the Firth of Lorne. That quarry attracted only slight attention outside its immediate vicinity, but elsewhere conservationists denounced 'the competitive destruction of Scottish mountains'.

Water and mountains figured in another way: in 1991 335,000 Americans came to Scotland to see them, a drop of 70,000 on the previous year as a result of the recession and the Gulf War, but Scotland's drop was only 17 per cent while the British figure slumped by 27 per cent. Tourism was then estimated to generate an income of £1.7bn and to employ 185,000 people. From time to time a friend who 'collects' mountains amazes me with his account of the number of people he meets on the high tops. When I was occasionally walking to the tops of mountains half a century ago I do not remember that I ever met a living soul. The visitors do not always hoof it now, for cable cars, installed primarily for skiers, take 'climbers' as well. Both mountains and water figured in the production of another export – electricity, but nuclear power came in to supplement them. It has been cheering to observe here and there a modest railway revival, with new stations and even some restored routes, to set alongside the 18% increase in 1991-2 of the number of passengers using Scottish airports.

There have continued to be signs of diversification, for example in the manufacture of computers at Erskine and Prestwick, ceramics in Glenrothes, some textiles, paper and paperboard (at Inverurie, Glenrothes, Aberdeen, Guardbridge, Inverkeithing and Inveresk), and various specialised forms of equipment in the 'industrial estates' which have mushroomed everywhere. For a time it seemed that the great recession of the early 1990s was hitting Scotland less hard than it was hitting some other regions of the United Kingdom, but by the autumn of 1992, with output falling, one could no longer be optimistic. About two-thirds of firms were working below capacity, and the undeniable (if limited) successes had to be set against incessant business failures. The situation and the prospects were authoritatively described as 'unrelieved gloom'.

The age-old occupations based on the products of Scotland's land and waters were faring better than manufacturing industry. In the fifteen years from 1960 to 1975, output per head in agriculture, forestry and fishing increased by 6.7% a year, when the comparable figure for manufactures was only 3.4%. A future for those fields seemed assured when there was a world-wide shortage of food for a rapidly increasing population. One innovation was the production of farmed venison (where, however, there was competition from New Zealand). But the European Community was producing food – and drink – far in excess of its own needs and it seemed to have a bias in favour of continental farmers. In consequence, after much talk of 'food mountains' and 'wine-lakes', the Common Agricultural Policy was amended in 1992, to reduce subsidies and give compensation to farmers for limiting cultivation. Moreover, the craze for 'conservation' involved a preference for 'nature reserves', 'wilderness areas' and 'sites of special scientific interest' which were to be protected as the habitat of flora and fauna and in which farmers were paid not to produce food. Even an entire county can be designated an 'Environmentally Sensitive Area' to conserve features 'vulnerable to changes in farming practice' and pay farmers to encourage 'environmentally beneficial farming practices'. Some saw this as 'stagnation' and 'ossification'. Land could now be viewed as a source not of food but of lavish conservational grants.

The pattern of landholding has meantime changed. The pressure of taxation, particularly death-duties, encouraged the sale of land, the capital value of land rose sharply while rents increased only modestly, and the security enjoyed by tenants discouraged land-lords from re-letting when tenants relinquished holdings. Thus the sale of land and investment of the proceeds at high interest rates provided the best return on capital. Then the increase in ownership meant that few farms were 'to let' and then only at high prices, making it difficult for anyone to start a career in farming without the substantial capital necessary for purchase. Costs of increasingly elaborate machinery rocketed too. In the 1940s about 76 per cent of the agricultural holdings were worked by tenant-farmers but by 1977 the percentage had fallen to 48, while the total number of holdings, over 74,000 in 1947 was little more than 30,000 in 1977.

Scottish fisheries were adversely affected in a different way: the powers of individual states to protect their own surrounding waters were curbed, and, after much evidence of over-fishing, operations were severely restricted by quotas, decommissioning vessels and limiting periods for fishing. The landings of fish in Scotland in 1978 were 426,000 tonnes, valued at £122m but the value for the first half of 1992 was almost exactly the same, in a period when there had been savage inflation. Closure of the North Sea and the Minches to herring fishing caused the percentage of herring in the total catch to fall from 9% in 1977 to 4% in 1978, which meant the virtual extinction of what had been an enormous industry. Some compensation was found in mackerel, the catch of which rose by 350%, but it was feared that that species would be the next victim of over-fishing. There was a great setback in fish-processing, which had been expanding, and a number of factories had to close. Compensation which looked promising came with a major innova-tion – the farming of fish, especially salmon (where Scottish prod-ucts received praise for their quality and a Label Rouge from France, which could give them the lead over strong competition from Norway, which was accused of 'dumping' and undercutting). It was claimed in 1992 that the revenue generated by the salmon industry outstripped the combined total from cattle and sheep farming in the Highlands. Catches of wild salmon, meantime, declined disastrously because, so it was said, of the interception of the fish by netting at sea before they reached the Scottish rivers. It was said in October 1992 that the Scottish fishing industry was lurching from crisis to crisis and that further restrictions would bring disaster.

The whole concept of the 'Highlands and Islands' as a unit is so mischievous that generalisation is misleading. The Highlands and Islands Development Board indeed continued its beneficence: in 1978, for example, it gave assistance to the amount of £13m and approved of 782 applications, which were expected to create or secure about 2,000 jobs. (In 1991 the Board was in effect merged with some other agencies to form Highlands and Islands Enterprise, which fitted into a network of local enterprise companies designed to encourage economic and social development plans and training.) The gross weekly earnings of male manual workers in the area averaged £91, as compared with £81 nationally, but this 'average' figure included payments to oil workers which often far exceeded £200. Equally, the long-term trend of depopulation was reversed in Shetland and Easter Ross, while in the Outer Isles and Sutherland (without any 'clearances') numbers still dwindled. (Throughout the whole country the percentage of people engaged in agriculture and fishing shrank in the 80s from 3.4 to 2.3.) The proportion of native stock was dwindling even outwith the tourist season, for incomers acquired houses as holiday homes or for retirement, at prices natives could not afford. To take another illustration, in 1992 the languishing Western Isles received from the government over £30m more than they paid, while Shetland received only £40m in return for paying £100m – without taking into account the £700m the government received from the petroleum revenue tax on the oil flowing through Sullom Voe.

As oil-related operations were limited geographically and likely to be short-lived, the problems of providing some areas with a sound economy not dependent on external subvention remained as intractable as ever. There was still much concern about the under-use or mis-use of land by tenants and landlords alike, about distances from markets and the cost of transport (despite shipping subsidies which have long been lavish in the west, but of only recent appearance and on a niggardly scale in the north). The greatest revolution in communications – greater even than the air services which came in the 1930s – has been the introduction of drive-on-drive-off ships, which offer safer transport for goods, enable travellers on either business or holidays to drive from door to door, and provide massive capacity. In 1939 the gross tonnage on the move each week between Aberdeen and the northern isles was little more than 7,000; now it is about 36,000.

Not all Scotland's economic misfortunes were the fault of the government. In some instances – for example the decline of coal production and the shrinking business of the Clyde Ports – the trouble had started before Mrs Thatcher had become Prime Minister. Shipbuilding, too, which in the 1960s had experienced a measure of recovery to something not very far from its pre-war level, had a disastrous decade thereafter and by 1979 order-books were almost empty. There was hope that a Conservative government, to remedy Labour's run-down of the national defences, would order naval vessels, but few such orders came to Scotland. Yards went down like ninepins until that once great industry vanished completely from the east coast and preserved only a precarious existence at one or two places on the Clyde.

It could hardly have been denied that some of the roots of the trouble lay far outside Scotland. But whereas there was some colour for blaming the government for the failures of nationalised industries and for their attitudes to Scottish interests, when an industry had been privatised the government protested that the actions of the private company must be based entirely on economic considerations. It was easier to blame the government than to suggest promising courses of action. The only recipe for economic depression usually offered is governmental intervention by investment or reinvestment. But the government has no money of its own and all it can do is to mulct firms which are profitable in order to inject money into firms which are not profitable, in other words penalise the successful in favour of 'lame ducks'. And there is not much point in subsidising firms to produce articles which no one seems to prefer to the products of foreign countries.

The administration was accused, not without reason, of insensitivity towards Scottish opinion, and its arrogant, strident personification in the almost aggressively English Mrs Thatcher did nothing to win Scottish voters. When she delivered 'the Sermon on the Mound' to the General Assembly the substance of her thought – essentially that those who accused her party of greed would do well to look at the Trade Unions with their incessant demands for less work and more pay, and that the political Left had no monopoly of the moral ground – was far from indefensible, but her histrionic attempt to identify herself with the Scots was stillborn.

Throughout 'the Thatcher years', Scottish unemployment figures remained noticeably above the UK level. In January 1979 the Scottish percentage was 8.7, the British 6.1; in 1983 the corresponding figures were 12.3 and 10.5 and in 1989 they were 9.3 and 6.3. The gap narrowed by 1991, when the British figure was 9.6 and the Scottish 10.9, and figures worked out early in 1992 suggested that the Scottish figure had dropped below the British, but there seemed no likelihood of a Scottish rate of less than 10 per cent. Within Scotland, as ever, there was a variegated pattern, with the percentage ranging form 16.7 in the Western Isles, 10.8 in the Highland region and 9.5 in Strathclyde, down to 6.7 in Orkney, 4.8 in Grampian, 4.5 in the Borders and 4.1 in Shetland. The changes were not only in the total figures: in the ten years from 1967 to 1977, the number of men at work had fallen from 1,312,000 to 1,196,000 and the number of women at work had risen from 768,000 to 872,000. In 1991 the wages of male full-time workers averaged £276.40 and of women £187.20. Employment in productive industries continued to decline, but the number engaged in professional and scientific services rose from 260,000 to 355,000. While politicians made the most of the high unemployment rates, there was little sign of the deep resentment which existed in the 20s and 30s, when there had been loud protests against 'women taking men's jobs' and 'Irishmen taking Scotsmen's jobs'. Somehow unemployment now seemed to bite less than it had done; but of course the expenditure on social security had risen from £265m in 1967 to £1,060m in 1977. On the other hand, that Scotland had become a less attractive place was suggested by the population figures. In only one previous decade – the dismal 1921-31 – had Scotland's population declined, but, after reaching an all-time maximum of 5¼m in 1971 there was a loss of ¼m by 1992. The decline would have been greater had there not been appreciable immigration from England.

The structure of local government, as reorganised in 1974-5 and inherited by Mrs Thatcher, caused some irritation but had to be accepted. In the Highlands and Islands the chief flaw was the attachment of most of the Highland county of Argyll to the predominantly industrial Strathclyde region, centred on Glasgow. The rest of the mainland Highlands were in the Highland region, although it included also Lowland areas around the Moray Firth and in Caithness. In the western and northern isles the distinct status of separate island authorities was an advantage. Shetland, in particular, showed admirable shrewdness in managing the revenues it derived from oil, and Orkney's distinctive ancient culture (one might almost say civilisation) flourished anew. The Outer Hebrides, previously divided between two counties, acquired their own Western Isles Council. This authority could not be credited with financial shrewdness, for it lost millions with the collapse of the Bank of Credit and Commerce International, but its existence gave a novel cohesion to a Gaelic stronghold. One consequence (based largely on propagandist lies about Gaelic being 'the original tongue of all Scotland') was to convince the government that Gaelic required a costly life-support machine, which was forthcoming in the shape of a subsidy of £9½m annually for Gaelic television (although the 1991 census showed only 65,000 Gaelic speakers). No other local authority even asked for assistance in ploughing a particular lonely linguistic furrow.

There was more dissatisfaction with local government elsewhere. The burden on ratepayers rose sharply: from 1974 to 1975 the general increase was 36 per cent, but whereas in Glasgow it was only 12 per cent, in some rural areas in the former counties it shot up by as much as 76 per cent, and by 1978 some householders were paying twice as much as they had paid in 1974. The inequity of the rating system, related as it was to property valuation and not to income, and sometimes imposing a heavier burden on a single pensioner than on a family of four or five wage-earners, was often admitted, but to find an acceptable alternative proved perhaps the most difficult problem in internal affairs. So far as the structure of local government was concerned, the Conservatives promised to reconsider and review it, but for years there seemed no prospect of anything more than tidying up some of the consequences of the sharing of some functions between regions and districts and of the division between regions and districts of some functions which were closely related, for instance social work, housing and education. It was only after the Conservatives, on their fourth consecutive term of office in 1992, committed themselves to bring in a single-tier system that they commissioned an investigation of the cost implications of such a move. It seemed that – especially if Scotland acquired an assembly or parliament – the ultimate solution was almost certain to be a single-tier structure, based on units somewhat resembling existing districts but more closely related than some of them were to real communities – as was true of the island groups which had in effect all-purpose authorities and were from their nature peculiarly cohesive. There were speculations about patterns ranging from 15 to 50 local authorities and one, for 15, was based partly on existing health authorities. There were few defenders of an arrangement whereby the largest region in respect of population – Strathclyde – contained half the people of the country and the largest region in respect of area – the Highland region – contained half the land surface.

Until fairly recently, local government in Scotland was less dominated by party politics than it was in England, for most candidates presented themselves to the voters on their own records and policies as individuals. Such 'Independent' councillors have become rare, and, especially in the larger authorities, the party system, often a polarisation of Labour and Conservative, prevails. This means that no attempt is made to reach a consensus, debates are a charade and decisions a foregone conclusion, made on party lines. This emerged with particular force in education. Because the Labour party was committed to coeducation and to non-selective schools, resources which might have gone to the improvement of old buildings in poor areas were diverted to the expensive adaptation for coeducational use of some recently built schools which had been designed for either boys or girls. Much was heard of the desirability of having a 'social mix' in schools, which meant the use of education as social engineering, but the 'comprehensive' school, drawing its pupils from the surrounding area, can be more homogeneous socially than the old 'selectives' were. The main effect of the abandonment of selectivity was to raise the value of houses in areas containing up-to-date schools. Councillors were not solely responsible for the misfortunes of education, because some of the reorganisation was blatantly designed to increase the number of 'promoted posts' and improve the 'career structure' of teachers, whose antics in having recourse to strikes and other forms of militancy – unthinkable a generation before – lost them the respect of parents and teachers alike. A few years ago in an Edinburgh bus I overheard remarks between two women in a seat behind mine. As we passed premises where a group of people were demonstrating the conversation went: 'It'll be some o' thae teachers.' Thus a once honoured profession is brought into disrepute. Purely educational considerations, and the good of the pupils, vanished from the forefront of policy. The Conservatives promised a rescue operation for grant-aided schools, but in practice simply abandoned the principle of grant-aid; schools which had previously relied partly on grants and partly on fees disappeared, to join the ranks of two types of schools – the independent and those maintained by local authorities. This led to a sharper division than before – both socially and educationally – between types of schools.

Meantime education was being expanded in various ways, though it is not clear if party policies were responsible. More children were remaining at school after reaching the minimum leaving age, and in 1990 the proportion of pupils leaving without any Certificate of Education qualification was reduced to about a third of what it had been in 1980. Apart from what the schools were doing, the number of colleges for further education rose, and in 1992 three colleges were raised to university rank – Napier in Edinburgh, Robert Gordon's in Aberdeen, and Paisley – while Queen's College in Glasgow was waiting in the wings for similar promotion.

The other field in which party politics could be mischievous was housing. The Labour party favoured council housing for all comers, irrespective of means, and it viewed with satisfaction a situation in which in the major districts of Scotland 58 per cent of houses were council-owned and in certain districts the percentage was as high as 84. A policy of keeping rents down bought so many supporters that the Labour party, it was thought, felt so confident that it had no need to take initiative on other issues. This, some believed, was the reason for the sudden success of the SNP in 1974, which shook Labour out of its complacency. The Conservatives on their side, though disapproving of universal subsidies, were too terrified of council voters to do much about it, though the Labour position was so strong that the Conservatives might have lost nothing by adopting a policy of reducing subsidies and raising rents.

Housing has to be seen against the background of the biggest revolution of recent years, in the changing levels of personal incomes. Chatter about 'the redistribution of wealth' obscured the extent to which the balance was gradually changing and differentials vanishing. It was evident for all to see that some families in council homes were better off than the supposed 'rich' who owned their dwellings. Even during the Labour government of 1974-9 private building began to overtake council building. It is not yet clear if the increasing affluence of the 'working classes' had led to much desire for property ownership or any other form of capital investment, but that something had to be done was shown by the fact that Glasgow accumulated a capital debt in its housing account of over a billion pounds, costing £150m a year in loan charges. There came to be something like general agreement that council houses should be offered for sale. The Conservative government elected in 1979 took steps towards not merely permitting (which Labour had done less than half-heartedly) but compelling councils to sell to sitting tenants who wanted to buy. This had considerable success, for the percentage of Scots who owned their homes rose from 36 in 1980 to 51 in 1990. Purchasers received advantageous terms, depending on the length of their occupancy. Some observers thought that it would be an economy for the local authorities to give the houses away and so be relieved of the cost of maintenance, for many tenants regarded every petty repair and replacement as a matter for the council. It was also argued that ownership would induce a new sense of responsibility and regard for amenity. It was difficult to follow the reasoning of those who thought that in some mysterious way the sale of houses would reduce the total housing stock, and easier to believe that the opposition to the policy of selling was simply a rationalising of the Labour fear of losing support if a large section of the population became less dependent on local authorities. On the other hand, it was also difficult to understand why the government did not permit, or encourage, local authorities to apply to the building of new houses (which could be let) the income from the sale of houses. One thing was clear, namely that it was nonsense to speak as if there was a serious overall shortage of housing. The fact was that prospective tenants, with more money and higher standards, were more selective than they had been, and the less desirable properties were left untenanted, often to be abandoned and destroyed. Another factor in this situation was the breakdown of 'the family' and especially of 'the extended family', as unmarried adults demanded their own 'pad' instead of living with their parents and as the amount of extra-marital cohabitation increased. In April 1979 the number of families on the waiting lists for council houses throughout Scotland – not of course by any means all of them homeless – was about 100,000, while the number of empty houses was estimated at 85,000.

The whole history of housing seems to be a series of paradoxes, of which the present situation is only the latest. Between 1800 and 1914 the population of Scotland rose by over $2\frac{1}{2}$m and not only were all those additional persons housed but there were plenty of houses to spare. In 1914 the Edinburgh Evening News sometimes had as many as thirty columns of advertisements of 'Houses to Let', and in Glasgow there were said to be 13,000 vacant houses. Since 1914 the population has increased only slightly, and there is a constant outcry of a housing shortage. Was private speculative building more successful than council housing? The shortage, too, has accompanied soaring wages, lavish pensions and allowances and a sharply improved standard of living among manual workers – the number of cars registered in the country increased by 28 per cent in the 'Thatcher years' of the 1980s.

On the other hand, taxation went a long way to impoverish old families. Ever since the end of the First World War estates up and down the country have had to be sold, and it is rare now to find a great mansion in use simply as a private residence: some have been demolished, others turned over to some institutional use, a few pay their way as show-places. Their precious contents have largely been dispersed. All in all, the prospect had been the loss of a great part of the nation's cultural heritage, of which few private individuals can now afford to be unpaid custodians. At last stirred to an awareness of the results of its fiscal policies, the government began, through the Historic Buildings Council (now subsumed under Historic Scotland), to make grants for the maintenance and restoration of historic buildings in private hands, and the establishment in 1980 of the National Heritage Memorial Fund had done something to secure their contents. Besides, one of the most cheering features of recent years had been the increased support given to the National Trust for Scotland, which has done a great deal to make possible the preservation and repair of fine houses, small as well as large, which characterised a society very different from that of the late twentieth century.

It might well be agreed that Mrs Thatcher's most unpopular measure was a substitute for rates assessed on notional values of property – a Community Charge, popularly miscalled 'The Poll Tax'. A poll tax is a tax not on property but on 'heads' – that is, persons. That the Community Charge was not as simple as that was only too evident to people who owned property in more than one local authority area and had to pay more than the single charge appropriate to a poll tax. Either by ignorance or misrepresentation 'The Poll Tax' was thought by some to be a tax on the right to vote at elections; and – this time, it may be charitably supposed, out of ignorance rather than malice – Scots were informed by agitators that 'we had a poll tax once before and it caused a rebellion' – a totally irrelevant allusion to an incident in English history in 1371. The introduction of the new charge was badly handled, with no attempt to phase it in gradually, but minds seemed to be closed to reason. It was in vain to appeal to the parallels of Vehicle Licence,

TV Licence, indeed postal charges – or for that matter the purchase of a loaf of bread – in none of which does 'ability to pay' enter. It was suspected that the real reason for dissatisfaction was that under the rates system there were so many rebates that a great many people were not making any direct payments at all to local government finance and now resented being compelled to make a contribution. It was an especial irritant that the new system was introduced in Scotland a year before it was introduced in England, giving rise to the cry that Scotland was being used as a guinea pig. Not only so, but – incredibly in view of numerous proofs that the Treaty of Union was a mere scrap of paper, many of whose clauses have been abrogated – the complaint was made that the differentiation of the two countries was a breach of that treaty. Many who were well able to pay refused to pay and were encouraged by politicians, while the legal machinery to enforce payment was ineffective and was sometimes met by violence. The consequences were deplorable from the point of view of damage to local authority finance, for it was calculated that after three years of the scheme £538m remained unpaid, representing an overall percentage of non-payment of 19%. But the psychological damage was even more serious, for it looked very much as if Scotland was going to become ungovernable. One wonders now if any method for local finance which can be devised in the future will prove acceptable and not encounter organised resistance.

A certain parallel to the row over the Community Charge arose in connection with what seemed the most innocent of issues, namely the testing of children's attainments at certain stages of their school careers. This time it would not have been a howler to say 'We had this before', because for generations it was understood that every child must 'pass his exams', and most parents welcomed information about how their children were doing at school. Equally, teachers eagerly scanned exam results from which their pupils' standards – and their own – could be assessed. Thus parents and schools alike might have been expected to welcome the testing of children, now according to nationally defined standards. But it had become fashionable to decry any kind of competition in intellectual attainments (though, oddly, competition was all the time intensifying in athletics), and to shield children from the knowledge that they would one day go out from school into a competitive world. Some thought that the opposition to 'testing' reflected anxiety arising from the revelations which occasionally emerged about falling standards in children's literacy and numeracy, and, especially as there was opposition also to plans for the assessment of teachers, the reluctance of some teachers to be further exposed might be understandable. The reasons for the opposition to 'testing' were far from being immediately apparent, but the subject was seized on by agitators, and a great many parents, encouraged by politicians, insisted on withdrawing their children from the tests. This again was a case of plain disregard of the law and a step towards anarchy. Once more the resisters got away with it, and threatened to make Scotland ungovernable. The law was being brought into disrepute.

To add to the Community Charge and the testing of children, a third government move which proved unpopular – this time more understandably – was the proposal for the 'privatisation' of water supplies, something which had already been introduced in England. As water was provided 'by nature' and was essential, the idea that profit should be made out of it and that supplies to non-payers should be cut off aroused a lot of emotion.

A government regarded as being so misguided as Mrs Thatcher's could not avoid losing support, and it was hardly surprising that, election by election – 1979, 1983, 1987 – the number of Conservative members representing Scottish constituencies shrank until in 1991 it had fallen to only nine. (In one election after World War II it had been 35.) Such an imbalance was not unprecedented in the history of the United Kingdom, for in 1874 the Conservatives held only seven of Scotland's 60 seats and in 1885 only ten out of 72. But, increasingly as the Conservative rout went on in the 1980s, the cry went up that the government had 'no mandate' to govern Scotland. This was a startling novelty in constitutional theory. Time and again in the past, when the Scottish (and sometimes Irish) vote had put into office a Liberal or Labour government which had no majority in England, the English had not complained that such a government had no mandate to rule them. The English had not even made capital out of the fact that in 1928 the Scottish vote had brought about the rejection of a new Prayer Book for the Church of England, and it has been rare for an Englishman to say to the Scots, 'For any sake go and be independent and leave the English to run their own country'. On the 'no mandate' reasoning, any constituency whose member does not belong to the majority party could claim that the government has no mandate to rule it. Or, indeed, had a Conservative government a mandate to govern certain parts of Scotland and not others? Moreover, the referendum of 1979 could have been taken to suggest that a Scottish parliament could have no mandate to govern Dumfries and Galloway, the Borders, Grampian, Tayside, Orkney and Shetland. The whole concept was nonsensical. Yet, immediately on the installation of Mrs Thatcher as Prime Minister in 1979, Labour-dominated Scottish local authorities and the STUC threatened to defy the London government because it had 'no mandate'.

Such propaganda, however illogical, was made much of by the SNP. The peak of ScotNattery after World War II had produced a Covenant, and a new peak in the '80s produced a self-appointed pressure group called Scottish Constitutional Convention, under the chairmanship of a Canon of Coventry Cathedral, which undertook to define 'devolution'. It was cold-shouldered by the SNP, which had declared for 'independence'. Then, although the SNP vote in 1987 had been only half what it had been in 1974, it was claimed early in 1992 that 50% of the people supported 'independence'. We no longer heard of 'Dominion Status', which all had understood, and now the cry was 'devolution', 'independence' or 'independence in Europe'; there was no clarification of the relations between a 'devolved' or 'independent' Scotland and its former U.K. partners in such matters as responsibility for the National Debt and national defence; we were not told even whether an independent Scotland would be a republic or a monarchy. While a degree of political autonomy was conceivable, it was not explained how economic autonomy could be meaningful in a world largely controlled by international or multinational companies. Few highlighted the fact that several of the businesses which were exporting successfully were foreign-owned. Silence on the fact that the whole field of economics and finance straddles state frontiers was the more striking in view of the revelations about the concentration of financial power which came just at this time, following the death of Robert Maxwell. Still hovering in the background was what had come to be known as the West Lothian Question because it had been formulated by Tam Dalyell, the MP for that area: assuming that Scotland gained devolution but Scottish MPs – to an undefined number – remained at Westminster, would England acquiesce in their having a voice in English affairs while English MPs had no voice in corresponding Scottish affairs? One wonders how many people who declared confidently one way or the other knew exactly to what they were saying 'Yes' or 'No'. On the other hand, those who preferred the status quo consoled themselves with the thought that it would take years to work out all the contentious details. However, the nationalist cause gained momentum from the fragmentation which was proceeding in the USSR and Czechoslovakia, and there should have been fervent prayers that Britain would not go the way of Yugo-Slavia.

Although not all who used the cherished slogan 'Independence in Europe' realised it, that phrase raised the whole issue of Scotland's position in the Community. Scotland had an experience in 1707 of being drawn into a larger economic unit, the United Kingdom, and her entry now (as part of the UK) into the European Community was accompanied and followed, as the union of 1707 had been, by debate over material incentives and deterrents. Scotland had been much less enthusiastic than the UK as a whole for entry into the 'Common Market': in the referendum of June 1975 the Scottish vote was 1,332,286 for and 948,039 against (nearly 5:4), compared with the UK's 17,378,581 for and 8,470,073 against (close to 2:1). Shetland and the Western Isles had majorities against (much as Norway, the Faroes and Greenland had remained outside the Community). Experience suggested that the Community resulted in higher food prices (introduced to accommodate continental agricultural interests) and might prove nearly fatal to Scottish fisheries, but it was undeniable that in simple financial terms the Scots were substantial gainers, receiving in 1979 £1 for every 40p. they contributed to the common purse. Grants and loans went to local authorities for water and sewerage schemes, for road-making, for construction work at the Hunterston plant and in connection with oil-related projects, and to many small industrial efforts. By its slogan 'Independence in Europe' the SNP may have meant to proclaim that it did not seek outright independence, but as the Community has developed it has become increasingly clear that membership of it is not compatible with full sovereignty, even in such matters as the ability to exclude plants carrying disease. The Community shows signs of interfering, in the interests of uniformity, in minutiae of every kind, in disregard of Scottish ways and Scottish wishes. There was some concern – at least temporarily allayed – about the level which might be fixed for duty on whisky; it was startling to learn that the rules of the Community had no category in which haggis could be comprehended and that the conditions in which Arbroath smokies were prepared risked being condemned as unhygienic. Westminster might have chastised the Scots with whips, but would Brussels chastise them with scorpions (1 Kings xii, 14)?

In the frantic debates which went on as feeling became more embittered and as another general election grew closer, there were wild claims and counter-claims. One claim was that an independent Scotland would have to raise over £5bn additional revenue to balance the books. As so often happens, a minor casualty was accuracy about the past. Some of the statements that were made caused one to wonder whether the work of historians was of any use at all, for it was obvious that whatever facts were produced hysterical fiction would still prevail over historical truth. Some went so far as to deny that Scotland had received any advantages at all from the Union – forgetting the benefits of Anglo-Scottish economic co-operation in the eighteenth century (see p. 213), forgetting that the Scots long enjoyed a 'common market' on which the sun never set, and even forgetting that in 1707 Scotland's wealth was only one fortieth of England's whereas two hundred years later it had increased to one seventh. Even when there was some truth in what was said it was apt to be presented in a context which distorted it. Much was made of the charge, stated in very succinct words, that 'the Union was carried by intimidation and bribery'. This, it happens, was proclaimed during the run-up to the election of April

1992, when the voters of Scotland were being bombarded by the propaganda of political parties which contained – what? Nothing but intimidation and bribery, for the incentives and disincentives held out by the parties amounted to nothing less. The truth is, to put it brutally, that it is precisely through intimidation and bribery that democracy works. Material considerations are always to the forefront, but the freedom to be swayed by them or to reject them is also always there, and the choice is freely made, as it was by the members of the Scottish parliament in 1707 and as it was by the Scottish voters in 1992, only 25 per cent of whom voted for the SNP's 'independence' while 75 per cent supported parties which had not rejected Union. Many hoary myths were dusted down. A single issue of *The Scotsman* (11 Feb 1992) contained a letter stating that 'all the signatories of the pro-Union lobby were paid for signing away this nation's sovereignty' and also another letter stating that 'the Episcopalians were against the Union as well, but so was almost everyone else in Scotland'. Elsewhere it was stated, yet again, that the petitions presented against the Union in 1707 indicated 'almost unanimous opposition', although anyone who takes the trouble to count the petitions finds that the number which came from the corporate bodies throughout the country was pitifully small. If there was indeed a majority against the Union, not many were prepared to record their dissent. The old myth was revived that in 1707 the sum of £20,000, actually distributed as modest reimbursements for expenses and to pay of a proportion of arrears of fees and salaries, constituted bribes. Money did indeed change hands (Lord Banff, for example, received £11 2s); but it has not been proved that the passing of money made anyone (except perhaps Lord Elibank, who got £50) change his mind. Indeed, there are few things harder to prove than bribery, because as it is sometimes difficult enough to read one's own mind in the twentieth century it can hardly be possible to be confident about others in the eighteenth. However, a few days before the 1992 election a band of demonstrators gathered in Parliament Square in Edinburgh and signed a 'cheque' for £20,000 which was to be sent to 'the English parliament' when Scotland achieved the independence which they so confidently expected. Nothing similar was done about the £400,000 which Scotland received in terms of the Union as an 'Equivalent' for undertaking a share of England's National Debt: to have saddled an 'independent' Scotland with that sum, plus accrued interest for nearly three centuries and an index-linked supplement for inflation would have bankrupted it right away! Fanciful ideas about corruption persist. One recent writer went so far as to imply that members of the Royal Commission on the Ancient and Historical Monuments of Scotland (who work hard and are unpaid) are victims of 'patronage' whereby the British government sways the political views of Scottish scholars.

The General Election of April 1992, which until the last minute seemed likely to produce a House of Commons where no party had an overall majority and where consequently there might be opportunities for minor parties to exert influence, was a major disappointment for the ScotNats, who had been confident that the Conservatives would be routed. Contrary to the expectations of even the most optimistic of Conservatives, that party enjoyed a three per cent swing in its favour and it gained two seats. As one editor saw it, 'they came back from the political dead'. Among Labour and SNP members there was immediately a lot of wild talk about 'disrupting the House of Commons', recourse to 'non-parliamentary means', 'angry and turbulent scenes', 'a summer of dissent' and 'a campaign of mass civil disobedience'. In view of what had happened over the issues of the Community Charge and testing in schools, the report that civil disobedience was 'gathering strength' did not seem entirely unrealistic, but little came of it. About 12 of Scotland's 49 Labour MPs formed a group called Scotland United, proclaiming 'We're not prepared to allow the Tories to rule us for another five years', protesting 'we're not calling for revolution', but pressing for actions which others characterised as mere 'futile gesture politics'. One possible non-parliamentary channel was of course a referendum, for which moderate voices called and which in May was supported in the General Assembly by a small majority (445 to 437). To mount a referendum, however, would cost money which was not now expected from the Treasury. It was suggested that the referendum should be arranged in conjunction with local authority elections in May and that it should be financed by local authorities, but when it was pointed out that such expenditure by them was likely to be challenged as illegal, the possibility of a referendum receded. Among politicians the voice was the familiar one between 'keeping the constitutional issue at the top of the UK agenda' or instead focusing on the continuing economic recession, and some Liberal Democrats doubted if the electorate, preoccupied with 'immediate day-to-day problems', would respond to 'one-issue pressure groups'. The government did not wholly rule out the possibility of a referendum, and moderates favoured one asking simply 'Are you in favour of a Scottish parliament?', whereas others wanted a 'multi-option' model, embracing status quo, devolution, independence in Europe. By the middle of June the majority of the Labour party had joined the majority of the Liberal Democrats in distancing themselves from Scotland United and deciding that the campaign for a Scottish parliament should have less immediacy. The summer seemed to have the general effect of cooling tempers, and preoccupation with 'the constitutional issue' faded in the light of events in the middle east and in Yugo-Slavia – not to mention the prurience about members of the royal family which some media kept at the top of the agenda – and there may even have been those who thought the Anglo-Scottish debate insignificant in relation to what was happening in Somalia. The Prime Minister, shortly before he was overwhelmed by complications both at home and abroad to which few denied the name 'catastrophe', visited Edinburgh in September 1992 to have a meeting with a number of Scots who were not (at least professionally) politicians. This may have given him an impression of the attitudes and aspirations typical among the considerable number of citizens who are not committed to stereotyped programmes and who are often heard to say, 'I never meet any Nationalists'. He was due back in Edinburgh in a few weeks, in his capacity as President of the EC, to act as host to the heads of other countries of the Community – a curious situation, out of which militant Nationalists hoped to do something for 'puir auld Scotland'.

Chronological Table

(The dates of the kings of Scots are given in the Genealogical Tables)

SCOTLAND	ENGLAND AND IRELAND	THE WIDER WORLD
		41–54 Emperor Claudius
	43 Roman Conquest began	79–81 Emperor Titus
80–85 Campaigns of Agricola		81–96 Emperor Domitian
		117–38 Emperor Hadrian
	c130 Wall of Hadrian	138–61 Emperor Antoninus Pius
c140 Antonine Wall		193–211 Emperor Septimius Severus
207–11 Campaigns of Severus		313 Christianity tolerated in Roman Empire
	c410 End of Roman rule	410 Rome fell to Goths
?c400 St Ninian	?432 St Patrick in Ireland	
c500 Irish 'Scots' arrived	?449 Beginning of Anglo-Saxon settlements	
		476 End of Western Empire
		547 Death of St Benedict
c550 Anglian settlement in south-east	597 Augustine landed in Kent	590–604 Pope Gregory the Great
597 Death of St Columba	616–32 } Ascendancy of	632 Death of Mohammed
c635 Columban mission in Northumbria	654–85 } Northumbria	
	663 Synod of Whitby	

Scotland	England	Europe
685 Angian defeat at Nechtansmere	735 Death of Bede	732 Mohammedan invasion of France checked at Tours
710 Pictish king adopted St Peter as patron	793 Scandinavian raids on England began	800 Coronation of Charlemagne as Emperor of the West
794 Scandinavian raids first mentioned	802–39 Egbert, king of Wessex, overlord of England	843 Treaty of Verdun: beginnings of France and Germany
844 Union of Picts and Scots	871–99 Alfred, king of Wessex	?872 Harald Fairhair unifies Norway
?872 Scandinavian earldom in Orkney	878 Peace of Wedmore: half of England subject to Scandinavians	910 Abbey of Cluny founded
		911 Scandinavian duchy in Normandy
c960 Edinburgh held by kings of Alba	954 England united under house of Wessex	987 Capetian dynasty began in France
	995–1017 Scandinavian conquest of England	1000 (?) Leif Erikson discovered America
	1014 Battle of Clontarf: defeat of Scandinavians in Ireland	
1018 Battle of Carham: Lothian confirmed to Alba	1042–66 Edward the Confessor	1046–72 Norman rule established in Naples and Sicily
1034 Strathclyde part of Scottish kingdom	1066 Battle of Hastings	

c1070 Malcolm III married Margaret	1066–87 William I	1073–85 Gregory VII (Hildebrand) Pope
1072 Malcolm III submits to William I		1077 Pope humiliated emperor at Canossa
1094 First extant charter	1087–1100 William II (Rufus)	1098 Foundation of abbey of Cîteaux
1097 Edgar put on throne by William Rufus		1099 First Crusade
1098 Expedition through western isles by Magnus Barelegs, king of Norway		
	1100–35 Henry I	1115 Foundation of abbey of Clairvaux
1117 onwards New religious orders introduced		1104 Archbishopric for Denmark (Lund)
1120s Burghs and sheriffs first mentioned		1122 Settlement of investiture controversy between pope and emperor
1138 Scots defeated at battle of the Standard	1135–54 Stephen	1148 Second Crusade
	1154–89 Henry II	1151 Archbishopric for Norway (Trondheim)
1175 English feudal over-lordship imposed	1169 Norman rule in Ireland began	1164 Archbishopric for Sweden (Upsala)
1189 English feudal over-lordship surrendered	1170 Becket murdered	1189 Third Crusade
1192 Scottish church's independence of England recognised	1189–99 Richard I	1198–1216 Innocent III Pope

287

1357 David II released	1356 King John of France captured at Poitiers	1358 Jacquerie in France
	1377–99 Richard II	1377 Pope returned to Rome
	1381 Peasants' Revolt	1378–1417 Schism between Roman and Avignonese popes
	1384 Death of Wyclif	1386 Swiss ensure independence by battle of Sempach
1395 Death of poet John Barbour	1399–1413 Henry IV	1397 Norway, Denmark and Sweden united
1396 Clan Fight at Perth	1400 Death of Chaucer	
	1400 revolt in Wales	1414 Council of Constance
1411 Battle of Harlaw	1413–22 Henry V	1415 Death of John Hus
1411 University of St Andrews		
	1415 Agincourt	
1424 James I returned from English captivity	1422–61 Henry VI	1431 Death of Joan of Arc
1426 First mention of 'session' for civil cases		
	1450 Cade's Rebellion	1453 Turks took Constantinople
	1453 End of Hundred Years' War	
1451 University of Glasgow	1455–85 Wars of the Roses	
1455 Overthrow of Black Douglases	1461–83 Edward IV	1469 Marriage of Ferdinand and Isabella united Spain
	1476 Caxton's printing press	
1468–9 Acquisition of Orkney and Shetland	1483 Edward V	
1472} Archbishoprics of St Andrews	1483–5 Richard III	1491 France acquired Britanny
1492} and Glasgow	1485–1509 Henry VII	1492 Columbus crossed Atlantic
149? Forfeiture of lordship of the Isles		

1568 Mary fled to England	1569 Northern Rebellion	1572 Massacre of St Bartholomew's Eve
1572–80 Rule of Earl of Morton		
1578 2nd Book of Discipline	1577–80 Drake circumnavigated the globe	1579 Union of Utrecht: Beginning of Dutch independence
1582 University of Edinburgh		1580 Portugal united with Spain
1586 League with England		
1587 County Franchise Act	1587 Execution of Mary, Queen of Scots	1588 Spanish Armada
1592 Presbyterian government authorised	1600 East India Company founded	1589 Henry IV, king of France
	1603–25 James I	1598 Edict of Nantes; toleration for French protestants
	1604 Hampton Court Conference	1607 Virginia colonised
	1611 Plantation of Ulster	1608 Champlain founded Quebec
1609 Statutes of Iona	1616 Death of Shakespeare	
1610 Episcopacy restored		
1614 John Napier invented logarithms		1618–48 Thirty Years' War
1616 Education Act		1620 Pilgrim Fathers
1617 Register of Sasines		
1618 Five Articles of Perth		
1625–49 Charles I, king of England and Scotland	1628 Petition of Right	
1633 Charles I crowned in Edinburgh. Education Act	1633 Laud Archbishop of Canterbury	
1637 Scottish Prayer Book	1634–8 Ship Money dispute	
1638 National Covenant		
1639–40 Covenanters at war with king	1640 Long Parliament met	1640 Portugal regained independence

Scotland	England	Europe
1643 Solemn League and Covenant	1642 Civil War began	1643–1715 Louis XIV King of France
	1649 Charles I beheaded; Commonwealth proclaimed	
1651 Charles II crowned at Scone. Cromwellian occupation	1649–50 Cromwellian conquest of Ireland	
	1652–4 Dutch War	
	1653 Protectorate	
1660 Charles II restored as king of England and Scotland		
	1665–7 Dutch War	1667 Louis XIV began aggressive wars
	1665–6 Great Plague and Fire	
1670 Negotiations for union between England and Scotland	1672–4 Dutch War	
1672 High Court of Justiciary established		
1682 Advocates' Library founded		1683 Second siege of Vienna by Turks
		1685 Revocation of Edict of Nantes
1685 Accession of James VII and II		1689 War of the League of Augsburg
1688–9 Revolution: James VII and II superseded by William and Mary		
1690 Presbyterianism restored	1690 Battle of the Boyne	
1692 Massacre of Glencoe	1694 Bank of England founded	
1695 Bank of Scotland and 'Darien Company' founded		
1696 Education Act		
	1701 Act of Settlement	
1702–14 Reign of Queen Anne	1702–13 War of Spanish Succession	1703 Foundation of St Petersburg
1707 Union of England and Scotland		

BRITAIN AND IRELAND

1709 Peter the Great defeated Swedes at Pultava

1712 Toleration for some Episcopalians. Patronage restored
1714–27 Reign of George I
1715 Jacobite Rebellion
1716 Septennial Act
1721–42 Ministry of Walpole

1724–43 General Wade in the Highlands
1725 Malt Tax Riots
1727 Board of Manufactures established
1733 First Secession
1736 Porteous Riot
1738 Beginning of Methodism
1740–86 Frederick the Great, king of Prussia
1742–8 War of Austrian Succession
1745–6 Jacobite Rebellion
1746 Office of Secretary for Scotland lapsed
1747 Abolition of heritable jurisdictions
1755 Webster's 'Census': population 1,265,380
1756–63 Seven Years' War
1757–61 Chatham's first ministry
1760 Carron Iron Works founded
1760 British conquest of Canada
1761 Second Secession: Relief Church
1764 Hargreaves invented spinning-jenny
1769 Arkwright invented water-frame. James Watt's steam engine patented
1770–81 Lord North's ministry
1776–83 American Revolution
1779 First spinning-mill
1779 Crompton's 'Mule'
1784–1806 Dundas Ascendancy
1784–1801 Ministry of Pitt the Younger
1785 Cartwright invented power loom
1788 Death of Prince Charles Edward
1789 French Revolution began
1790 Forth and Clyde Canal opened
1792 End of penal laws against Episcopalians

1793 War between Britain and France

1804 Napoleon Emperor of the French

1805 Battle of Trafalgar

1815 Battle of Waterloo. Belgium and Holland united. Norway and Sweden united

1821–9 Greek War of Independence

1825 Independence of Spanish American mainland complete

1830 Belgium independent

1837 Telegraphy invented by Morse

1801 Union of Great Britain and Ireland

1807 Slave Trade abolished

1819 'Peterloo Massacre'

1825 Stockton–Darlington railway

1833 Abolition of slavery in British dominions

1838–50 Chartist Movement

1840 Penny postage introduced

1845–8 Famine in Ireland

1793 Relief Act for Roman Catholics

1793–4 Political Trials

1796 Death of Robert Burns

1801 First official census: population 1,608,420

1803 Commissioners for Highland Roads and Bridges

1807 Sutherland 'Clearances' began

1812 *Comet* steamship

1820 'Radical War' rebellion

1822 First visit of a Hanoverian king, George IV. Caledonian Canal open

1828 Invention of hot blast

1831 Glasgow–Garnkirk railway

1832 First Reform Act. Death of Sir Walter Scott

1833 Municipal Reform

1843 Disruption

1845 Potato famine. New Poor Law

1846 Repeal of Corn Law		
1847 United Presbyterian Church formed		1848 Revolutions in France and other European countries
		1854–6 Crimean War
1853 National Association for Vindication of Scottish Rights	1856 Bessemer's steel process invented	1857 Indian Mutiny
1867 Second Reform Act		1861–5 American Civil War
		1868 Suez Canal opened
		1870 Unification of Italy complete
		1871 German Empire established
1872 Education Act		
1884 Third Reform Act		
1885 Secretary for Scotland appointed. Scottish Home Rule Association	1886 Irish Home Rule proposed. Liberal Party split	1885 Canadian Pacific Railway completed
1886 Crofters Act		1899–1902 South African War
1889 County Councils established		1903 Beginning of aeroplane flight
1895 Parish Councils established		1905 Norway became independent
1900 United Free Church formed		1914–19 World War I
1906–13 Home Rule Bills	1911 Parliament Act	1915 Panama Canal opened
1906 First Labour MPs	1916 Easter Rebellion in Ireland	
1921 Population 4,472,103	1921 Irish Free State established	
1928 National Party of Scotland formed	1922 Wireless broadcasting began	
1929 Union of Church of Scotland and U.F. Church. Local Government Act		
1939 St Andrew's House became headquarters of administration	1947 Coal industry nationalised	1939–45 World War II

1948 British Railways nationalised
1948 Electricity nationalised
1949 Gas nationalised

1950 Stone of Scone
removed from Westminster

1950-68 Korean wars

1951 Steel nationalised
1953 Steel denationalised

1953 Ascent of Everest
1955 EEC established
1956 Suez crisis
Hungarian rising

1958 Dounreay reactor working
1961 Polaris submarines in Holy Loch
1963 'Beeching cuts', on Railways
1964 Forth Road Bridge

1965-75 Vietnam War
1967 'Six Day War'
1968 'Prague Spring'
1969 First Men on Moon

1967 *Queen Elizabeth 2* launched

1970 First victory of SNP
at General election

1971 'Decimal Day'

1973 Kilbrandon Report

1973 UK joined EEC
1973-6 'Cod War' with Iceland

1974 Eleven SNP MPs
1974-5 Local government
reorganised

1974 Labour government

1975 Sex Discrimination and
Equal Pay Acts
Referendum on EEC

1978 Bill for Scottish Assembly passed
Sullom Terminal in operation

1979 Referendum on proposed Assembly SNP members drop to two Assembly Bill repealed	1982 'Falklands War' 1984-5 Great Pit Strike 1985 Unemployment over 3,300,000 1986 Anglo-Irish Agreement British Telecom set up Gas privatised	1985 Gorbachev in power in USSR 1986 Channel Tunnel approved Chernobyl disaster 1988-90 Democratisation in Baltic States and Russian satellites 1989 Tiananmen Square massacre, China Commons 1990 Germany unified
1989 Community Charge introduced	1989 British Steel set up Television of House of began 1990 Electricity privatised Violent 'Poll Tax' riots in London Mrs Thatcher resigned	1990-1 Break-up of Yugo-Slavia Dissolution of USSR 1991 Yeltsin President of Russia
1992 Ravenscraig closed		1992 Gulf War Separation of Czechs and Slovaks

Genealogical Tables

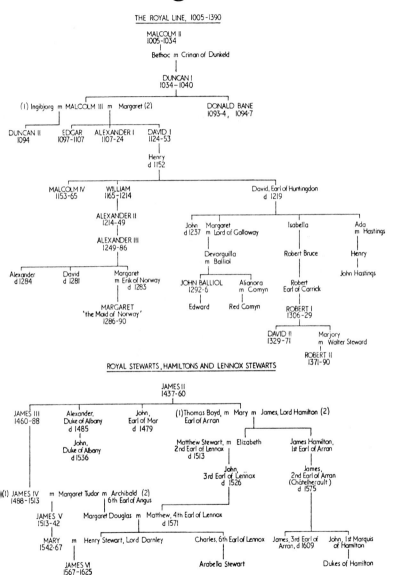

THE ROYAL LINE, 1005-1390

MALCOLM II
1005-1034

Bethoc m Crinan of Dunkeld

DUNCAN I
1034-1040

(1) Ingibjorg m MALCOLM III m Margaret (2)   DONALD BANE
1093-4, 1094-7

DUNCAN II   EDGAR   ALEXANDER I   DAVID I
1094   1097-1107   1107-24   1124-53

Henry
d 1152

MALCOLM IV   WILLIAM   David, Earl of Huntingdon
1153-65   1165-1214   d 1219

ALEXANDER II   John   Margaret   Isabella   Ada
1214-49   d 1237   m Lord of Galloway   m Hastings

ALEXANDER III   Devorguilla   Robert Bruce   Henry
1249-86   m Balliol   John Hastings

Alexander   David   Margaret   JOHN BALLIOL   Alianora   Robert
d 1284   d 1281   m Erik of Norway   1292-6   m Comyn   Earl of Carrick
                      d 1283
                                        Edward   Red Comyn   ROBERT I
MARGARET   1306-29
'the Maid of Norway'
1286-90   DAVID II   Marjory
                                                    1329-71   m Walter Steward

                                                                  ROBERT II
ROYAL STEWARTS, HAMILTONS AND LENNOX STEWARTS   1371-90

JAMES II
1437-60

JAMES III   Alexander,   John,   (1)Thomas Boyd, m Mary m James, Lord Hamilton (2)
1460-88   Duke of Albany Earl of Mar   Earl of Arran
             d 1485   d 1479
                                          Matthew Stewart, m Elizabeth   James Hamilton,
             John,   2nd Earl of Lennox   1st Earl of Arran
             Duke of Albany   d 1513
             d 1536   James,
                                          John,   2nd Earl of Arran
                                          3rd Earl of Lennox   (Châtelherault)
                                          d 1526   d 1575
(1) JAMES IV m Margaret Tudor m Archibald (2)
   1488-1513   6th Earl of Angus

   JAMES V   Margaret Douglas m Matthew, 4th Earl of Lennox
   1513-42   d 1571

   MARY   m Henry Stewart, Lord Darnley   Charles, 6th Earl of Lennox   James, 3rd Earl of   John, 1st Marquis
   1542-67   Arran, d 1609   of Hamilton

        JAMES VI   Arabella Stewart   Dukes of Hamilton
        1567-1625

297

GENEALOGICAL TABLES

THE STEWARTS AND THE DOUGLASES

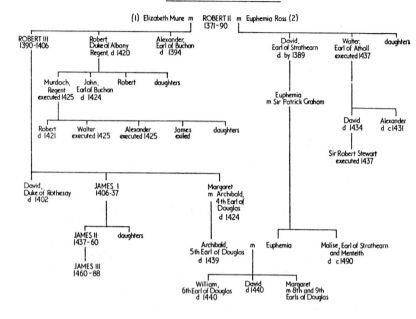

THE SUCCESSION TO THE ENGLISH THRONE

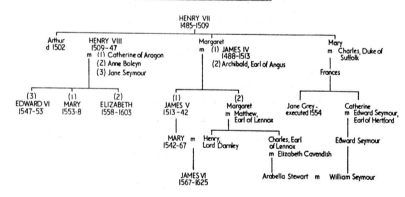

Recommended Reading

The four-volume *Edinburgh History of Scotland* (Oliver & Boyd 1965-75, revised and reprinted by The Mercat Press 1987-9) and the eight-volume *New History of Scotland* (Edward Arnold, 1981-3, reprinted by Edinburgh University Press) meets most needs. An outstanding work is a vast single-volume by eight distinguished authors, *The Scottish World* (Harry N. Abrams, Inc., New York 1981). A new edition and translation in nine volumes of the medieval *Scotichronicon* (ed. D.E.R. Watt and others, Aberdeen University Press, in progress) provides a wonderful guide as far as the fifteenth century.

Among literally many hundreds of monographs, several of them produced in the last thirty years, it is impossible to do more than single out the following, all based on sound scholarship: R.L.G. Ritchie, *The Normans in Scotland* (Edinburgh University Press, 1954); Andrew Fisher, *William Wallace* (John Donald, 1984); G.W.S. Barrow, *Robert Bruce* (Eyre and Spottiswoode, 1976); Leslie J. Macfarlane, *William Elphinstone* (Aberdeen University Press, 1986); Norman Macdougall's *James III* and his *James IV* (John Donald, 1982,1989); G. Donaldson, *The Scottish Reformation* (Cambridge University Press, 1960); the various works of Maurice Lee and David Stevenson on the sixteenth and seventeenth centuries; P.W.J. Riley, *The Union of England and Scotland* (Manchester University Press, 1978); T.C. Smout, *History of the Scottish People 1560-1830* (Collins, 1969); Caroline Bingham, *Beyond the Highland Line* (Constable, 1990); Bruce Lenman, *The Jacobite Risings in Britain* (Eyre Methuen, 1980).

Three reference books: G. Donaldson and R.S. Morpeth, *A Dictionary of Scottish History* (John Donald, 1977); Ian Donnachie and George Hewitt, *A Companion to Scottish History* (Batsford, 1989); David Daiches (ed.), *A Companion to Scottish Culture* (Arnold, 1981).

Index